THE WRECK OF REPARATIONS

THE WRECK OF REPARATIONS

BEING THE POLITICAL BACKGROUND
OF THE

LAUSANNE AGREEMENT 1932

by

JOHN W. WHEELER-BENNETT

HOWARD FERTIG

NEW YORK · 1972

First published in 1933

HOWARD FERTIG, INC. EDITION 1972
Published by arrangement with George Allen & Unwin Ltd.

Preface to the Howard Fertig, Inc. edition copyright © 1972
by John Wheeler-Bennett

Library of Congress Cataloging in Publication Data

Wheeler-Bennett, Sir John Wheeler, 1902–
   The wreck of reparations.

   Reprint of the 1933 ed., which was issued as no. 8 of Information series.
   Bibliography: p.
   1. Lausanne. Conference, June 16–July 9, 1932. 2. European War, 1914–1918—Reparations. 3. Debts, External—Germany. I. Title. II. Series: Information series, no. 8.
D648.W5   1972   940.3'1422   70–80602

For sale only in the United States of America and its
dependencies.

PRINTED IN THE UNITED STATES OF AMERICA
BY NOBLE OFFSET PRINTERS, INC.

DEDICATION TO

MAJOR-GENERAL SIR NEILL MALCOLM, K.C.B., D.S.O.

My Dear Sir Neill,

I am so glad that you have allowed me to dedicate a book to you because I have always felt that you have been so intimately connected with my work from the time that you wrote the Introduction to my first book in 1925 till you did the same for my sixth, last year.

You once urged me, in writing of Germany and the great problems affecting her, not to trust entirely to the study of documents but to go to the country and see the position for myself. As a result of following your advice I have had exceptional opportunities for weighing up the problems of disarmament and reparations in both Germany and France and have thus been able to gain an amazingly increased perspective.

This present book, moreover, is more particularly yours as we have so often discussed its contents together in distant lands. In it I hope and believe you will find many of the views which we hold in common and which I have imbibed from you. We have both believed that the policy of the "clean-slate" was the best and most practical method of settling the Reparation Problem, and for that reason the hopes of both of us have been disappointed at Lausanne. But is it not possible to believe with old John Brown that "The end is not yet," and that possibly the slate may yet, in fact, if not in theory, be wiped clean? Isn't this perhaps what has really, almost unknowingly, been achieved at Lausanne?

Finally, it was owing to you in very great measure that the book was written at all. When I had finished my last book on *Disarmament and Security* I was in such bad health that I determined to give up altogether this kind of work. But both privately, and publicly in your Introduction, you advised me not to do so, and the present book is the result. So at least you must share moral responsibility!

I have so much to thank you for that this dedication seems inadequate.

Ever yours,

JOHN WHEELER-BENNETT

A14 Albany
Piccadilly, W.1

PREFACE TO THE
HOWARD FERTIG, INC. EDITION

THIS book, first published in 1933, is a reluctant sequel to that entitled *The Reparation Settlement* which I wrote, with the collaboration of Hugh Latimer, in 1930 and which traced the history of the Reparation Problem from its genesis at the Peace Conference of Paris to what proved to be not its final but its penultimate stage at the Second Hague Conference of 1930. In writing of the Young Plan and the Hague Agreements we permitted ourselves a certain lack of credulity in the claim made for them that they provided "a final liquidation of the outstanding questions left over from the War," but we also expressed our hopes that they would endure for a sufficient period to make a lasting contribution to some later readjustment. We had no conception, however, that for reasons at once economical, financial and political, they would be virtually still-born and that it would be necessary to write a sequel to the original work, chronicling the collapse and shipwreck of all that in which high hopes had been reposed.

Indeed, one of the most remarkable aspects of the economic and financial crisis of 1931—which overwhelmed

amongst other devastation the structure of the Young Plan
—was its extraordinary suddenness and the appalling rapidity with which one catastrophe followed another. When
one considers the comparative calm in which the first five
months of the year passed, the amazing chaos of the last
seven months stood out in sharp contrast.

This present book, therefore, follows the story of the
Reparation Problem from the Hague Agreement of August
1929 to the Lausanne Agreement of July 1932. It is the
history of just three years, but it saw greater changes than
almost any other of the previous postwar years. For during
these years peoples were called upon in time of peace to
make sacrifices and undergo privations which, heretofore,
had been inseparably connected in their minds with times
of war; and it was this fact, among others, that made this
period of such engrossing interest and importance.

At the end of it all we were faced with yet another "final"
settlement in the Lausanne Agreement and this time, *nolens
volens*, it *was* final. For if anything certain emerged from
the Lausanne Conference it was that reparations were at an
end; that never again would Germany ever pay anything
more.

There were many fascinating and disquieting aspects of
the story. The virtually irresponsible manner in which
Pierre Laval used the French gold reserves as an instrument of national policy has found its parallel in later years,
and once again the willful myopia of Western European
statesmanship failed to make to the wisdom and integrity of
Brüning in German leadership those economic and final
concessions which they ultimately made to the irresponsible
and volatile von Papen—again a case of "appeasing the
wrong Germans."

Though the book ends with the fate of the Lausanne
Agreement and the Inter-Allied war debts in the air, it is a
matter of fact that both Reparation and Allied indebtedness
payments were dead from this hour. The diplomatic welter
of the Conference of Lausanne in the summer of 1932

proved, in effect, to be the last occasion on which a "civilized" attempt was made to reach an agreement amongst the powers. Thereafter international affairs passed into the phase of appeasement in the face of the use of force and blackmail, which was in itself but a prologue to the tragedy of war.

JOHN WHEELER-BENNETT

GARSINGTON MANOR
OXON
June 1969

NOTE

For the purposes of this book the sterling rate of exchange has been taken at the par value previous to September 20, 1931 (i.e. £1 = 20 marks, 124 francs and 4·86 dollars).

J. W. W.-B.

CONTENTS

THE WRECK OF REPARATIONS

CHAPTER I

THE TORNADO BREAKS

1

IT was claimed for the Young Plan of 1929 and the Hague
Agreements of 1930, by which it was made operative, that
they provided a final liquidation of the reparation problem.
In effect, however, they provided no such thing, but formed
merely another, if a final, example of the economic impractic-
ability and the political futility of reparations.

It would be erroneous, however, to believe that either the
experts who drew up the Young Plan or the statesmen who
signed the Hague Agreements did so in anything but the best
of good faith.[1] Fallible, as even experts and statesmen, in
company with the rest of human nature, must be, they failed
to gauge accurately the movement of the world-wide economic
depression and, in consequence, their labours, thus based upon
the shifting sand of optimism rather than the rocky foundation
of reality, failed to produce the desired result.

The Young Plan, with its rising series of annuities, contemplated not only a relatively short depression, but a steady
expansion of world trade, not merely in volume but in value,
in which the annuities payable by Germany would become a
factor of diminishing importance. In reality the exact opposite
took place. Not only did the economic depression become
intensified in gravity, but from the time the Young Plan came

---

[1] This opinion would be hotly contested by many eminent German authorities,
who hold that in both the case of the Dawes and of the Young Committees
the fundamental considerations were political and not economic. It is alleged
that the experts were handicapped from the start by the knowledge that
whatever their findings might be they must not decide on a possible total
amount of reparation payments below a certain sum set in advance by the
politicians as the lowest minimum to which they would agree.

into effect in May 1930 the trade of the world has shrunk and
the exceptional fall in gold prices which has occurred in the
last three years itself added to the real burden not only of the
German annuities but of all payments fixed in gold.

In place of the final liquidation hoped for from the Young
Plan a state of affairs developed which brought the world to
the brink of financial and economic ruin.

2

Fully to appreciate the situation to-day it is necessary to cast
a brief glance backwards across the intervening years between
the Peace Conference of 1919 and the Hague Conference of
1930. These twelve years fell naturally, as far as reparations
were concerned, into two periods, before and after the year 1924.

The first of these periods was distinguished by a singular lack
of common sense on the part of both debtors and creditors.
The bitter and obstinate evasiveness of Germany, the implacable
insistence of France, combined to bring about a deadlock, and
it was not until Germany had passed through the depths of
national bankruptcy, and the mark had ceased to exist as a
medium of exchange, that both sides began to approach the
problem from a practical point of view.[1]

During this period there were certain men of sound sense,
amongst them notably Lord D'Abernon, the British Ambassador in Berlin, who were endeavouring with great anxiety to
remove the whole question of reparations to the commercial as
opposed to the political field and to have it dealt with, not by
the professional politician or the theoretical economist, but by
the practical business man.[2]

These wise counsels eventually prevailed when in 1924 the
Dawes Plan and the London Conference placed reparation payments for the first time upon a business footing, that is to say

[1] For a detailed account of this period in the history of reparations see
Information on the Reparation Settlement, by J. W. Wheeler-Bennett and
H. Latimer (George Allen & Unwin, 1930) (hereafter cited as *Reparations*),
ch. iii, pp. 41–54.
[2] See *An Ambassador of Peace*, by Viscount D'Abernon (London, Hodder &
Stoughton, 3 vols., 1929–1930).

based not merely upon Allied desires for reparation but on Germany's capacity to pay, assisted by an international 7 per cent. Dawes Loan to Germany from which that country received £40,000,000. International confidence was sufficiently restored to enable States amongst the former Allied Powers to begin funding the debts they had made among themselves during the War. Paradoxically enough it was at this same moment that the untenability of certain attitudes in the matter of indebtedness began to become apparent.

From 1922 onwards the United States has, with the one magnificent exception of the Hoover Moratorium of 1931, studiously refused to recognize any connection between inter-Allied debts and reparations. Yet it was not until an agreement had been made in the matter of reparation payments that France and Italy were able to consider the repayment of their American debts. The attitude of Great Britain had been made clear as far back as 1922, when in the Balfour Note she agreed to take no greater sums in reparations and war debts due to her than she was required to pay to the United States.[1] The Anglo-American Debt Funding Agreement of January 1923 had been concluded in this light. Moreover, from 1924 onwards the restoration of international confidence in Germany led private finance houses in Great Britain and the United States almost to implore the German State and municipal authorities to accept short-term credits. This anxiety to lend was met by a corresponding keenness to borrow on the part of these authorities, in accordance with the advice given by many experts. It became, therefore, dangerously easy to obtain short-term credits out of proportion to security. The unforeseen sequel to this policy occurred in the summer of 1931, when these credits were found to be "frozen" and their extension, therefore, inevitable.

The authors of the Dawes Plan were under no misapprehension as to the nature of their work. It was essential that

[1] The wisdom of the policy enunciated in the Balfour Note has more than once been called in question. Its sin was one of omission rather than commission, since no mention is made as to the currencies in which debts are to be repaid to Great Britain.

some method should be evolved for reparation payments and for the restoration of confidence in Germany, but the economic experts fully realized that the plan which they put forward could only be in the nature of a temporary measure and that, at a later date, some more definite and, if possible final, agreement should be arrived at. This view is clearly expressed in the following quotation from the Report of the Dawes Committee:[1]

"We would point out finally that our plan does not, as it could not properly, attempt a solution of the whole reparation problem. It foreshadows a settlement extending in its application for a sufficient time to restore confidence, and at the same time is so framed as to facilitate a final and comprehensive agreement as to all the problems of reparation and connected questions, as soon as circumstances make this possible."

Though Mr. Parker Gilbert, the Agent-General for Reparation Payments (appointed under the Dawes Plan), in his Reports for 1927 and 1928 expressed the view that it would be to the advantage of all parties to reach a final settlement by mutual agreement,[2] the moment for taking this next step did not arrive until the autumn of 1928, when on the strong initiative of Mr. Gilbert and as a result of negotiations at Geneva in September, it was agreed to endeavour to reach a final settlement in the matter of reparation payments and the occupation of the Rhineland.[3] To this end a committee of experts was appointed early in 1929, who in the June of that year gave to the world what has become known as the Young Plan.[4]

The main principle of the Young Plan was the final determining of the amount payable by Germany and the completion of the gradual conversion of the whole subject of reparations from a political to a commercial obligation. The Plan included the formation of a Bank of International Settlements which was to act as a trustee and clearing-house through which the

[1] See *Reparations*, p. 59.
[2] *Ibid.*, pp. 67–68.   [3] *Ibid.*, pp. 69–84.
[4] For details of the discussions of the Committee of Experts and an analysis of the Plan itself see *ibid.*, pp. 85–105.

transfer of the annual payments from Germany to her creditors should pass.

The final sum fixed for Germany's reparation debt was agreed at RM. 110,735,700,000 (£5,536,785,000) to be paid in sixty annual payments terminating in 1988. The annuities were to be at first on a rising scale beginning at RM. 1707·9 million (£85,395,000) for the first completed year, 1930–1931,[1] increasing to a maximum of RM. 2,352·7 million (£117,635,000) in 1965–1966, and decreasing to RM. 897·8 million (£44,890,000) in 1987–1988, giving an average annuity of RM. 2,050·6 million.

The annuities themselves were of two different kinds, "conditional" and "unconditional." The German Government had the right, after giving 90 days' notice, to declare a postponement of the payment of conditional annuities for a period not exceeding two years, if it was their opinion "that Germany's exchange and economic life may be seriously endangered" by continued payment. In such case the Government might apply to the Bank of International Settlements for the appointment of a Special Advisory Committee to inquire into and consider her financial position. Having done so the Committee should indicate to the Creditor Powers and to the Bank what steps should be taken.

There was no proviso within the Plan for the postponement of the unconditional annuities. And, a fact which was even more important, there was no provision, such as had been included in the Dawes Plan, for the revision of the Plan in the event of unforeseen circumstances.

The Hague Conference of 1929, by setting up committees to report to a later meeting, paved the way for the putting into force of the Young Plan.[2] In addition, agreement was reached as to the date of the termination of the occupation of the Rhineland, which had been the price of Germany's acceptance of the Plan.[3]

---

[1] The first annuity dated from September 1, 1929, to March 31, 1930. Subsequent annuities dated from April 1st to March 31st. The first annuity amounted to RM. 676·9 million.

[2] See *Reparations*, pp. 106–123.   [3] *Ibid.*, pp. 124–125.

The Hague Conference of 1930 succeeded not only in adopting the Plan with modifications,[1] but in working out, in accordance with the recommendations of its authors, a means of determining Eastern European as well as German reparations indebtedness.[2] The Conference also added to the provisions for postponement contained in the Plan a certain system of "sanctions" to be put into force in the event of an unjustified default on the part of Germany, or, in the words of Annex I of the Hague Agreement of 1930, in case a future German Government "might commit itself to actions revealing its determination to destroy the New Plan."[3] Under this system, if one or more of the creditor Powers believed Germany guilty of such an intention, the matter should be submitted to the Permanent Court of International Justice. In the event of an affirmative decision by the Court, Germany should acknowledge that it was legitimate, in defence of the integrity of obligations resulting from the Young Plan, that the creditor Power, or Powers, might reserve their full liberty of action.[4]

The division of the annual payments under the Young Plan, based on the "average" annuity of £100,000,000 and divided into the "unconditional" and "conditional" categories,[5] was agreed upon as shown in the table on page 27.

With the object of assisting immediate payments the German International 5½ per cent. Young Plan Loan amounting to some £60,000,000 was floated in 1930.

Such was the Young Plan, from which so much was popularly hoped, as it was launched on May 17, 1930. On this day the Bank for International Settlements opened its doors at Basle. The final evacuation of the Third Rhine Zone was begun. For

---

[1] See *Reparations*, pp. 137–147.
[2] *Ibid.*, pp. 150–165. The actual Agreement was not signed until August in Paris.
[3] *Ibid.*, pp. 143–144, 147–149.
[4] This wording is reminiscent of Part VIII, Annex II, para. 18 of the Treaty of Versailles, on which France based and justified the legality of her occupation of the Ruhr in 1923. See *Reparations*, p. 24. For an interesting comparison of the conflicting French and German interpretations of this provision, see *The End of Reparations*, by Dr. Hjalmar Schacht (London, Cape, 1931), pp. 119–130.
[5] The year of the payment most closely approximating to the "average" annuity was not to be reached until 1941–1942. The annuity for the year 1931–1932, that affected by the Hoover Moratorium, was scheduled at £82,000,000.

a while the world was lulled into a sense of false security;
reparations were settled at last—prosperity was "just round
the corner." It was but the calm which precedes the breaking
of a tornado.

	Unconditional	Conditional	Total
	£	£	£
France	25,000,000	32,000,000	57,000,000
Great Britain ..	2,250,000	20,000,000*	22,250,000
Italy	2,100,000	12,000,000	14,100,000
Japan, Yugoslavia, Portugal, etc.	650,000	6,000,000	6,650,000
Total	£30,000,000	£70,000,000	£100,000,000

* From this sum £2,665,000 was earmarked for the Dominions.

3

Germany accepted the Young Plan only with the greatest
reluctance. It is difficult to say whether in his innermost heart
Herr Stresemann believed that his country could meet the
obligations assumed under the Young Plan, but he was fighting
a gallant but losing battle with death, and had set his heart on
seeing the Rhineland freed from foreign occupation before he
died. Though he did not live to see this actually completed,
the Evacuation Agreement signed at the Hague in August 1929
was the last international document to which Herr Stresemann
put his name. In the following October he died, and when the
Hague Conference reassembled in January 1930 it was Dr.
Curtius who represented Germany.

Of the original German members of the Young Committee,
Dr. Vögler had resigned rather than sign the Report, and
although Dr. Schacht, then President of the Reichsbank, signed,
he proceeded almost immediately to inaugurate a campaign
against the Plan as amended at the first Hague Conference.
During the interval between the two Hague Conferences

(December 5, 1929), Dr. Schacht issued a memorandum printed in German, English, and French, at the official printing press of the Reichsbank, vehemently attacking the Government on two scores: first, their acceptance of the modification of the Young Plan; and, secondly, the inadequacy of their financial policy.[1] He had, he wrote, signed the Plan under the dual impression that its recommendations would be accepted in their totality by all the Powers, and that Germany's financial and economic policy would be set in order. In effect neither had been done. The amendments to the Plan made by the Conference, with the consent of the German delegation, involved Germany in heavy additional sacrifices "which altogether ran into milliards . . . to be taken over without any noteworthy *quid pro quo* which was not fully assured to us under the Young Plan."[2]

As regards the financial policy of the Government, Dr. Schacht declared that the promised tax reduction and reorganization of States finances (Reich, State, and Commune)[3] had not been carried out and that, on the contrary, prices were rising and would continue to rise. The savings from the introduction of the Young Plan (as opposed to the Dawes payments) would not result in a decrease of taxation, and would not even cover the deficit in the Budget. He demanded that, before the Government finally accepted the Plan, they should put the finances of the country in order.

Dr. Schacht's bombshell, though it resulted in the resignation of the Finance Minister and endangered the position of the Chancellor, had the salutary effect of forcing the Government to introduce a system of taxation and economies instead of adding to Germany's external indebtedness by means of an external loan which had been their original intention. It further

[1] See *Reparations*, pp. 129–136. For text of memorandum and Reichstag speeches in reply to it see *Documents on International Affairs*, 1929 Oxford) University Press, 1930), pp. 91–98. See Schacht, pp. 95–118.
[2] The figure amounted to some RM. 1,080 million ¡(£54,000,000), exclusive of the amount sacrificed by Germany in her renunciation of her claims to former German property in Poland, under the Polish-German Treaty of October 31, 1929.
[3] The organization of German national finances had been severely criticized in the Report of the Dawes Committee of 1924.

brought home to the Reichstag, which did not know its own mind, the need for sound financial reforms. Dr. Schacht's intervention restored the Treasury position in part, and at the same time imposed upon the Government a policy which the Agent-General for Reparation Payments had repeatedly advocated in his Reports.

Dr. Schacht continued his campaign of opposition to the amended Plan. Some time after resigning his office he proceeded on a lecture tour in the United States in the winter of 1930, wherein from coast to coast he prophesied the collapse of the Young Plan and the inevitable necessity of a moratorium, thereby causing considerable embarrassment to the German Government and no little damage to German credit on Wall Street.

By reason of the extreme reactionary nature of his political affiliations there has been a tendency to discount Dr. Schacht's expressions of opinion.[1] Whatever his politics may be, it cannot be denied that from the beginning, and almost alone among his fellow economic and financial experts, Dr. Schacht has preached the impossibility of carrying out the Plan which he himself helped to formulate. It must also be admitted that in the main his prognostications have been disastrously justified by the course of later events, and readers of his book *The End of Reparations* will agree that, apart from political propaganda, what Dr. Schacht wrote in April 1931 the world is thinking and saying to-day.

Meanwhile in Germany the ratification of the Young Plan met with very great opposition throughout the country. A referendum on a "Bill against the Enslavement of the German People," organized in December 1929 by Herr Hugenberg and the Nationalist Party, though sufficient favourable votes were

---

[1] Though declaredly a supporter of the National Opposition, Dr. Schacht, with considerable agility and foresight, avoided a definite identification with any one political party of the Right. He supported the referendum campaign of Herr Hugenberg and the Nationalists in December 1929, and has frequently endorsed the repudiation policy of Herr Hitler and the Nazis. During the political crisis of June 1931 he was mentioned as one of the potential "Economic Directorate" which the German Peoples' Party hoped to place in power in the event of Dr. Brüning's defeat and resignation.

not recorded for the measure to become law, resulted, nevertheless, in six million votes being secured in favour of the Bill,
which provided for the repudiation not only of the Young Plan
but of all reparation obligations.[1] Great popular pressure was
brought to bear on President von Hindenburg in order to
persuade him not to sign the Bill of ratification, and perhaps
the most courageous action in the veteran Field-Marshal's
career was his persistence in honouring the signature of his
Ministers, in spite, perhaps, of his own personal misgivings
and certainly in opposition to his own personal desires. "It
was little known or appreciated outside of Germany through
what depths of unpopularity the former idol of the German
people passed at this critical juncture."[2]

On March 13, 1930, the same day that his signature of the
Bill of Ratification made the Young Plan and the Hague
Agreements law as far as Germany was concerned, Marshal
von Hindenburg issued a Manifesto to the German People
which had in it a ring both of statesmanship and patriotism.[3]

"After a thorough and conscientious examination of the Young
Plan Laws, I have with a heavy but resolute heart put my signature
to the Agreement. Having listened to all the arguments for and against
the Plan, and having carefully considered both points of view, I have
come to the conclusion that, in spite of the heavy burden the new
Plan will place upon Germany's shoulders for many years to come,
and in spite of the serious objections which may be raised against some
of its provisions, the Young Plan represents, in comparison with the
Dawes Plan, an improvement and relief and a step forward economically and politically along the hard path of Germany's re-establishment
and liberation. In view of my responsibility for Germany and Germany's
future, I could not consent to a rejection, since the consequences of such
an action would be incalculable for German commerce and finance and
would lead to serious crises, exposing our country to considerable dangers.

"I am fully aware of the fact that mere acceptance of the Young
Plan does not free us from all anxiety for the future; nevertheless I
confidently believe that the course upon which we have now embarked
and which brings to German Occupied Territory its longed-for freedom,
and to us all hope for further progress, will prove the right one."

---

[1] See *Reparations*, pp. 126–129. For texts of Bill see *Documents on International Affairs*, 1929, p. 81.
[2] See *Hindenburg*, by Dr. G. Schultze-Pfaelzer pp. 326–340.
[3] For text see *Documents on International Affairs*, 1930, edited by J. W.
Wheeler-Bennett (Oxford University Press, 1931), pp. 93–94.

4

The success, or even the practical value, of the Young Plan was dependent upon the presumed increase in the volume and value of international trade and a general improvement in the economic state of the world. These conditions formed both the basis and the reason for the system of increasing annuity payments for which the Plan provided. From this point of view, therefore, the Young Plan may be said to have been stillborn, since the political, economic, and financial condition of the world has grown rapidly and progressively worse.

Even before the Hague Conference of 1930 had given the Young Plan legal form, the New York Stock Exchange crash in October and November 1929 had heralded a new and graver phase of the economic depression. In 1930 a wave of political and economic unrest spread over Latin America, causing Governments and Dictatorships to rise and fall with bewildering rapidity and bringing with it a material decrease in the volume of trade. Economic distress and financial embarrassment became vividly apparent in Australia.

In Europe the economic depression became intensified and the situation was further exacerbated by political complications. The Briand Memorandum of May 1930 was at one and the same time an endeavour on the part of France to bring the States of Europe into some self-protective economic federation and a final attempt to bring about a reaffirmation of the international *status quo* created by the Treaty of Versailles.[1] But if France expected the passive acquiescence of Germany in this project she was gravely mistaken. The nation-wide opposition to the Young Plan which had manifested itself in the early part of the year found freedom of action and expression at the German General Election of September 1930. The German reply to the Briand proposal was contained in reality not in the official note and commentary of June 1930. It was to be found in the

[1] For text of the Briand Memorandum see *Documents on International Affairs*, 1930, pp. 61–73. See also *Bulletin of International News*, vol. vii, no. 6, September 11, 1930.

fact that the twenty-four political parties, regardless of their partisan colouring, went to the polls in September with the same main plank in the electoral platforms—treaty revision. The result of the Election, which brought the Nazis to the Reichstag as the second largest Party with 107 members, was the manifestation of a great movement of national awakening in Germany, which proceeded to grow in strength and importance. Germans of all ages, but more particularly the youth of Germany, became persuaded of the futility of Herr Stresemann's Policy of Fulfilment with its League membership and its granting of concessions in the vain hope that these might beget counter-concessions in return, and showed in numbers which steadily increased at every subsequent local election[1] a disturbing preference for Herr Hitler's Policy of Repudiation.

Neither the political nor the economic conditions in Germany were improved by events which occurred at Geneva at the close of 1930. The Preparatory Disarmament Commission, which had been sitting at irregular intervals since 1926, completed its labours in December with the adoption of a draft disarmament convention. The fact that this document did not attempt to provide for the reduction of the armaments of the ex-Allies to a figure proportionate to that imposed upon the ex-enemy States by the peace treaties, coupled with the fact that these latter States (vide Art. 53) were called on by the terms of the document virtually to reaffirm the said disarmament treaty provisions, rendered the draft convention unacceptable to Germany. She therefore reserved her right

---

[1] For example, the election in Brunswick (March 1, 1931), Oldenburg (May 18, 1931), Hessen (November 15, 1931), and others. By the winter of 1931 the Nazis were the largest single party in the country, and at the close of the year Herr Hitler claimed that his party had a registered membership of more than 900,000.

It should be noted that the enthusiastic support given by German youth to the National Socialist Party is not attributable to a sublime confidence in its political programme, which is more effervescent and self-contradictory than practical in character, but rather to the fact that alone amongst the German political parties the Nazis offer opportunities to young men and make appeal to the spirit of enthusiasm and adventure innate in youth.

See an article "Germany and the League," Bulletin of International News, vol. vii, no. 17, February 12, 1931.

to state her case before the plenary disarmament conference to which the convention was to be presented as a model.[1]

The discussions at Geneva and the consequent Press comments caused unfortunate repercussions in France and Germany and the year closed with as gloomy a record as could at the moment be conceived.

But if the economic storm which had arisen in 1929 had reached the proportions of a hurricane in 1930, it gained the force and fury of a tornado in 1931. Future historians may well denominate this the Black Year, or the *Annus Terribilis*, for no nation in the world was wholly exempt from calamity in some form or another. Yet it is strange to record that the first six months were a period of sullen depression, with little to indicate that amazing events were to happen in the second half of the year. Markets continued to fall, trade to shrink, but there was no apparent reason to believe that the crisis, inevitable though it certainly was, would arrive so quickly, or that events would develop with such extraordinary swiftness after it had occurred.

In Great Britain, for example, the only warning note struck during the early part of the year was by the then Chancellor of the Exchequer, Mr. Philip Snowden, who on February 11th, during the debate on the setting up of the Economy Committee, issued the following warning to the House of Commons:

"I say with all the seriousness I can command that the national position is grave; that drastic and disagreeable measures will have to be taken if the Budget equilibrium is to be maintained and industrial recovery is to be made. . . .

"Recovery from the present crisis will involve some temporary sacrifices from all, and those best able to bear them will have to make the largest sacrifices."[2]

This speech was said at the time to be one of the gravest made by any Chancellor of the Exchequer for fifty years, and Mr. Snowden's warning was found to be amply justified when the fiscal year closed on April 4th with a deficit of £23,000,000

[1] See *Disarmament and Security since Locarno*, by J. W. Wheeler-Bennett (George Allen & Unwin, 1932), pp. 78–102.
[2] See Hansard (House of Commons Debates), February 11, 1931.

instead of the estimated surplus of £2,000,000, and the expenditure for the coming year was estimated at £823,500,000, showing an increase of £16,000,000.[1]

A more complete negation of the economic conditions essential for the successful functioning of the Young Plan than those obtaining in Europe in the early summer of 1931 it is impossible to imagine. It was no longer the question of sceptical critics of the Plan, "Will Germany default?" Europe waited with bated breath, asking itself, "When will Germany default?"[2] This question was instantly followed by a second and equally vital one, "If Germany defaults, what about the payment of inter-Allied debts?" It was conceivable that the European States, all partners in misfortune, might reach an agreement amongst themselves for a temporary postponement, but what about payments due from Great Britain, France, and Italy to the United States? Should not the European attitude towards America be, "Forgive us our debts as we forgive our debtors"?

Such thoughts were very naturally uppermost in the minds of the Sixth Congress of the International Chamber of Commerce, which President Hoover opened at Washington on May 4th. The discussions disclosed some interesting factors. The Administration at Washington and the French Delegation to the Congress were at one in their anxiety to prevent a discussion on the effects of international indebtedness on the depression which might lead to the adoption of a resolution on the subject. This Franco-American desire to "side-track" a debate was based in each case on conflicting reasons. The Administration, while anxious to develop the connection between the reduction of international indebtedness and the reduction of armaments, was not prepared to abandon the traditional American ostrich-like disbelief that reparation payments and inter-Allied debts were inextricably commingled. France, on the other hand, while only too anxious to establish the recognition

---

[1] Mr. Snowden's warning had, however, little or no deterrent effect upon his colleagues' spending propensities, and the Government continued to pursue a thoroughly unsound and extravagant policy. See below, p. 97 *et seq.*
[2] The position of Germany is discussed in the following chapter, see below, p. 37 *et seq.*

of the latter doctrine, was entirely unprepared to accept any thesis which might tie her hands at the forthcoming Disarmament Conference.[1]

Thus in his opening speech, President Hoover emphasized the "economic interdependence" of the world, but quickly proceeded to make clear that the United States would not contemplate any change in its attitude towards international debts and international credits.[2] Sweeping aside as "contributory causes" such factors as competitive over-production, under-consumption, and economic nationalism, Mr. Hoover found the basic causes of the world-wide depression to be the tax burdens, instability and lack of confidence which had followed in inevitable sequence the Great War, and which were being perpetuated and kept alive by the maintenance of huge armaments and preparation for, or fear of, a further clash. Co-operation then, the President argued, between the European countries and between Europe and the United States, co-operation undertaken with a view to ameliorating the economic depression, was futile, and would continue to be futile until such a time as actions had been successfully taken to reduce armaments.

But the Congress which had met with a specific purpose of considering the underlying causes of the world economic depression and searching for a possible remedy was not thus to be baulked of discussion of one of the most important factors. Delegates from the debtor States, notably Sir Alan Anderson, Signor Pirelli, the Italian industrialist, and Dr. Carl Bergmann, formally German representative on the Reparation Commission and author of one of the most important works on this subject,[3] not only differed from Mr. Hoover's analysis of the situation, but trenchantly emphasised the existing "disequilibrium" between creditor and debtor countries as a real cause of, and its removal a very real cure for, the existing depression.

[1] It seems to have occurred to neither party that in practice both their theories were correct and were perfectly capable of reconciliation. "On earth the broken arc, in heaven (?) the perfect round."
[2] For text of speech see *Documents on International Affairs*, 1931, edited by J. W. Wheeler-Bennett (Oxford University Press, 1932), p. 109.
[3] *The History of Reparations*, by Dr. Carl Bergmann (Ernest Benn, London, 1927).

Dr. Bergmann indeed urged the Congress to make a definite pronouncement on the subject, arguing that the questioning of the recent reparation settlement was not only justified but rendered imperative by the sudden and fundamental change of all underlying economic conditions which the world had undergone.

Though they failed to prevent a discussion of the subject of international indebtedness, French and American influences were more successful when it came to framing a general resolution to be adopted by the Congress. Here a definite pronouncement was avoided, the final draft adopted on May 9th merely stating:

"International obligations have been made definite in amount and in terms between nations. The integrity of such obligations is always fundamental to the maintenance of industrial credits and the expansion of trade and industry. The observance of this essential principle, however, is not inconsistent with an impartial examination of the effect of these obligations on international trade if warranted by changed economic conditions."[1]

The remainder of the Resolution was so worded as to leave the matter open and to allow the United States Government time in which to see how things would turn out. The gentlemen in Washington had not long to wait, for hardly had the delegates to the Congress returned to their respective countries when the revelation of the grave difficulties of the Austrian Kreditanstalt began a period of unparalleled economic eruptions throughout Europe,[1] which, though it gave them "little time to see how things would turn out" forced Mr. Hoover's Administration to make a very drastic change in the traditional American attitude towards international indebtedness.

[1] On May 11, 1931, it was divulged that the Kreditanstalt, the leading bank in Austria, had suffered losses amounting to more than £4,000,000 in 1930. Despite the provision of new capital exceeding the amount of the losses, foreign creditors continued to withdraw their credits. The Austrian Government guaranteed the liabilities of the bank, and an international committee representing the leading central banks was formed to secure agreement among all the foreign creditors to continue their credits to the bank. On June 16th the Bank of England made a provisional interim advance of £4,486,000 at par to the Austrian National Bank pending negotiations for an international loan to the Government to provide it with funds for the guarantee of the liabilities of the Kreditanstalt. Difficulties over the Government guarantee demanded by the creditors caused the fall of the Government on June 16th. After long negotiations with the new Cabinet, an agreement was at last reached on November 28, 1931, as to the constitution and duties of the new executive committee of the Kredit-Anstalt, which was to consist of three Austrians and two foreigners.

CHAPTER II

THE STAR IN THE WEST[1]

1

HAVING negotiated the Young Plan, weathered the two Hague Conferences, and piloted the necessary Laws through a recalcitrant Reichstag in the face of grave popular opposition, the Müller Government resigned on March 27, 1930, and Dr. Brüning succeeded to the Chancellorship with a Cabinet based chiefly on support of his own Centre Party, the Social-Democrats, and the German Peoples' Party.[2]

Dr. Brüning came to the helm of the German ship of State when that vessel was beset with fierce storms both political and economic. The death of Herr Gustav Stresemann in October 1929 had removed the controlling influence which had so successfully guided the foreign policy of the country for the past seven years at the moment when it was most needed. His successor, Dr. Curtius, was not of the calibre to cope adequately with the difficulties which loomed ahead. It behoved the Chancellor to be to a very great degree his own Foreign Minister even before he actually assumed the portfolio in October 1931.

But the immediate problems were economic, and here, indeed, the Chancellor found a *damnosa hereditas* in the shape of an accumulated deficit of RM. 1,284,000,000 (totalling £64,200,000) from the years 1925–1930,[3] and was faced with

---

[1] Figures in this chapter are taken from the Report of the Basle Committee of Financial Experts (the Layton–Wiggin Report, August 18, 1931), the Report of the Special Advisory Committee, December 23, 1931, the *Economist*, June 13, 1931, and the *Bulletin of International News*, June 18, 1931 (vol. vii, no. 26).

[2] The Centre Party is entirely Catholic and derives much of its membership from the Christian Socialist Trade Unions.

[3] From 1926 onwards German expenditure had consistently exceeded revenue, a state of affairs to which the Agent-General had frequently drawn attention in his Annual Reports. One contributing cause of this development is the unsatisfactory financial relation of the States and Communes to the Reich

the prospect of a further deficit of RM. 700,000,000 (£35,000,000) for the year 1930–1931. Since by reason of opposition in the Reichstag no Budget had been voted by July, the Chancellor took the extreme step of advising the President to utilize his power under Article 48 of the Constitution of the Reich to prorogue the Reichstag and promulgate an Emergency Decree, designed, by the imposition of fresh taxation and economies, to produce RM. 543,000,000 (£27,150,000), and save, or otherwise gain, RM. 217,000,000 (£10,850,000).

The means of procuring the additional revenue and economies were as follows:[1]

1. A temporary decrease from $4\frac{1}{2}$ per cent. to $3\frac{1}{2}$ per cent. in unemployment contributions, together with certain reforms in the scheme's administration.

2. A special levy of $2\frac{1}{2}$ per cent. effective September 1930–April 1, 1931, on officials' salaries which exceeded RM. 2,000 per annum, after the reduction of RM. 20 per month in respect of each minor child.

3. A similar charge on recipients, other than widows and orphans of Reich and State pensions, on wages of public employees not insured against unemployment, and on 60 per cent. of the fees received by those members of the Supervisory Board of any undertaking who did not participate in the management.

4. A surcharge of 5 per cent. on the 1929 assessment to income-tax of incomes exceeding RM. 8,000 per annum.

5. A 10 per cent. surcharge on the income-tax of unmarried persons, and a reimposition of 25 per cent. by which the tax was reduced in 1927.

The continued trade depression rendered all calculations at fault, and whereas the July Decree had budgeted for 1,600,000 unemployed, the number at the close of the year had swelled to no less than 4,384,000, of which the number in receipt of benefit alone amounted to 2,500,000.

Continued shrinkage of trade and increase of unemployment, coupled with the diminished international confidence in the political stability of Germany which resulted from the Nazi

which, though it is responsible for raising most of the revenue, has little control over the expenditure.

An excellent study of the German economy and reparations has been contributed by Mr. Jules Mencken to the *Survey of International Affairs* for 1930 (see pp. 528–551).

[1] See the *Economist*, June 13, 1931.

and Communist gains in the September elections, produced towards the end of the year a situation in which recourse to further emergency measures became necessary. Accordingly, on December 1st a second Decree was issued, after a struggle in the Reichstag during its preliminary discussion, when a combined Nazi and Communist Motion for Repeal was rejected by 38 votes.[1]

The new Decree reduced by 6 per cent. the wages and salaries of Civil Servants above 1,500 marks (£75); the duty on beer was doubled, that on raw tobacco raised by 125 per cent., and smaller increases were imposed on cigarettes, cigars, etc. The income-tax on larger incomes was raised, and finally Budget expenditure was strictly limited for the next three years to RM. 10·6 milliards (£530,000,000). An understanding was reached with the Communes and States whereby they also reduced the salaries of their public employees, and the total anticipated saving to the Reich, States, and Communes under this head was RM. 480,000,000 (£24,000,000).

But, like the redoubtable Mrs. Partington, who attempted to keep the Atlantic Ocean at bay with a mop,[2] all the efforts and contrivances of the German Government to keep abreast of the rising tide of economic depression proved inadequate. During the first six months of 1931, although German imports fell off, her exports also fell to a great extent, and her commodity surplus (including deliveries in kind) though still favourable, decreased to RM. 1 milliard (£50,000,000) to which was added RM. 0·1 milliard (£5,000,000) for invisible exports. This failed to cover her external obligations (interest on commercial debts of RM. 0·4 milliard (£20,000,000) and reparations RM. 0·9 milliard (£45,000,000) by RM. 0·2 milliard (£100,000,000). In addition, there was also a very heavy drain on capital funds.[3]

Furthermore, a marked decrease of revenue derived from taxation, on the one hand, and increase of unemployment on

[1] The December Decree did not become operative until February 1, 1931.
[2] And to whom Sydney Smith, during his campaign for the Reform Bill, likened the House of Lords after their rejection of the Bill in 1831.
[3] See the Layton–Wiggin Report.

the other, demanded supplementary expenditure amounting to some RM. 418·2 million (£20·910 million), of which about RM. 300 million (£15,000,000) was directly due to unemployment.

It was inevitable that the alternative lay either in a foreign loan or in further taxation and economies. As the only State capable, at the moment, of lending money to Germany was France, it was particularly foolish of the German Foreign Office to throw the bombshell of the proposed Austro-German Customs Union into the French camp. This move, in March 1931, not only destroyed any hope of a foreign loan, but also alienated much foreign sympathy from Germany. It was the crowning blunder of Dr. Curtius's career.[1]

Based on the calculations of the December Decree the 1931 Budget was, at the beginning of June 1931, faced with the prospect of a deficit of RM. 940,000,000 (£47,000,000), and it was to meet this that Dr. Brüning made a supreme and final effort.[2] On June 6th there was issued a third Emergency Decree calculated to produce RM. 306,000,000 (£15,300,000) in economies, and RM. 268,000,000 (£13,400,000) in taxation. Economies included cuts in Departmental expenditure, a decrease in the rates of certain war pensions and a reduction of from 4 to 8 per cent. (in addition to the 6 per cent. imposed by the December Decree) in official salaries. The tax on sugar was doubled and that on mineral oils and petroleum increased.

Notwithstanding the above measures the Emergency Employment benefit (*Krisen-Fuersorge*) of RM. 245,000,000 (£12,250,000), and RM. 140,000,000 (£7,000,000) for provision of work, was still left uncovered. In an effort to meet this total a roughly graduated Crisis-Tax was introduced designed to yield the necessary RM. 385,000,000 (£19,250,000).[3]

---

[1] See below, p. 76.
[2] The deficit was made up as follows:
   Reich revenue deficit, RM. 495,000,000 (£24,750,000), to which must be added RM. 79,000,000 (£3,950,000) for supplementary expenditure, bringing the eventual total to RM. 574,000,000 (£28,700,000); allowance to States and Communes, RM. 440,000,000 (£22,000,000).
[3] Crisis-Tax (*Krisen-Steuer*) was intended to extend corresponding sacrifices to private employers, employees, members of professions, and independent workers. It was in two parts: (1) An additional tax graduated from 1 to 5 per

From this summary of the first of these Emergency Decrees covering the period December 1930–June 1931, it will be clear that the German people had been taxed to the utmost. Salaries of Civil Servants had been cut to a point 10 to 13 per cent. lower than during the years 1927–1930, and the salaries of Reichs Ministers had been decreased by 30 per cent. In addition, the amount being raised outside the Budget was equivalent to an additional levy of some 24s. per head per annum. The German Treasury had come to the end of its tether. The acute industrial depression and the diminished incomes of taxpayers had had their effect. It was imperative that some relief should be obtained, for the imposition of further taxation would not only certainly produce a serious political crisis, but might well result in an attempted *coup d'état* from the Right or Left. Indeed, had not Dr. Brüning, with the consent of the President, prorogued the Reichstag in March until the following October a crisis could not have been so long postponed, and the only alternative to Dr. Brüning was Herr Hitler and a Government of Repudiation or so all believed at that time.

Such was the situation on the eve of the Chequers Conference.

2

The original invitation extended to the German Chancellor and Foreign Minister by Mr. MacDonald to visit England was for the beginning of May, and the original topic of discussion had been disarmament. The political *brouhaha* caused by the proposed Austro-German Customs Union, however, occasioned the postponement of the visit until June 5th. By that date the subject of disarmament had been superseded in importance by the immediate problem of Germany's financial position.

No one could find fault with the tactics of Dr. Brüning. No one could accuse him of failing to take full advantage of the opportunities presented by the situation. For some weeks

cent. on wages and salaries from RM. 300 (£15) to RM. 3,000 (£150) a month; (2) an additional tax of from ¾ to 4 per cent. on annual incomes from RM. 3,600 (£180) to over RM. 1,000,000 (£50,000).

past he had been urgently advised to declare the inability of Germany to meet her reparation payments even without giving the 90 days' notice required under the Young Plan. Wiser counsels had deprecated the taking of so drastic a step (the effect of which on French public opinion could readily be guessed) until after the Chequers Conference. The Chancellor himself shared this view.

He therefore timed the publication in Berlin of the third Emergency Decree for the morning of June 6th, the day on which the conversations with the British Ministers at Chequers actually began. The Decree was accompanied by a Manifesto to the German people by President von Hindenburg, which, though it coupled an appeal for support and further sacrifice with a promise that this was the final effort of the Government to balance the Budget, was also in the nature of a notice to the world at large that Germany had reached a limit to her privations. It was, furthermore, a warning that the Decree represented the last straw which could be placed with any degree of safety upon the back of the German camel—a penultimate straw.

The Manifesto declared:

"We have made every effort to fulfil obligations resulting from a lost war. We have, too, made use of foreign help for this purpose to a large extent. That is no longer possible. The mobilization of the last forces and reserves of all sections of the population gives the German Government the right, and renders it its duty to its own people, to declare to the world: The limit of the privations which we can impose on our nation has been reached! The assumptions upon which the New (Young) Plan was based have been proved erroneous by the course taken by world developments. The alleviation, which it was the intention of all concerned that the New Plan should bring to the German nation and which at first it gave promise of doing, has not been brought by it. It is clear to the Government that the economic and financial situation of the Reich, which is menaced in the extreme, inevitably compels the relief of Germany from the intolerable reparation obligations. The economic recovery of the world is also involved."[1]

This, then, was the text of the discourse which Dr. Brüning delivered to his hearers at Chequers, and the sting was in the

[1] For full text of Manifesto see *Documents on International Affairs*, 1931, edited by J. W. Wheeler-Bennett (Oxford University Press, 1932), p. 111.

tail. It was not Germany alone, but Europe and the world
which was in danger. Was Europe about to commit suicide
for the sake of the Young Plan? Was the basis of the policy
of reparation to be changed from the capacity of the debtor
to pay, to the power of the creditor to extract? These were
the questions which required an answer in Berlin where the
Brüning Administration was already known as "The Starvation
Government."

At Chequers the German position was put to the British
Ministers as a frank admittance of self-evident facts. In no
sense was it in the nature of an ultimatum. The conversations
had no immediate result, yet they at least enabled those at
the head of affairs in this country to gain a first-hand knowledge
of the position which they could never have received from
ambassadorial dispatches and consular reports.[1]

The German Ministers left England on June 9th in the
North German Lloyd liner *Europa*. On board they found the
American Ambassador in Berlin, Mr. Sackett, who had
abandoned his original intention of disembarking at Cherbourg
in order to meet the Chancellor at Southampton. They dined
and conferred together on board, and on arrival at Bremerhaven
next day Mr. Sackett accompanied the Chancellor's party in
the special train. So that on his arrival in Berlin Dr. Brüning
was fully conversant with the official view in Washington. At
the moment this was not encouraging.

The Chancellor at once found himself in the vortex of financial
and political crises. The condition of Germany had already
occasioned withdrawals from the Reichsbank, which had lost
RM. 200,000,000 (£10,000,000) in gold and foreign exchanges
during the first week of June, and this drain continued. Moreover, the German Peoples' Party, representative chiefly of big
industrial interests, took the opportunity of exploiting the
unpopularity of the latest Emergency Decree to press for the

---

[1] The information given to the British Ministers at Chequers led to their
taking up the question of the German situation, in co-operation with officials
of the Treasury and the Bank of England, with the United States, and
materially contributed to the subsequent proposals made by Mr. Hoover
on June 20th.

dropping of Dr. Curtius (their own nominee) and Dr. Wirth from the Cabinet and its reconstruction further to the Right.[1] As an alternative they threatened to join with the Nazis, Nationalists, and Communists in demanding the immediate convocation of the Reichstag to discuss the Decree before it became operative on July 1st. It was known that Dr. Brüning would resign rather than do this, and in this case it was hoped to place an "Economic Dictatorship" at the head of affairs.[2]

It had been confidently hoped that the Government would declare a moratorium on its external indebtedness as soon as the Chancellor arrived in Berlin, and this hope had in part mitigated the criticism of the Decree. The fact that he returned from the Chequers Conference empty handed intensified the opposition against him. For a week the crisis dominated Berlin, rumours were rife, officials anxious. Would Dr. Brüning resign? What would happen then? Were the Nazis planning a *coup*? Could the Reichswehr be trusted? These, and many other queries, were the daily bread of the foreign observers in the days of that critical week. An end was put to the immediate anxiety on June 16th, when the Chancellor met the Standing Committee of the Reichstag and won two decisive victories. The first involved the reassembly of the Reichstag, and was won against the united opposition of the Nationalists, the Nazis, the Communists, and the German Peoples' Party; the second was gained in face of the opposition of these same four parties, with the Social Democrats in support, in refusing similarly to convene the Budget Committee.

For the moment the situation was eased, but this demonstration of lack of national unity in the face of acute national danger dealt a heavy blow to foreign confidence in Germany. The week of crisis cost the Reichsbank a further milliard of

[1] The German Peoples' Party had, since the death of Herr Stresemann, moved, under the leadership of Dr. Dingeldey and General von Seeckt, progressively towards the Right, a process which was completed in August 1931, when the Party joined with the National Opposition and the Communists in supporting the Stalhelm Referendum for the Prussian elections.
[2] Of which the potential membership was said to be Dr. Schacht, Herr Krupp von Bohlen, Herr Springorum, the steel magnates; Herr Henckel, the champagne manufacturer; Dr. Vögler, who had resigned from the Young Committee in 1929; and General von Seeckt.

marks in withdrawals, which tended to increase rather than diminish in volume.

Yet it is extraordinary to note how little appreciation there was of the gravity of the situation. For example, on June 5th, Berlin announced officially that the statement made recently in a London newspaper as to Germany's inability in the near future to continue reparation payments was "a pure invention and totally devoid of foundation." Yet on the following day President von Hindenburg's Manifesto said just this. In Paris, M. Briand, speaking on June 9th in the Chamber, said of the Young Plan, "*il ne peut pas être question de le déchirer ni de le modifier. Il a le caractère d'une Convention définitive,*" and within a month that same Plan had been modified with the consent of France herself. The correspondent of a London weekly, writing from Berlin on June 11th, stated *à propos* of the losses of the Reichsbank in the first week of June, "The position of the Reichsbank is so strong that the withdrawals are causing no embarrassment"; yet within a fortnight it was necessary for an international rediscount credit of £20,000,000 to be placed at the disposal of the Reichsbank "to help it over the end of the month." Finally, in Washington, the Under-Secretary of State was announcing as late as June 14th that before taking any action the United States must be convinced that Germany's financial and social structure was in danger of complete collapse. Moreover, President Hoover, on the following day, speaking in the heart of the Middle West, was re-emphasizing the theory he had advanced to the International Chamber of Commerce in May, namely, that the basic causes of the world-wide depression were attributable to "the malign inheritance in Europe of the Great War," and had nothing to do with America. The change of official attitude in this latter country was the most striking of all.

The feeling was general throughout Germany that a complete financial collapse was inevitable within a few days, and if the declaration of a moratorium could be postponed until July 1st, that was the latest date possible. The stock-market fell to an alarming extent and the German people went to

bed on Saturday, June 20th, with a sense of impending
catastrophe which had never seemed so near since July 1914.
They awoke on Sunday, June 21st, to the reading of the
Extrablatt issued to convey to the public the news of the
Hoover Proposal.

The Star in the West had risen.

3

History has been provided with few such examples of complete and rapid political *volte-face* as that achieved by President
Hoover between June 15 and 20, 1931. On the first of these
dates he was telling his Indianapolis audience that both the
causes and the cure of the world-wide economic depression
lay outside America. On the second, he took a step which was
not only a complete negation of this theory, but which for the
moment reversed the policy of the United States towards
international indebtedness.

Since its "withdrawal" from Europe, as a result of the refusal
to ratify the Treaty of Versailles, the United States had
studiously refused to regard international war debts as a whole.
There were on the one hand the reparation payments due to
the Allies from Germany and the debts contracted between
the Allied Powers themselves, and on the other there were the
debts owed by the Allied Powers to the Associated Power,
America, who had raised the necessary funds by issuing Liberty
Loan Bonds to the American public. In the first of these
categories the United States would admit no interest at all.
If Germany or the Allied Powers defaulted amongst themselves, *tant pis pour eux*, but this must not interfere with the
Allied payments to America.

The moral argument against this attitude, i.e. that the loans
made by America constituted the more substantial part of her
contribution to the Allied victory of 1918, may be discarded
for political purposes. But what cannot be overlooked is the
fact that the Debt Funding Agreements which the majority of
the Allied Powers negotiated with the United States from

1925–1928[1] were only possible of conclusion after the reparation problem had been placed on a business basis by the Dawes Plan of 1924. These agreements had been based, certainly as far as the European negotiators were concerned, on Germany's capacity to pay, and if that broke down their own capacity ceased also.

There is another and more recent aspect of the American attitude towards war debts, and their connection with disarmament. For some considerable time there had been a large and influential section of American opinion which held that if the European nations would economize on their war estimates, they could not only balance their budgets but meet the payments of the American debts also, and this view had been expressed by the President to the International Chamber of Commerce. There were even those who would meet a cut in armament budgets by a corresponding cut in debt payments; but there was strong and justifiable opposition to any cancellation or revision of war debts by the United States which would release funds for further expenditure on European armaments.

All these arguments had been considered and debated during the Washington Congress of the International Chamber in May, but perhaps the most cogent argument advanced against any immediate action by the United States was that communicated privately and unofficially to members of the Congress; namely, that any move towards modification of the attitude of the United States towards war debts would have to be preluded by an intensive campaign for the education of American public opinion. With this consideration in mind the rapidity of Mr. Hoover's movements between June 18th and 20th is the more remarkable.

On June 14th the President left Washington to tour the Middle West. A plan had been forming in his mind as early as June 5th, when he had discussed it informally with Secretaries Mellon and Stimson on the eve of the former's departure

[1] The Anglo-American Debt Agreement was signed in 1923 and is in a class by itself.

for Europe. Later, on June 8th, he had even sought the opinion of the Cabinet upon it.[1] But there is no indication at the time of Mr. Hoover's departure, nor indeed for some time after, that the Administration had any intention of taking any immediate action. Certainly when Ambassador Sackett sailed from New York in the *Europa* on June 4th, he had no message of hope to give to Dr. Brüning when he joined the Chancellor's party on the 9th; and as late as June 14th, that is to say, in the midst of the critical week in Berlin, when withdrawals of American credits were daily draining the Reichsbank's store of gold, and the political fate of Germany was hovering in the balance, the Under-Secretary of State expressed the view that in the event of a serious threat of catastrophe in Germany, the Administration might be compelled to consider the advisability of making a temporary change in its attitude towards war debts, but that before any action could be taken, evidence must be forthcoming that the financial and social structure of Germany was in danger of complete collapse. Though it might be asked what further evidence the Administration required, the general tone of the statement was of one envisaging an almost remote contingency.

Mr. Hoover was profoundly shocked and disturbed at the signs of very real distress in the Middle West with which he met during his tour. This would seem to have brought home to him the extent of the depression in his own country,[2] and convinced him of the urgency of remedying these conditions. On his return to Washington on June 18th, the President found awaiting him reports from Mr. Andrew Mellon, United States Secretary of the Treasury, on the conversations which

[1] A group consisting of Mr. Owen D. Young, Mr. Eugene Meyer, Mr. Ogden Mills, Mr. Mellon, Mr. Harris, and others had been for some time past urging some such action on the President.

[2] With a singularly Puckish medley of irony and paradox, Nature had ordained that 1931 was to be a year of bumper crops and harvests. In America immense surpluses of wheat and cotton accumulated, but the market dropped lower and lower. Wheat in Chicago at one moment touched c. 44⅝ per bushel, while cotton fell to c. 5·32 per lb. Rather than sell at those prices, farmers poured their surplus grain into the street, or, in some cases, used it as a means of barter. Similarly, planters were officially advised to burn a third of their cotton crop.

he had held in London with Mr. MacDonald, Mr. Arthur Henderson, and Mr. Montagu Norman, Governor of the Bank of England. During these conversations the situation as outlined by Dr. Brüning at Chequers was placed before Mr. Mellon, together with the more recent developments in Berlin, and all of this was faithfully reported to the President.

Mr. Mellon's reports would seem to have provided the Administration with the necessary amount of conviction that, in the words of the Under-Secretary of State, "the financial and social structure of Germany was in danger of complete collapse," and that the vast commitments and interests of the United States, in that country, including some $1,250,000,000 in short-term credits and long-term loans estimated to amount in the aggregate to $4,000 million, were endangered. Moreover, if Germany were allowed to collapse, the rot would not end there, other of those foreign markets so essential for America's well-being would be closed also, and the distress in the Middle West, which had so shocked the President, would be greatly increased.[1]

Mr. Hoover decided to move, and move quickly. On the evening of his return, Thursday, June 18th, he held a long conversation with Mr. Stimson, the Secretary of State, and during the next day and Saturday got into touch, either directly or by telephone, with Republican and Democratic leaders in both Houses of Congress. He also conferred by transatlantic telephone with Mr. Mellon, who confirmed the grave tenor of his reports and emphasized the need for swift action. A series of Cabinet meetings were held during these two days, and the Ambassadors of various foreign States were called into conference.

---

[1] It is interesting to speculate as to why it was left to Mr. Mellon to supply the final evidence at the eleventh hour. Had the American Embassy in Berlin not realized the steadily increasing gravity of the situation? Or was the State Department unable to appreciate the importance of the reports sent to it? There was ample evidence at the time of Dr. Brüning's return to Berlin on June 10th that "the financial and social structure of Germany was in danger of complete collapse," and had the Hoover Proposal been antedated by only a week it would undoubtedly have had a very much more beneficial effect, and would have achieved more than a tardy recognition that default was inevitable.

The step which the President was contemplating was a bold one, involving as it did the complete reversal of the ten-year-old policy of the United States. It was essential therefore that the leaders of the political parties should be acquainted with, and, if possible, their approval gained for, the proposed action in advance. Moreover, the exigencies of the situation were such as to preclude the intensive educational campaign without which it was said that any modification of the traditional attitude of the United States could not take place,[1] and in lieu of this the facts must be presented to the American public from the proper angle.

These facts briefly were as follows: unless immediate relief were forthcoming, the collapse of Germany was inevitable, in which case American interests in that country would be endangered. Some of the foremost financial houses and banks of New York were threatened with bankruptcy in the event of a wholesale default by Germany, and it was imperative that immediate and drastic action must be taken by the United States.

On the evening of June 19th, after twenty-four hours of almost continuous negotiation, President Hoover felt that he had reached a point where a preliminary statement might be of value. In addition, his negotiations with so many parties had set on foot a crop of rumours which it was as well to scotch at the outset. The President therefore announced that he had conferred with the leaders of both political parties

"with regard to certain steps we might take to assist in economic recovery both here and abroad. The conversations have been particularly directed towards strengthening the situation in Germany. No definite plans or conclusions have been arrived at. . . . Any statement of any plan or method is wholly speculative, and is not warranted by the facts."

The reaction of the American Press to this preliminary *ballon d'essai* was anxiously awaited at the White House. On

[1] Those who had held this view have been amply justified during the Congressional debate on the ratification of the Hoover Moratorium in December 1931. Had the consent of Congress been required before putting the Moratorium into being instead of afterwards, it would never have been obtained. It was only extorted in the face of a *de facto* situation.

the whole it was not unfavourable, and the feeling was voiced very representatively by the *New York Times* on June 20th in a leader entitled "No Splendid Isolation," in which it welcomed and approved the tone of the Presidential statement:

"We cannot stand apart and think we shall suffer no harm. Our commitments abroad are too vast for that, too vital the need of foreign trade for our congested producer of raw materials and food and manufactured articles. It is to-day as if there was but a single nervous system for the entire civilized world. A 'short' at one exposed filament instantly sends tremors running through the whole framework."

The favourable reception by the Press and the successful progress made in his consultations with political leaders, which continued throughout the day and were described as "most gratifying," assured Mr. Hoover that he was at last in a sufficiently strong position to take the final step. Indeed, this was essential, for further secrecy was impossible, and the situation in Germany had become so acute that if external relief did not arrive immediately financial collapse and political chaos were inevitable.

Before taking the final step Mr. Hoover informed the German Chargé d'Affaires, Rudolf Leitner, that he must receive from some high and impartial authority in Germany an appeal for assistance which would justify his action in certain quarters. A cable was therefore sent to President Hoover by President von Hindenburg on June 20th, and though it actually arrived just after the President had made public his proposal, it served its turn later on the course of the Senate debates on ratification.[1]

On the evening of June 20, 1931, therefore, President Hoover made "the boldest, most far-reaching, and swiftest stroke of his whole career,"[2] and one which Mr. MacDonald at the London Conference described as "an act of rare courage and statesmanship." The President proposed:[3]

"The postponement during one year of all payments on inter-Governmental debts, reparations, and relief debts, both principal and

---

[1] For text see *Documents on International Affairs*, 1931, p. 114.
[2] *The Times*, June 22, 1931.
[3] For text see *Documents on International Affairs*, 1931, p. 115.

interest, of course not including the obligations of Governments held by private parties. Subject to confirmation by Congress, the American Government will postpone all payments upon the debts of foreign Governments to the American Government payable during the fiscal year beginning July next, conditional on a like postponement for one year of all payments on inter-Governmental debts owing to the important creditor Powers."

Herein, as far as Europe was concerned, lay the meat of the proposal. But this was only half the President's task, and the remainder of the statement was devoted to an explanation intended for American public opinion, of the reasons for the action taken. Mr. Hoover referred to the world-wide depression which had affected the countries of Europe "more severely than our own" and to the burden of war debts, which, "supportable in normal times, weighs heavily in the midst of this depression." Various factors such as the fall in foreign commodities, the lack of confidence, and the abnormal drain of gold to the United States, had diminished the buying power of other States for American exports, and were the underlying causes of unemployment and lower prices to farmers in the United States.

"The essence of this proposition is to give time to permit the debtor countries to recover their national prosperity. I am suggesting to the American people that they be wise creditors in their own interest and be good neighbours."

Then followed an emphatic assurance that the President did not approve "in any remote sense, the cancellation of debts to the United States of America." But the basis of the debt settlements was "the capacity, under normal conditions, of the debtor to pay." The situation then existing was abnormal, and the President continued:

"I am sure that the American people have no desire to attempt to extract any ounce beyond the capacity to pay, and it is our view that broad vision requires our Government to recognize the situation as it exists. This course of action is entirely consistent with the policy we have hitherto pursued."

The final paragraphs of the Presidential statement contained a reminder that the United States had nothing to do with reparations and that it was not merely a European problem which was being discussed, but a question of world prosperity, and concluded with an expression of hope—an assurance to the American people that the inter-relationship of disarmament and war debts had not been ignored—that

"inasmuch as the burden of competitive armaments has contributed to bring about this depression, we trust that, by this evidence of our desire to assist, we shall have contributed to the goodwill which is so necessary to a solution of this major problem."[1]

The importance of this statement can scarcely be exaggerated. Although Mr. Hoover pled consistency with previous policy and reaffirmed that the United States had nothing to do with reparations, he had nevertheless renounced on behalf of the American people any "desire to extract any ounce beyond the capacity to pay," and had at the same time accorded a tacit recognition to the fact that this capacity to pay on the part of Europe was dependent on a similar capacity to pay on the part of Germany.

The reaction of Great Britain, Italy and Germany to Mr. Hoover's offer, in the first flush of its enthusiasm and pleasure, was one of unmixed relief, and this was evidenced in the favourable response of stock-markets in every capital to a remarkable degree, the general rise being maintained for some days. This did much to mitigate, for the time being at least, any opposition to the proposal in the United States, where it was agreed that both psychologically and materially the actual gain from the improved conditions on 'change more than covered the loss of the actual sum of money (some £50,000,000) the receipt of which by the United States had been postponed under the Hoover Plan.

Mr. Hoover's own stock rose enormously on the world exchange of public opinion, where the courage of his action gained the more general recognition and approbation because of his lost popularity in the United States, the comparative proximity of the party nominations to the Presidential elections, the deficit on the coming Budget, and the necessity of making up by taxation the deficiency of £50,000,000 of war debts.

To Germany the Hoover proposal came like a reprieve to a condemned man on the gallows, and the Chancellor hastened on June 23rd to express his gratitude to the President and his willingness to discuss matters with French statesmen. The political situation had temporarily improved and the financial panic was stayed when, on June 25th, it was announced that a rediscount credit of £20,000,000, in which the Bank for International Settlements, the Federal Revenue Bank of New York, and the Banks of England and France had participated, had been placed at the disposal of the Reichsbank on June 16th to meet payments at the end of the month.

It almost seemed as though a new era was opening for Germany, especially as within a week's time the Hoover proposal had been accepted by Great Britain, the Dominions and India, Italy and Japan.[1]

4

But in this chorus of approval there was a discord of some voices in a major key. France, Belgium, Greece, and Yugoslavia failed to harmonize in the Hoover symphony. To take them in the reverse order: Yugoslavia complained that to accept the proposal would be to sacrifice 10 per cent. of her Budget, and felt that this "could not be inherent in the intentions of its initiator."[2] The Greek Government pointed out that, like

---

[1] British approval was given on June 22nd, and the Italian on June 24th. Italy did more than accept. She put the moratorium into virtual operation on July 1st without waiting for the result of the Franco-American negotiations then in progress in Paris. On June 30th the Italian Government informed those States from whom payments to Italy were due that, pending further developments, it did not expect any payments from them, and those to whom Italian payments were due that the amount was being put aside. In view of the fact that Japan owed no debts to the United States, no official communication was sent to her from Washington, but it was announced on June 26th that the Japanese Cabinet cordially welcomed President Hoover's proposal and was prepared to co-operate in putting it into operation.
[2] It was estimated that the difference to the Yugoslav Budget would be 406 million dinars (reparation receipts), less 176 million dinars (debt payments) = 230 million dinars (approximately £836,000).

Yugoslavia, its reparation receipts were derived mainly from non-German sources and suggested that they should be excluded from the Hoover Proposal.[1] Belgium made a reservation regarding the German Marks agreement of July 12, 1929,[2] and France expressed the opinion that whilst most laudable in intent, the arrangement of an "all in" war-debt moratorium was not quite so simple as Mr. Hoover seemed to think. Public and official opinion in France were at once on their guard against any arrangement which might impair the integrity of the Young Plan, and herein lay the rift in the lute.[3]

The Hoover Proposal's essential value lay in its psychological effect. With the object of ensuring this, Mr. Stimson issued on June 22nd an appeal for speed in accepting. He explained that in view of this consideration the delay caused by the summoning of an International Conference to discuss the proposal would only nullify its benefit. He also stated that the American offer was open only on condition that it was accepted by every one of the Governments concerned. The impression gained in France from this somewhat blunt statement was that the United States was attempting to force them to accept an ultimatum. France already felt aggrieved that she had not been consulted before the Plan was announced. Furthermore, the fact that all doubt as to the inclusion in the Proposal of the unconditional, as well as of the conditional annuities, had been removed by an authoritative announcement to this effect, had already damped the initial approval which the French Government had telegraphed to Washington, as soon as the first news of the Plan arrived. It also had its bearing upon the "sympathetic examination" which had been promised. In order to counteract this impression Mr. Stimson issued a further

---

[1] In subsequent negotiations in London, Greece was persuaded to forgo all her reparation receipts, both German and non-German, with the exception of those payments made by Hungary referring to damages during the period in which Greece was neutral.

[2] It was agreed by the London Committee of Experts that the payments due from Germany to Belgium under this agreement "should not be interrupted."

[3] The following account of the negotiations which resulted in the Franco-American Agreement of July 6, 1931, is reprinted in part from an article in the *Bulletin of International News*, July 2, 1931 (vol. viii, no. 1).

statement on June 24th, before the French reply had been received, in which he referred to the "many details which must be filled in after careful study, and conversations" which must "necessarily be carried on in the regular way through diplomatic channels and not through the Press." Though something was done by this announcement to sooth French susceptibilities somewhat ruffled by the informal method of announcement, it early became apparent that the knowledge of the inclusion in the plan of the unconditional portion of reparations had altered the French attitude to the scheme.

Suggestions appeared in the *Temps* that if America found it inadmissible that debts owing to her, for the continuance of a war waged in a common cause, should not be paid, *a fortiori*, France found it inadmissible that reparations due to her, to cover actual damage suffered by her, should not be paid. The *Temps* went on to suggest that a formula might be found to maintain intact the actual payments of the unconditional annuity while indirectly meeting German needs. The general feeling was that there should be no tampering with the Young Plan. The principle of reparation payments had been embodied in the peace treaty, and, it was pointed out, the large sums expended by France for the restoration of her devastated areas and the compensation of war victims had been specially considered when the Young Plan was drawn up. In addition to these facts, the actual financial sacrifice entailed was noted, and the fact that the chief burden of the sacrifice would fall on France was unfavourably commented upon.

On June 24th the text of the French reply to Mr. Hoover was finally approved at a meeting of the Cabinet and dispatched to the French Ambassador at Washington. Pending the publication of the text complete unanimity was apparent in the comments of the French Press to the effect that the Young Plan should be preserved as

"the sole remaining guarantee for the ultimate reimbursement of France for money provided amid the direct financial difficulties and actually spent in restoring war damage."

M. Léon Blum, writing in the *Populaire*, the official Socialist paper, declared:

"If it is proposed, either directly or indirectly, now or in the future, to wreck the principle of reparations and the obligations thereby implied, then we are obliged to say 'No.' "

A resolution to the effect that the essential principle of the right to reparations should be respected and should be harmonized with the needs of European solidarity was passed at a Socialist-Radical Party meeting.

In the afternoon of June 26th the French Chamber met to hear and discuss the text of the Government's Note to the United States. It had already met in the morning, when expenditure amounting to some £19,000,000 for the completion of the fortifications on the Eastern Frontier had been passed. M. Laval read the Note, which opened with an expression of cordial agreement with the high sentiments which had inspired the Proposal, and went on to refer to the concessions already made by France to Germany—the successive reductions in the German debt, the evacuation of the Rhineland in exchange for the complete and final settlement of reparations, and the present sacrifice which was asked. In order to meet the suggestion of President Hoover the French Government was prepared —subject to the approval of the French Parliament—"that France shall refrain as a provisional measure and during a period of one year from retaining any payment it shall receive from the Reich."

The Note proceeded to refer to the Young Plan and the "solemnity by which it recognized the final and non-postponable annuities, by which the necessary permanence of the principle of reparations was shown." If, in the proposed suspension of payments, the unconditional were treated in the same way as the postponable annuities "there would be a grave risk of shaking confidence in the value of signatures and contracts."

"To suspend the German payments of the unconditional annuity, even though the service of the Young Plan Bonds already placed continues, would run directly counter to a fundamental principle and the stipulations expressly made. The Government therefore feels that

moral considerations of the highest order demand that, even during
the period of delay suggested by President Hoover, the payment of
the unconditional annuity shall in no way be deferred."

The French Government, the Note continued, was anxious to
collaborate to the widest extent in any measure taken to
alleviate the present crisis, but considered that it should point
out that "a general suspension of payments by itself would
offer an insufficient remedy." Restrictions of credit and the
withdrawal of foreign funds were largely the causes of the
crisis, and the solution of Germany's difficulties seemed to lie
not "only in a diminution of the Budget charges of the Reich,
but also in an extension of credit."

"For this reason the French Government declared itself prepared, if
Parliament approves, to put at the disposal of the Bank for International Settlements a sum equal to the French share of one year's unconditional annuity, except for such sums as may be necessary for the
fulfilment of the remaining contracts for deliveries in kind now in
process of execution, which should themselves be of help to Germany
on the economic side.

". . . The sums thus paid to the Bank for International Settlements
can be used immediately for the improvement of German credit and
of the credit also of the countries of Central Europe, notably those in
which the suspension of the execution of the Young Plan for a year
might lead to economic or financial difficulties. It goes without saying
that the sums thus used would be released at the end of the period
of one year suggested as the limit of the provisional suspension of the
Young Plan.

"The French Government also considers that all necessary precautions
should be taken that these sums, as well as those savings which result
from reductions in the Budget of the Reich as the result of the year's
suspension, shall be used only for economic purposes, measures being
taken to prevent the financing of dumping. Finally, it would be advisable
to arrange before the expiry of the period of one year that there should
be an examination of the measures to be taken by Germany for the
resumption of payments. The proposals of the French Government,
and such adjustments as will be suggested by the putting into effect
of the American proposal, which will necessarily be the subject of a
later exchange of views, appear to be perfectly compatible with the
dominating idea of President Hoover's proposal."

The penultimate paragraph of the Note referred to the charges
for the restoration of the devastated regions which are left
uncovered during the period of suspension and to the fact that

the French public debt had attained an amount four times greater than that of the Reich, and that "French effort towards financial re-establishment pursued and realized with her own resources for a period of four years, must not be endangered."

The Reply concluded with an affirmation of solidarity between the French and United States Republics.

"They have the right to hope that their international goodwill will be repaid by respect for treaties and the restoration of confidence between peoples—both essential to the future of peace."

A stormy debate ensued and it was not until half-past six on Saturday morning, June 27th, after an all-night sitting, that the Chamber eventually approved the text of the Government's reply by 386 votes to 189, in the form of a resolution that

"the Chamber, approving the French Government's reply to the proposal of the President of the United States, relies upon it to assure both the intangibility of the unconditional annuities agreed to at the Hague by the Powers signatory to the Young Plan, and the requirements of a policy of peace and economic co-operation."

The Government had to struggle hard for victory, and was only saved from defeat by the last-minute decision of the Socialists, who voted solidly for it.[1]

On June 30th the Senate approved the text of the Reply by 197 votes in favour to 5 against, while drawing attention to the fact that

" . . . the respect for treaties and conventions constitutes the sole sound basis of international relations," and recalling "the sacrifices and concessions of every kind consented to by France during the last 13 years for the maintenance of the peace of the world and for the re-establishment of European concord and economic life. . . . "

During the debates the following points indicative of French opinion emerged. In the first place there was a feeling that the Plan was conceived and launched after Anglo-American-German conversations from which France was excluded, and that there appeared to have been an attempt to force France

---

[1] This last-moment decision of the French Socialists to support the Government was greatly influenced by the advice of Dr. Breitscheid, a leader of the German Social-Democrat Party and of the Labour and Socialist International.

to subscribe to such a plan without proper consideration, thereby depriving her of the opportunity of gaining the credit of being generous. Secondly, France had saved herself by her thrift and was now asked to save Germany from the consequences of her extravagances, there being a doubt as to whether the remedy suggested would be effective. Thirdly, there was the suspicion that Germany might use the money saved for new armaments[1]—and successive Nazi and Stahlhelm demonstrations had alarmed French opinion—or for financing a new economic policy of dumping. Lastly, there was the thought that France, who suffered so much at the hands of Germany in the war, was now being asked to rescue her, and that the method suggested involved the violation of the sanctity of contractual obligations. The Young Plan, as the French Note pointed out, was regarded by France as her last remaining guarantee, and it was feared that if it were once tampered with, a disastrous precedent would be set up which might lead eventually from temporary to complete suspension.

The receipt of the French Note caused considerable disappointment in Washington, and in making public its text on June 26th, Mr. Stimson issued a statement which for the time being was intended to take the place of an official reply. While emphasizing, in view of the expressed concern of the French Government, the fact that the President's Plan did not propose the reconsideration of any international agreements, the official statement continued that there were suggestions contained in the French Note regarding the method by which postponement of payments was to be accomplished, which did not coincide with the full measure of relief to the debtor nations envisaged in the President's Proposal. The suggestions must be subject to further discussion with a view to modification.

Mr. Mellon had crossed from London to Paris on the day prior to this statement, and on the morning of June 27th, together with the United States Ambassador, Mr. Walter

---

[1] To meet this objection, Dr. Brüning sent a note on July 2nd to the United States Government giving an assurance that the money saved by the suspension of reparation payments would not be applied in any way to increasing Germany's military strength.

Edge, began discussions with M. Laval, M. Flandin (Minister
of Finance), and M. Briand, who had been empowered by the
vote of the Chamber, taken early that same morning, to enter
into negotiations. On the same day Mr. Stimson sailed from
New York for Europe.

The course of the Paris negotiations was not a smooth one,
and on several occasions draft agreements submitted by cable
and telephone to Mr. Hoover were rejected by him. Uneasiness
of public opinion in America caused Mr. Castle, Under-Secretary
of State, to state authoritatively on June 29th that no agreement had been reached and that no proposals would be accepted
which did not fall completely within the spirit and purpose of
the President's offer. On the following day the French Government secured a vote of confidence in the Senate in a debate,
during which M. Laval described the situation as the most
delicate which had arisen since the war, adding: "Reparations
must not be called in question. The Young Plan and the Hague
Agreements must be maintained; they represent the complete
and final settlement of reparations."

July 1st, the date set by Mr. Hoover for the coming into
force of the moratorium, came and went without agreement
being reached, but on that day the American negotiators
presented a memorandum to their French colleagues which
had the effect of crystallizing the situation somewhat. The
Memorandum stressed the psychological value of the Plan and
pointed out that it was intended to benefit the whole world,
and should be considered in this larger sense rather than in
terms of dollars and cents. It mentioned the two fundamental
points on which the two Governments agreed: firstly, that
France would forgo for one year the retention of all payments
from Germany, and, secondly, that "while affording complete
relief to Germany" the principle of the continuity of the unconditional annuities should be preserved by arranging for these
annuities to be paid into the Bank for International Settlements
and immediately reloaned to Germany.

There were, however, four points of difference, as follows:

1. The French proposal to reloan the equivalent of the

unconditional annuities to German industrial firms, not to German Government.

2. The French suggestion that the Bank for International Settlements should reloan these sums to other countries of Central Europe besides Germany. (This, it was pointed out, violated the principle of the suspension of all inter-Governmental debts as Germany would have to pay into the Bank a sum of which the complete total would not be reloaned to her.)

The United States Government was absolutely definite in its objection to these two points. There remained—

3. The period during which the suspended payments should be refunded. (The United States Government suggested a period of twenty-five years, but was willing to negotiate for a shorter period on the basis of the French proposal that no repayments should be made for the next two years.)

4. The question of the Guarantee Fund of RM. 500,000,000, which France was obliged[1] to pay into the Bank for International Settlements in the event of a German moratorium for the purpose of relieving other creditors during the period

[1] The provision in the Young Plan for the establishment of a Guarantee Fund is included in Annexes VII and VIII. In Annex VII it is recommended by the experts responsible for drawing up the Plan that out of the unconditional annuity of RM. 660,000,000 the amount of RM. 500,000,000 shall be allocated to France, subject to the provision of a Guarantee Fund by the French Government in accordance with the arrangements set out in Annex VIII.

Paragraph 3 of Annex VIII states: "On the coming into force of this plan France will give to the Bank for International Settlements an undertaking to deposit in a Trust Fund, on the demand of the Bank for International Settlements, foreign currency to a total value of RM. 500,000,000."

Paragraph 5 of Annex VIII explains the use to which this Guarantee Fund, on which interest at the maximum current rate offered by the Bank for International Settlements for long-term deposits is paid, is to be put.

Upon postponement of transfer of any payment due from Germany, the Bank for International Settlements shall take the following steps:

(a) Offer to the creditors, other than France, *devisen* up to the amount necessary (but not exceeding RM. 500,000,000, divided if necessary proportionately) to ensure to each of them receipts in *devisen* equal to the amounts they would have received had the non-postponable annuity been distributed in the same proportions as the total annuity.

(b) Debit the Trust Fund with the amount of *devisen* actually utilized.

(c) Receive from each creditor in exchange for *devisen* accepted under paragraph (a) an assignment in favour of the Trust Fund of an equivalent amount of the annuity, transfer of which has been postponed.

Paragraph 6 provides that when Germany effectively transfers the postponed amounts, the Bank will credit to the Trust Fund its share thereof.

of the suspension of postponable annuities. (The United States Government took serious exception to the French suggestion that the Funds paid into the Bank and reloaned to Germany during the suspension period should be credited to the Guarantee Fund, "just as if France had actually made the deposit, thus relieving France of any future obligations in respect of the Guarantee Fund." The suggestion was unacceptable, as it involved a substantial departure "from not only the spirit but the substance of the President's offer," and seemed to "seriously impair the spirit of the declaration of France that she wishes no benefit from the payment.")

The final paragraphs contained a plain warning to France that the failure of the Hoover Plan would unquestionably result in Germany's declaring a moratorium under the Young Plan, and France was urged to compare the sacrifices which she was now called upon to make voluntarily with the state of affairs which would exist if the Plan broke down.[1] It concluded with an appeal to France to help to find a means to remove these differences.

The American Memorandum had the effect of bringing matters definitely to a head, and there followed some days of hectic and secret negotiations, during which the only point which emerged was that the American representatives were prepared to concede the maintenance of the principle that payment by Germany of the unconditional annuities under the Young Plan should continue, provided that the relief to Germany should be real and complete during the limited period contemplated.[2]

[1] Had the Young Plan been allowed to break down and the Hoover moratorium not been in operation, France would have suffered a much greater loss, even if in turn she had invoked the moratorium clauses in her debt agreements with Great Britain and the United States. For these clauses only provide for a partial postponement—in the case of Great Britain to the amount of not more than one-half of any half-yearly instalment for not more than three years, and in the case of the United States to that portion of any half-yearly instalment which exceeds £4,000,000 for not more than three years.

[2] During the period of these negotiations the French Senate was indulging in an outbreak of jingoism. On July 2nd it rejected the Government proposals for the naval construction programme, which had been cut by the Chamber by more than 50 per cent. and totalled some £4,000,000 instead of £8,799,680 as originally proposed. The Senate also adopted a motion calling on the

Finally, on July 5th, after prolonged discussions between the negotiators themselves and the French Council of Ministers, and a dramatic personal appeal by Mr. Hoover by telephone, the latter body approved the text of a statement giving the outline of the arrangements arrived at with Mr. Mellon and Ambassador Edge. On reading it neither of the latter felt that it represented faithfully their views on all points, and modifications were suggested. These were accepted by M. Laval, and the amended draft was cabled to Washington for the President's approval. The main points in the draft were as follows:

"1. France renounces all German payments for one year, while the principle of the continuity of the payments of the unconditional annuity is recognized, and complete assistance is given to Germany.

"The U.S. consider that this point is settled by the stipulation laying down that the payments received from the German Railways shall be put at the disposal of the Railways on the following conditions:

"The payments shall be effected as before, and the payments destined for the different beneficiaries shall be returned to the German Railways for such use as they may judge necessary, including direct and indirect loan to the German Government. The contribution of RM. 660,000,000 from the Railways will continue to be paid into the Bank for International Settlements, according to the stipulations incumbent on the German Railways.

"The Young Plan provides for an unconditional annuity of RM. 612,000,000 payable by Germany to the Bank for International Settlements for the annuities covering the service of the Young Plan, but not covering the service of the Dawes Loan. In order to maintain intact the continuity of the unconditional payments, the payment of the Railways during the year of the moratorium shall be made to the Bank for International Settlements, in order to cover the obligation of Germany.

"The loan shall be on the account of and at the risk of the creditors sharing the unconditional annuity. Probably the difference between the RM. 660,000,000 and the RM. 612,000,000 will be used to meet the service of the Dawes Loan, it being understood that Germany shall supply the additional sum provided for the service.

"2. The French Government suggests that a loan of 25,000,000 dollars on the unconditional payments be made to the nations of Central

---

Government for the immediate laying down of "a cruiser designed to reply to the construction of the *Deutschland*," a proposal which had already been postponed by the Chamber. On July 4th the Senate voted an additional appropriation of nearly £20,000,000 to complete the line of fortresses on France's eastern frontier, a project on which over £11,000,000 had already been spent.

Europe, particularly those whose Budget is affected by the moratorium of the Young Plan.

"The American Government does not accept this idea, but thinks that the French Government would consider that a credit from the Central Banks would fulfil adequately the purpose of the French suggestion.

"The American Government points out that a credit from the Central Banks cannot be the object of an agreement between Governments.

"3. A divergence of views exists on the subject of the duration of payments of the conditional and unconditional annuities benefiting by the moratorium. The American Government thinks that the French Government would accept postponement of all payments for two years after the year of the moratorium and would agree to these payments being effected thenceforward in ten years, yearly or half-yearly, provided that certain other questions be settled in a satisfactory manner. This arrangement satisfies the U.S. Government.

"4. As to the Guarantee Fund, the Note points out that the French Government indicates the possibility of leaving this Fund outside the discussion as far as the U.S. Government is concerned.

"5. As to the payments in kind, the U.S. Government is still of the opinion that a solution of the problems arising from the contracts of 1931–1932 should be discussed later on between the experts of the interested Powers. As the solution must be found in the spirit of the proposal of President Hoover, after an agreement has been reached between the two Governments interested in the main question, the other questions do not seem to be such as to justify a delay in the final agreement, because these questions imply technical difficulties in connection with the Young Plan of which the U.S. Government is not a signatory.

"The U.S. Government suggest that these difficulties be reserved for a commission of Treasury experts of the nations interested provided that they are settled in the spirit of the President's proposal."

President Hoover cabled his approval of this draft agreement in principle, and the following day, July 6th, was spent in further negotiations and in drafting the final text for signature. Late in the evening, this task was completed and the agreement was initialled by MM. Laval and Flandin on behalf of France, and Mr. Mellon and Mr. Edge on behalf of the United States.[1]

The agreement in its final form was as follows. After announcing its approval in principle of the President's proposal, the French Government agrees:

"1. That the payment of all war debts and reparations shall be suspended for one year, from July 1, 1931, until June 30, 1932.

---

[1] For text see *Documents on International Affairs*, 1931, p. 117.

"2. That the German Government shall continue the payment of the unconditional annuities during this period.

"But the French Government agrees, in so far as it is concerned, that the payments thus made by Germany shall be invested by the Bank for International Settlements in guaranteed bonds of the German Railway. These bonds will be repayable, like all the suspended payments, in ten annuities from July 1, 1933, and they will be at the disposal of the German Government. The repayments will begin one year after the year of the Hoover Year, and not two years as at first suggested by America.

"3. That the suspended payments shall bear interest in accordance with the conditions suggested by the U.S. Government and shall be repayable in ten annuities beginning in the year 1933–1934."

It was recognized that the following three points did not directly concern the United States Government, i.e.

"1. That of help to Powers other than Germany.
"2. That of the French Guarantee Fund in the event of a moratorium, if asked for by Germany after the end of the Hoover Year.
"3. That of deliveries in kind."

As to these the French Government made a unilateral declaration in the following terms:

"(a) Concerted action shall be taken by the principal Central Banks through the Bank for International Settlements to organize assistance for those European countries which are particularly affected by the proposed suspension of payments.

"(b) There shall be a previous agreement between France and the Bank for International Settlements to the effect that France shall not be called upon to complete the Guarantee Fund required by the Young Plan, except by equal monthly payments at the demand of the Bank for International Settlements, and following the effective transfer of the payments made by Germany.

"(c) So far as concerns deliveries in kind and other technical adjustments necessitated by the application of the American proposal and the French agreement, a committee of experts shall be appointed by the interested Powers to reconcile actual needs with the spirit of President Hoover's proposal.

"(d) France reserves the right of demanding of the German Government the indispensable assurances concerning the employment for exclusively economic purposes of the sums by which the Budget of the Reich will profit."

Both parties seemed to be satisfied with this somewhat equivocal compromise. President Hoover expressed his gratification that his proposal had now been accepted by "all the important creditor Governments." While M. Laval informed the Press that while the agreement aimed at "consecrates a hard sacrifice for our country . . . it will be remarked that the Government has not allowed to lapse the sacred rights of France to reparation."

Throughout the course of the negotiations one cannot but be struck by the accuracy and precision with which France judged the situation. With acute perception she foresaw that the Hoover Plan was not an end in itself, and that in all probability Germany would be forced to demand a moratorium at the conclusion of the Hoover Year. French statesmen therefore wished to place themselves in as strong a position as possible against such an eventuality. Fully realizing that the Young Plan was doomed, by insisting on the recognition of its sacrosanctity they washed their hands of any part in the responsibility for its demise, and at the same time secured a bargaining factor when the time should come for the final "show-down." At least one reason for the prolongation of the Franco-American negotiations is believed to be that the French Government was engaged in successfully "holding the fort" until French banks had completed their withdrawals from Germany, though the greater part of these had been made in 1930.

Thus was agreement reached in putting the Hoover Plan into operation; but at what a price? The protracted negotiations had relieved the President's proposals of very much of their immediate psychological value. In effect the proposal came much too late to achieve more than a tardy recognition that default was inevitable.

The Star in the West had betokened but a false dawn.

5

The Committee of Financial Experts, for which provision had been made in the Franco-American Agreement of July 6th, sat in London from July 17–August 11, 1931,[1] and was composed of representatives of Belgium, France, Great Britain, Germany, Italy, Japan, Australia, Canada, Czechoslovakia, Greece, India, New Zealand, Portugal, Poland, Rumania, and South Africa.

It was the task of the Committee to devise machinery to be set up to bring about the suspension of payments, more particularly the deliveries in kind, occasioned by the operation of the Hoover Plan. The Report of the Committee, signed on August 11th and approved by the Governments concerned on the same date,[2] showed that an agreement had been reached providing that the suspended Young Plan and inter-Allied debt payments due to and by France, Italy, and Great Britain should be repaid by ten equal annuities from July 1, 1933, to include principal and interest not exceeding 3 per cent. from the same date.[3] The payments for the service of the Dawes Loan of 1924 and the Young Loan of 1930 would continue to be made without charge. The unconditional annuity would also continue to be paid, provided it was reloaned at once to the German State Railways.

The Committee was faced with certain practical difficulties in dealing with the application of the Hoover Plan to deliveries in kind, the main anxiety being to avoid a serious dislocation of current contracts.[4] A series of recommendations was made on this point, and it was agreed that existing credits for these deliveries would be used "in accordance with the regulations

[1] The Protocol and Declaration concerning Payments due by Italy to Great Britain was not signed until August 13th.
[2] See British White Paper, Cmd. 3947. See also *Documents on International Affairs*, 1931, p. 133.
[3] In June 1932, as a result of the policy adopted by the United States Congress, which insisted on the repayment of European postponed sums at a rate of 4 per cent., it was agreed in the Berlin Protocol (June 6, 1932) to increase the rate of interest for the repayments of European war debts and the German annuity from 3 per cent. to 4 per cent.
[4] Deliveries in kind were made to private French firms who did not pay cash against them to their own Government, but on terms of extended credit, whereas on the German side the German Government paid cash to the firms who made the delivery. A large part of this portion of reparation payment was not made in the form of manufactured goods delivered, but of carrying out of construction of public works, such as railways, canals, and hydro-electric schemes. The interruption of such works under process of construction it was the endeavour of the Committee to avoid.

for deliveries in kind as far as they will suffice for continuing the execution of certain approved contracts."[1] Any arrangements for the continuation of deliveries in kind against such contracts would have to involve no charge on the German Budget during the year July 1, 1931–June 30, 1932.

As regards non-German reparations, agreement was reached on the measures for the suspension for one year of payments due by Czechoslovakia and Bulgaria under the Hague Agreements of July 20, 1930, and by Hungary under the Paris Agreement of August 28, 1930. It was, however, agreed in principle that the payments to Funds A and B should be continued.[2]

Alone of the dissenting voices raised at the first receipt of Mr. Hoover's proposal, Yugoslavia remained adamant, and her representative in a declaration to the Committee expressed his inability to sign the report or adhere to the protocol giving effect to the Hoover Moratorium, unless and until "a definite means of compensating the Yugoslav budgetary deficit and of assisting the monetary situation of the National Bank could be provided."[3] Belgium, as has already been stated, reached an agreement with Germany for the continuance of payments under the Marks Agreement of July 12, 1929.

There remained the question of Relief and Reconstruction Loans, and as to this the Committee was informed that the Governments represented on the International Relief Credits Committee had decided in principle to suspend the amounts due during the Hoover Year in respect of Relief Bonds on the same principles as those already adopted in the case of inter-Governmental debts.[4]

It is now possible to give a brief survey of the profit and loss resulting from the Hoover Moratorium as put into opera-

[1] For Regulations of Deliveries in Kind see British White Paper, Cmd. 3763. Treaty Series No. 2 (1931).
[2] Fund A is the "Agrarian Fund" created by the Hague Conference of 1930 from which the Agrarian claims of the Succession States had to be met. Fund B, constituted at the same time, to cover the Succession States in the matter of liabilities arising from the seizure or liquidation of Hungarian property. See *Reparations*, pp. 158–163.
[3] The Yugoslav Government officially acquainted the United States Government of its inability to participate in the Hoover Moratorium on August 15th.
[4] This agreement required, and secured, the additional approval of the Governments of Denmark, Holland, Norway, Sweden, and Switzerland.

tion by the agreements reached in London on August 11th.[1,2]

[1] The Protocols applying the Hoover Moratorium to the reparation payments of Bulgaria and Hungary were not signed until January 22, 1932. By a special agreement signed between Bulgaria and Greece in Athens on November 11, 1931, the payments which Greece has to make to Bulgaria under the Molloff–Caphandaris Agreement are set off against an equal sum from reparation payments due by Bulgaria to Greece, and the remainder of those reparations payments due to Greece during the Hoover Year are to be paid during ten years in accordance with the London Protocol.

[2] The fact that Hoover Year ran from July 1, 1931–June 30, 1932, cuts across the Budget years of 1931–1932 and 1932–1933 in all cases except that of the United States. The same applies to the annuities under the Young Plan, which run from April 1st to March 31st, and to the various debt-funding agreements. The calculation is further complicated by the different periods of payment, varying from one month to six. The following figures are reprinted from a special supplement, "Reparations and War Debts," published by the *Economist*, January 23, 1932:

	Suspended Receipts	Suspended Payments	Net Loss (−) or Gain (+)
	£	£	£
United States	53,600,000	—	− 53,600,000
Great Britain	42,500,000*	32,800,000	− 9,700,000
France	39,700,000†	23,600,000	− 16,100,000
Italy	9,200,000	7,400,000	− 1,800,000
Belgium..	5,100,000	2,700,000	− 2,400,000
Rumania	700,000	750,000	+ 50,000
Yugoslavia	3,900,000	600,000	− 3,300,000
Portugal	600,000	350,000	− 250,000
Japan	600,000	—	− 600,000
Greece	1,000,000	650,000	− 350,000
Canada	900,000	—	− 900,000
Australia	800,000	3,900,000‡	+ 3,100,000
New Zealand	330,000	1,750,000	+ 1,420,000
South Africa	110,000	(340,000)*	− 110,000
India	228,000	836,000	+ 608,000
Egypt	90,000	—	− 90,000
Germany	—	77,000,000	+ 77,000,000
Hungary	—	350,000	+ 350,000
Czechoslavakia ..	10,000	1,190,000	+ 1,180,000
Bulgaria	150,000	400,000	+ 250,000
Austria	—	300,000	+ 300,000

* On receipt of President Hoover's proposal the British Government at once offered the Dominion Governments and the Government of India the option of postponing their payments to Great Britain for the period of the Hoover Year. With one exception all accepted with gratitude. South Africa, however, while voicing its appreciation of the British offer, did not avail itself of it, but, nevertheless, forewent its share of reparation payments.

† Exclusive of £3–4 million for service of Dawes and Young Loans.

‡ Excluding annual sinking-fund payment of £814,000, which Australia had already the option to suspend for two years.

The following table shows the effect of the agreements reached by the London Protocol of August 11, 1931, on the payments at the rate of 3 per cent. interest which will have to be made by the principal Powers from 1933–1943:[1]

	Receipts	Payments	Net Annual Deficit or Receipt
	£	£	£
United States	6,300,000	—	+ 6,300,000
Great Britain	5,000,000	3,800,000	+ 1,200,000
France	4,700,000	2,800,000	+ 1,900,000
Italy	1,100,000	900,000	+ 200,000
Belgium..	600,000	300,000	+ 300,000
Germany	—	9,000,000	− 9,000,000

By the Berlin Protocol of June 6, 1932, however, it was agreed that payments should be made on a 4 per cent. basis, with the result that the following are the final figures:[2]

	Receipts	Payments	Net Annual Deficit or Receipt
	£	£	£
United States	6,600,000	—	+ 6,600,000
Great Britain	5,240,000	4,040,000	+ 1,200,000
France	4,900,000	2,900,000	+ 2,000,000
Italy	1,130,000	910,000	+ 220,000
Belgium..	630,000	330,000	+ 300,000
Germany	—	9,500,000	− 9,500,000

6

For Germany the Star in the West did, in many respects, betoken a false dawn; for to Germany more than to any other country concerned the psychological value of the Hoover Plan lay in its immediate application. The expression of surprise and

[1] See *Economist* Special Supplement, January 23, 1932.
[2] Figures supplied by the *Economist* Information Bureau.

relief, which one could not but notice taking the place of gloom and depression on the faces of the Sunday crowds as they read the extra editions of the newspapers on June 21st, found its reflection in every phase of German life, political, financial, and economic. The new-found hope and enthusiasm were sustained during the next few days by the immediately favourable reaction of Great Britain and Italy to the President's proposal. But at the back of everyone's mind was the thought, "What will France do?"

As the negotiations dragged on in Paris and July 1st came and went, still leaving the suspense unrelieved, so proportionately did the atmosphere of despair and impending calamity descend once more upon Germany, the more intensified by reason of its brief alleviation, until by the time the Franco-American Agreement was reached on July 6th, the problem which Mr. Hoover's plan was intended to solve had reappeared in a form more acute than before.

Germany was in no condition to face the renewed crisis, which came at the culmination of a period of increasing lack of confidence in the mark on the part of German and foreign creditors alike and an accentuated flight of capital abroad in the form of foreign exchange. The period dated from the result of the elections of September 1930 and the increasing uneasiness at the growing strength of the National Socialists.[1] Since that time Germany had lost nearly two-thirds of her short-term credits, amounting to some 2·9 milliards of marks,[2] and the total losses to her economic system were estimated by the Finance Minister, Herr Dietrich, on July 7th as at between

[1] The flight of capital had already started before the elections of 1930. The German "balance of payments" published on July 9, 1931, showed that the net inflow of short foreign money (under twelve months) in 1930 was no more than 24 million marks, as compared with 1,092 million in 1929 and 1,575 million in 1928. In 1928 and 1929 there was a net purchase of securities from Germans by foreigners of 430 and 185 million respectively, but in 1930 this changed to a net purchase by Germans from foreigners valued at 162 million marks.

[2] Annex 5 to the Layton–Wiggin Report showed the difference between the short-term credits in Germany on March 31, 1931, and the middle of July 1931 to be a loss of RM. 1,246 million. At the same time the short-term claims of German banks were computed to be RM. 520 million. The figure quoted for the amount of short-term credit withdrawals during the period January–July 1931 is that given by the Basle Advisory Committee.

three and four milliard marks worth of foreign exchange
(£150–200 million). Of these withdrawals about 60 per cent.
were taken out of Germany by American investors, about
10 per cent. by French, and the remaining 30 per cent. by
Germans themselves through purchases of foreign currency.[1]

The financial panic, which had died down during the days
immediately succeeding the granting of the rediscount credit
of £20 million (RM. 400 million) to the Reichsbank on June 16th
was renewed in aggravated form during the first week of July,
and on July 7th the Reichsbank had to meet foreign exchange
requirements of between RM 40 and 60 million (£2–3 million).
On the same day the Government took its first step in dealing
with this new crisis. It conscripted all German business houses
with a capital of £250,000 and upwards, to the number of
1,000, and compelled them to participate in a guarantee of
RM. 500 million to the Gold Discount Bank, with a view to
placing that institution in a position to negotiate for new foreign
credits from private as distinct from central banks. On the
following day (July 8th) President Hindenburg signed a decree
legalizing this plan, but any beneficial effect which it might
have had on the situation was more than counteracted by the
announcement that the North German Wool Company (*Nordwolle*) of Bremen had failed for RM. 200 million, having as one
of its principal creditors the Darmstädter und National Bank
(*Danat*), the position of which was endangered.[2]

On this same day, July 8th, Dr. Luther, President of the
Reichsbank, flew to London and to Paris in search of credits,
in particular the renewal of the rediscount credit of £20,000,000
which fell due on July 16th, and if possible an increase in that
credit. In both capitals he was singularly unsuccessful and

[1] See *Bulletin of International News*, July 16, 1931 (vol. viii, no. 2).
[2] The failure of the *Nordwolle* also brought about the collapse of the Schroeder
Bank of Bremen, which involved the Government of the Free City alone in
a loss of more than RM. 24 million. These two catastrophes temporarily
paralysed the Free City of Bremen and caused a very large number of private
bankruptcies. In addition, the Beamtenbank, in which were the savings of
the majority of the Government officials and employees, closed its doors.
This situation was merely symptomatic of financial conditions throughout
Germany during the summer of 1931, when bank failures and the collapse
of business concerns became everyday affairs.

returned on July 11th to find conditions considerably worse than on his departure. The demand for foreign exchange on the Reichsbank, which on January 10th had amounted to RM. 40 million, rose on the 11th to RM. 100 million, and the Government decided to prevent by decree the export of German capital.

But before this could take effect an unexampled banking crisis broke. The *Danat* Bank closed its doors on July 13th, having been involved in the losses of the *Nordwolle* to the extent of RM. 29 million marks, and it was rumoured that another of the D. Banks, the Dresdner Bank, might follow its example.[1] The Government at once promulgated a decree closing all banks, stock exchanges, and post office clearing branches for two days (July 14th–15th), and on the following day extended this measure to private liabilities.[2] The mark on July 13th touched 31 to the £ at one period, but later rallied to 22½. It was not quoted on July 14th–15th on the exchanges, and travellers holding marks had difficulty in negotiating them in foreign countries. On the 16th, however, there was a brisk demand for marks in London, German firms buying by telephone in the London market.

The Reichsbank raised the discount rate from 7 to 10 per cent. on July 15th, and the Lombard rate from 8 to 15 per cent.[3] But despite every effort made by the Government and the Bank to cope with the situation—and there were many emergency decrees issued during this period placing very stringent restrictions on the German people as to any use of money—all proved fruitless, and the gravest consequences seemed inevitable. The

[1] The Danat Bank, in a reorganized form and with a Government guarantee of all deposits, reopened on August 3rd. On the same day the Government also gave assistance to the Dresdner Bank by taking up RM. 300 million of the preference shares issued to increase the bank's capital. Later, in March 1932, in the course of a general banking reorganization under the auspices of the German Government, the Danat Bank was merged with the Dresdner Bank, thereby terminating eighty years of independent existence.
[2] On reopening on July 16th, banks, etc., were allowed to pay out not more than 100 marks daily, and exchange bureaux might only sell foreign currencies up to the amount of 100 marks per week per person or firm; this restriction continued until July 23rd.
[3] These rates were again raised on July 31st to 15 per cent. and 20 per cent. respectively, and reduced as from August 12th to 10 per cent. and 15 per cent.

only ray of hope was the decision on July 15th of the Bank for International Settlements and the various central banks participating to renew the rediscount credit of £20 million for a further period of three weeks, and the decision of British and American banks, made public on July 17th, to renew short-term credits to Germany as they matured.

The statesmen of Europe were seriously alarmed at the new situation in Germany. Informed officially by the German Government on July 11th of the gravity of the position, they watched with dismay the rapidity with which conditions became steadily worse. On July 15th the British Government hurriedly issued invitations for a Conference of Ministers to meet in London on July 20th, and Mr. Henderson, the Foreign Secretary, left for Paris. Mr. Stimson arrived from Rome the same afternoon, and throughout the next two days the heads of the British and American Foreign Offices, assisted by their respective Ambassadors, conferred with MM. Laval, Briand, and Flandin as to what proposals should be set before the German Chancellor on his arrival on July 18th.

As these preliminary conversations progressed it became evident that there were two openly conflicting schools of thought, the American and the French. The first of these envisaged an undertaking by the banks to maintain the existing volume of credits in Germany "for an adequate period of time," and that the German Government should exercise complete control, through the Reichsbank, over all foreign exchanges and should exercise preferential withdrawals. The American proposals also included measures for funding some of the short-term loans into long-term ones and for the super-vision of such an operation by the Bank for International Settlements, in order to secure co-operation, first, in making inquiry into the immediate further credit needs of Germany, and secondly, in consultation with banking interests in various countries, in providing for the renewal of the existing volume of outstanding short-term credits.

The French proposals were of a very different nature. They included the prompt grant to Germany of a short-term credit of £100 million by the Central Banks of Great Britain, France, and U.S.A. to enable the Reichsbank to maintain the stability of the mark and assist towards the recovery of trade. This credit would be for a period of one year and would be replaced on maturity by a long-term loan of an equal amount to be redeemed in ten years, and to be used for consolidation purposes. This loan would be guaranteed by the same three countries, with the addition of Belgium and Italy.

The loan, however, would be subject to certain economic pledges and political guarantees. The first of these would involve the pledging of the German Customs Revenue as security to the Bank for International Settlements, which would act as Trustee for the loan,[1] and the assurance by Germany that she would undertake to resume the Young Plan annuity payments at the termination of the Hoover Year (i.e. July 1, 1932).

It was in the second category of "Securities" that a more sinister note was apparent. France, it will be remembered, had at the time of the Franco-American Agreement of July 6th reserved the right to exact from Germany "the indispensable assurances concerning the employment for exclusively economic purposes of the sums by which the Budget of the Reich will profit";[2] she adopted the same policy now. The "political guarantees" to be given by Germany included the abandonment of the Austro-German *Zollunion*;[3] the cessation of all

---

[1] The Customs Revenues had already been pledged as a collateral guarantee for the Dawes Loan of 1924 and as a "negative" guarantee of the Young Plan annuities.

[2] See above, p. 66.

[3] On March 19, 1931, the German and Austrian Governments had initialled a protocol in Vienna for the establishment of a Customs Union between their two countries. The effect was most detrimental to German credit and to the political situation in Europe. The proposal at once revived the fear of the Little Entente regarding a possible *Anschluss* and the suspicions of France that Germany was aiming at the establishment of an economic hegemony in Central and South-Eastern Europe. The question came before the Council of the League of Nations at its session in May 1931, and was referred, at the proposal of the British Government, for consideration to the Permanent Court of International Justice on the ground that it might violate Article 88 of the Treaty of St. Germain and the Austrian Protocol No. 1 of 1922. At the time of the Paris Conversations the matter was therefore *sub judice* (see *Disarmament and Security*, pp. 334–335; *Survey of International Affairs*, 1931, Part IIIA; and *Documents on International Affairs*, 1931, pp. 1–16).

work or the second "pocket-battleship," the *Ersatz Lothringen*, due to be launched in 1934;[1] the declaration of a political moratorium" for the ten-year period of the long-term loan, during which all agitation for treaty-revision must cease; the dissolution (by force if need be) of such semi-military organization as the Stalhelm;[2] and last but not least, the acceptance by Germany of the permanency of the eastern frontier.[3]

With a bluntness that was almost brutal, Mr. Stimson, who had kept in close touch with President Hoover by transatlantic telephone, informed M. Laval on July 18th that the United States Government considered his proposals "impracticable," and that in any case it would have nothing to do with political entanglements. In this he was supported by the British representatives.[4]

When Dr. Brüning, with Dr. Curtius, joined the discussions later in the day the French proposals in a modified form were placed before him and he, confident of American support, unhesitatingly rejected any form of "political guarantee." In any case, the German Chancellor had somewhat of a different conception of the nature of the Paris conversations than that

[1] The *Deutschland*, the first of the 10,000-ton "pocket-battleships" to be built by Germany in accordance with the provision of the Treaty of Versailles, had been launched on May 19, 1931, and had caused considerable commotion in naval circles, particularly in France. Within the restrictions imposed by the Treaty, German naval architects had succeeded in creating a war vessel which was superior in every way to anything in its own class. It could sink anything that could catch it and could escape from anything that could sink it. The anxiety of France was reflected in the debate in the Senate on July 2nd. (See above, pp. 63–4. See also *Disarmament and Security*, pp. 336–337; and *Survey* for 1931, p. 71.)

[2] The *Stalhelm* rallies at Coblenz in the summer of 1930 and at Oels in June 1931, which disclosed the fact that this organization could at surprisingly short notice mobilize 130,000 men at a given point, had occasioned considerable anxiety to the French and Polish Foreign Offices respectively.

[3] France, having failed at Locarno to persuade Herr Stresemann to accept as permanent the German frontier with Poland and Czechoslovakia, has allowed no opportunity to pass without endeavouring to extract this undertaking from Germany, as, for example, the proposals put forward by France during the autumn and winter of 1928 in the course of the preliminary negotiations preceding the setting up of the Young Committee (see *Reparations*, pp. 62–64).

[4] It is to be believed that Mr. Henderson was not personally inimical to the French proposals, and was even inclined to try to persuade Dr. Brüning to make some concessions on the lines indicated. Like President Hoover, however, Mr. MacDonald kept in daily communication with his lieutenant, and was strongly opposed to any form of "political guarantee" being required of Germany.

entertained by the French. He regarded them as entirely preliminary to the forthcoming London Conference, a series of
conversations designed to facilitate an exchange of views and
to see whether a more friendly atmosphere could not be created
through personal contact. On this basis he was more than
anxious to participate, but he firmly refused to enter into any
agreement which might tie his hands in London. Thus the most
that the official *communiqué* of the 19th could say was that
the French and German statesmen "were agreed to recognize
the importance of this meeting." The French view was contained in the words "The representatives of the French
Government declared that, under reserve of certain financial
guarantees and measures of political appeasement, they would
be ready to discuss later the terms of financial co-operation
within an international framework." The phrase "political
appeasement" marks the only modification which M. Laval
would concede.

Mr. Stimson had crossed to London on July 19th for the
purpose of a preliminary exchange of views with the British
Prime Minister before the opening of the Conference next day.
He found that the terms which he had put forward in Paris
were very much in accordance with the line of policy which
had been approved by the British Cabinet, and therefore when
the Conference opened the British and American delegations
were united in their proposals.

The London Conference opened on July 20, 1931, at the
House of Commons and was attended by the representatives
of Seven Powers, Mr. MacDonald, Mr. Henderson, Mr. Snowden
(Great Britain); MM. Laval and Briand (France); Signor Grandi
(Italy); Drs. Brüning and Curtius (Germany); Mr. Stimson,
Mr. Mellon, and General Dawes (U.S.A.); Mr. Matsudaira
(Japan); and M. Renkin (Belgium).

The French Government was apprehensive as to the suit-
ability of the London atmosphere to the discussion of far-
reaching plans for the assistance of Germany, involving political
considerations and conditions, and M. Laval urged that the
scope of the Conference should be confined to the measures to

be taken to deal with the immediate financial crisis.[1] The
Conference therefore sat for three days in great secrecy, and
after much labour the mountain produced a mouse. For by
no possible means could the *communiqué*, on the results of the
Conference issued on July 23rd, be considered proportionate to
the galaxy of statesmen who were gathered together. The
document read as follows:

"The recent excessive withdrawals of capital from Germany have
created an acute financial crisis. These withdrawals have been caused
by a lack of confidence which was not justified by the economic and
budgetary situation of the country.

"In order to ensure the maintenance of the financial stability of
Germany, which is essential in the interests of the whole world, the
Governments represented at the Conference are ready to co-operate,
so far as lies within their power, to restore confidence.

"The Governments represented at the Conference are ready to
recommend for the consideration of the financial institutions in their
respective countries the following proposals for relieving the immediate
situation:

"1. That the Central Bank credit of £20 million recently granted
to the Reichsbank, under the auspices of the Bank for International
Settlements, be renewed at maturity[2] for a period of three
months.

"2. That concerted measures should be taken by the financial
institutions in the different countries with a view to maintaining
the volume of credits they have already extended to Germany.

"The Conference recommends that the Bank for International Settlements should be invited to set up without delay a committee of
representatives nominated by the Governors of the Central Banks
interested to inquire into the further credit needs of Germany and to
study the possibilities of converting a portion of the short-term credits
into long-term credits.

"The Conference noted with interest a communication from Dr.
Brüning relative to the joint guarantee recently placed by German
industry at the disposal of the Gold Discount Bank.[3] The Conference
is of the opinion that a guarantee of this description should make it

---

[1] In any case, the United States Acting Secretary of State had announced
on July 15th that the American representative at the London Conference
would in no case allow the United States to become involved in any political
situation in connection with the extending of financial aid to Germany, and
that the Federal Reserve Board would not consider any credit to Germany
except in collaboration with all the Central Banks, including that of France.
[2] August 6, 1931.   [3] See above, p. 73.

possible to provide a sound basis for the resumption of the normal
operation of international credit.

"The Conference considers that, if the measures are carried through,
they will form a basis for more important action to follow."

It will be noticed that all mention of a long-term loan and
of political guarantees was absent from the Conference *communiqué*. M. Laval had abandoned the latter only because
insistence on his demand would have prevented anything more
definite from being done. He had, however, another ace up his
sleeve. On July 21st, in the midst of the Conference, the Quai
d'Orsay published a memorandum on disarmament which,
though it bore the signature of M. Briand, was known to be
the work of the then Minister of War, the late M. Maginot.
In effect the memorandum was a reiteration and re-emphasis
of the views expressed by the French representatives at the
final session of the Preparatory Disarmament Commission in
November and December 1930, and put forward the conditions
on which France would consider the reduction of her armaments
at the forthcoming Conference in February 1932. These were
two in number, namely, the acceptance by Germany of the
perpetuation of the *status quo* created by the disarmament
clauses of the Treaty of Versailles; and the granting to France
of further general measures of security against political
aggression.[1]

The publication of this memorandum at this particular
juncture, two months earlier than was expected, left no room
for illusions as to whether French policy had undergone any
modification as a result of the situation in Germany. It more
than off-set any political benefit which might have derived
from the London Conference.

The results of the Conference were indeed meagre and consisted mainly in giving official recognition to conditions already
in existence. Thus, the decision to prolong the rediscount
credit to the Reichsbank had already been taken by the banks
concerned on July 15th, and as regards the recommendation
to maintain the existing volume of short-term credits, the

[1] See *Disarmament and Security*, pp. 343–345; and for text, *Documents on
International Affairs*, 1931, p. 43.

accepting houses and private banks, both in London and New York, had announced their intention on July 17th to renew these, as far as a general decision can be made on a matter which is the concern of a large number of private firms and individuals. In any case, this common decision did not amount to much more than making a virtue of necessity, as any precipitate measures to withdraw these credits would result either in prohibitive measures by the German Government or else in the collapse of the German financial structure, in the course of which the credits would be lost. In other words, the outstanding short-term credits to Germany had been "frozen" not so much by an agreement reached at the London Conference, as by economic compulsion.[1]

Easily the most valuable and far-reaching decision taken by the Conference was that to recommend the Bank for International Settlements to set up a Committee of Financial Experts nominated by the Central Banks to inquire into Germany's credit position on all its aspects, for the report of this Committee has proved one of the powerful factors in the Wreck of Reparations.

[1] See *The Times*, July 24, 1931, and *Bulletin of International News*, July 30, 1931 (vol. viii, no. 3).

CHAPTER III

THE WISE MEN OF BASLE

1

OF the several national attitudes assumed towards the latter phase of the reparation problem, none was more helpful than that of Great Britain. Germany and France, as the principals, may be left out of account, and, of the remaining five Powers, Italy was so fiercely vehement as partially to defeat her own ends, while the contribution of the United States was diminished by the fact that it was difficult to know whether or not the Congressional voice would contradict the Presidential. Throughout 1931 Great Britain pursued a policy of definite constructive helpfulness and allowed no opportunity to slip by for utilizing this policy. The Anglo-German Conversations at Chequers in June and the Seven-Power London Conference in July, though virtually barren of results, were genuine efforts to do the best possible thing under singularly difficult circumstances.

The return visit to Berlin on July 27th–29th of Mr. MacDonald and Mr. Henderson was a further step taken in pursuance of this policy and was singularly well-timed. Germany as a whole had been disappointed at the results of the London Conference, though the whole country had approved the Chancellor's attitude in refusing a long-term loan on French terms. It was therefore very welcome to Germany that the British Prime Minister and Foreign Secretary should visit Berlin, not only to return the Chequers visit, but to discuss the best means of giving effect in a constructive manner to the decisions taken by the London Conference and, in the words of Mr. MacDonald, "to show the world that our confidence in Germany is undiminished." He added that it was Great Britain's firm belief that if Germany continued her efforts to get on her feet again and did not give way to desperation the other peoples would help and not allow her to go under, for a free and self-respecting Germany was indispensable for civilized society.

The visit of the British statesmen, together with the agreements arrived at with the Central and private Banks both before and immediately after the London Conference, had a salutary effect upon the German financial position. Confidence, both foreign and internal, returned in large measure, and by August 3rd the Reichsbank returns showed that in a week the gold and foreign exchange cover had increased by RM. 100 million and stood at 36·1 per cent. the gold circulation; a week later, on August 10th, the cover had risen to 38·2 per cent., having increased by over RM. 62 million, to a total of RM. 1,672 million.

There remained one further psychological effect of the crisis. Conversations in Paris, London, and Berlin with foreign statesmen had convinced the German Chancellor that to a very great extent, at least for the present, the recovery of Germany lay in her own hands and must be brought about by measures of self-help. The most that could be expected in the shape of external assistance would be that already extended in the rediscount credit and non-withdrawal of short-term loans. This view was communicated by Dr. Brüning to the German people in a broadcast message on August 4th, in which he asked for restraint after the reopening of the banks next day, and said quite definitely that for some time the question of a foreign loan lay outside the bounds of political possibility. Germany would have to help herself.

Two days later (August 6th) the first of the measures recommended by the London Conference was put into effect when it was announced that all parties to the £20 million rediscount credit to Germany had agreed on its prolongation for a further period of three months.

2

The London Conference had recommended:

"That concerted measures should be taken by the financial institutions in the different countries with a view to maintaining the volume of credits they have already extended to Germany."

The sum involved amounted to RM. 6·3 milliards (£315 million), of which about RM. 2·4 milliards (£120 million) were in the hands of United States Banks and RM. 2·0 milliards (£100 million) in English Banks. The other nationalities concerned were Dutch, French, Swiss, and Swedish.

Coincidently with the visit of the British statesmen to Germany the Anglo-American creditors of Germany took action. Mr. Tiarks (of the J. Henry Schroeder Bank of London) and Mr. Gannon (of the Chase National Bank of New York) conferred in Berlin with Dr. Melchior, representing the German debtors, and reached, on July 30th, an understanding in principle on "the silent prolongation" of their credits for a period of six months, but retained the right to remove a part of them from one German bank to another through the medium of the Gold Discount Bank. This draft agreement was to be submitted for approval to the bank themselves.

This action was taken independently of the other short-term creditors. However, on August 14th representatives of all the creditor banking groups concerned and of the German banks met at Basle at the suggestion of the Committee of Experts appointed by the Bank for International Settlements on the nomination of the Central Banks as recommended by the London Conference. This action on the part of the Committee was prompted by the impression that negotiations between the short-term creditors and debtors had better proceed on a uniform method rather than piecemeal.

After five days' study and consideration both sides arrived, on August 19th, at an agreement which they would recommend to the numerous creditor banks and bankers for their acceptance. The agreement provided for the continuation of credits to German debtors up to the total amount then outstanding for a period of six months from the date of the signing of the Agreement, subject to an arrangement being made with regard to the existing Central Bank credits. Provision was made for an individual and direct agreement, in an approved standard form in every instance, between the German debtor and the foreign creditor. The form of this agreement was so drafted as not to interfere in any way with the normal relations previously existing between the parties, and while it involved certain specific assurances, it was essentially based on the broad foundation of mutual confidence.

The creditors were fully alive to the fact that it was in their own interest to give every assistance to ensure the stability of the Reichsbank, and for this reason it was agreed between them and their debtors that the immediate release of their Reichsbank balances, amounting to some RM. 740 million (£37 million) should be only partial and that the remainder should be gradually released during the term of the Agreement.

It was agreed that 25 per cent. of the existing German credits in marks should be immediately liquidated and 15 per cent. each month until the balance had been eliminated. A proviso was, however, made that these payments should be postponed if the Reichsbank could show that such withdrawals would endanger the currency.

The German debtor banks feared these mark credit withdrawls, as they exceeded the total free gold holdings of the Reichsbank, but acceptance of the creditors' terms was inevitable, as otherwise the external debt moratorium would have been prolonged and made formal, thus eliminating all hope of obtaining new credits in the future.

The Agreement further provided for two forms of additional security to the creditors participating, (1) to associate a direct responsibility on the part of the final creditors taken with that of the debtor banks itself; and (2) an undertaking by the Deutsche Golddiskontbank to take over or to guarantee, within certain limits, the indebtedness to foreign creditors; thus lending the important support of the Golddiskontbank's resources and prestige to the obligation. Provision was also made for the securing by Government decree, or otherwise, that foreign creditors of German banks should receive equal protection to that of creditors residing in Germany.

On their side the German debtor banks undertook to endeavour to utilize all encashments received from their clients in buying immediately the requisite foreign exchange

for remittance to the respective foreign creditors in (or towards)
the replacement of the respective outstanding acceptances.

For the adjustment of any differences arising as to the
interpretation and execution of the Agreement, the Bank of
International Settlements, at the request of all the parties concerned, and in view of its international functions, agreed to set
up a special Committee with full power to deal with such cases.

In short, in return for realizing 25 per cent. of their deposits
immediately and 15 per cent. per month latterly, the creditor
banks agreed to renew their credits. It will be noticed that
neither was representation given to, nor cognizance taken of,
private investors. This would hardly seem to be a means of
encouraging future private investment.

Such was the "Standstill" Agreement of 1931, and although
adopted at Basle on August 19th, it was nearly a month later
(September 17th) that the Bank for International Settlements
was able to announce that it had been signed by all of the
eleven creditor national groups and the German banks. The
Agreement was therefore declared to be in force as from September 1st, 1931, and would consequently expire, unless renewed,
on February 29, 1932.

3

"The Conference recommends that the Bank of International Settlements should be invited to set up without delay a committee of
representatives nominated by the Governors of the Central Banks
interested, to enquire into the further credit needs of Germany and to
study the possibilities of converting a portion of the short-term credits
into long-term credits."

So ran the official *communiqué* issued by the London Conference
on July 23rd, and on the following day Mr. MacDonald, in his
capacity of President of the Conference, received a telegram
from the Chairman of the Bank, Mr. Gates W. McGarrah, assur-
ing him that the Bank was proceeding "without delay" to
examine the best and most expeditious methods of giving effect
to those recommendations of the Conference which fall within
its powers and sphere of action. A week later, July 31st, the

Bank announced that the membership of the Committee of Experts had been completed and that the first meeting had been called for August 8th at the offices of the Bank at Basle.

The Committee was composed as follows:

Professor Alberto Pirelli, appointed by the Governor of the Banca d'Italia.

Dr. Rudolf Bindschedler, appointed by the Governor of the Schweizerische Nationalbank, Bern.

M. P. de Groot, appointed by the Governor of the Amsterdamsche Bank.

M. Emile Francqui[1,2] appointed by the Governor of the Banque Nationale de Belgique.

Sir Walter Layton, C.H., appointed by the Governor of the Bank of England.

Dr. Carl Melchior,[3] appointed by the President of the Reichsbank.

M. Emile Moreau,[2] appointed by the Governor of the Banque de France.

M. Oskar Rydbeck, appointed by the President of the Riksbank of Sweden.

Mr. T. Tanaka, appointed by the Governor of the Bank of Japan.

Mr. Albert Wiggin, appointed by the Governor of the Federal Reserve Bank of New York.

At the initial meeting on August 7th, Mr. Wiggin was unanimously elected to take the chair, thus preserving the tradition of an American chairman of expert Committees of Inquiry into reparations and kindred subjects, and the Committee began its work with a statement by Dr. Melchior on Germany's financial position. This statement, supported by a most valuable array of documents and figures supplied by the Statistical Office of the Reich, placed the Committee in possession of a number of facts which threw a great deal of light on the economic developments of the post Dawes Plan Years.

These figures included an estimate of Germany's balance of payments; a statement on the origin and employment of net foreign exchange received by Germany from 1924 to 1930; the estimated movement in Germany's international capital position; an estimate of foreign investment in Germany and of German's investments abroad; an estimate of the total of short-term foreign commitments and short-term foreign claims of

[1] Member of the Dawes Committee of 1924.
[2] Member of the Young Committee of 1929.
[3] Alternate on Young Committee of 1929.

German banks; a statement on the geographical distribution of German long-term foreign loans; a statement on the position of the Reichsbank; the ordinary Budget estimates of the Reich for 1930 and 1931; and general indices of German economic activity.

The figures of balances of international payments were especially interesting. They showed that in only two of the six years had Germany had an "active" visible trading balance, i.e. in 1926, when the favourable balance was RM. 160 million (£8 million) and in 1930, when it was RM. 840 million (£42 million). It was also noticeable that up till 1929 when the Dawes annuities were reduced), the growth of reparations liability was accompanied by an increase in the interest require-ments for the service of the commercial debts. Another interest-ing fact disclosed was that, whereas Germany paid, in all, RM. 9·4 milliards (£470 million) in reparations during 1925–1930, she received from loans approximately RM. 15·0 milliards (£750 million), of which about RM. 7·4 milliards (£370 million) was in the form of long-term loans and RM. 4·4 milliards (£220 million) in short-term credits, the balance being un-classified. The lending on a large scale came to an end in 1929, and during 1930 the inflow was negligible, but the fact that exports were large and were valued at 1·5 milliards (£75 million) more than imports prevented a financial crisis. By the beginning of 1931, however, capital was definitely leaving the country, but even so, the favourable trade balance covered reparation payments amounting to RM. 860 million (£43 million) during the first half of the year. The amount left for payment of interest was, however, less than RM. 400 million (£20 million), and the country only got through those six months by borrowing a further RM. 640 million (£32 million), of which RM. 160 million (£8 million) was on short-term. As against this withdrawals of short-term credits during January to July inclusive totalled RM. 2·9 milliards (£145 million).

Germany's foreign indebtedness during the seven years under review grew faster than her foreign assets by RM. 18·2 mil-liards (£910 million). This net influx of capital, together with RM. 3 milliards (£150 million) received for shipping services, etc., i.e. 21·2 milliards in all (£1,060 million), enabled her to pay interest on her commercial debt totalling RM. 2·5 milliards (£125 million), to pay reparations amounting to RM. 10·3 milliards (£515 million), to add to her holdings of gold and foreign currencies to an extent of RM. 2·1 milliards (£105 million), and to pay for a surplus of imports over exports of 6·3 milliards (£315 million).

In four of the seven years[1] her borrowings were so large that they exceeded by a large sum her debt service and reparations payments together. Capital was drawn into the country by high rates of interest, to an amount greater than was paid out, and only in two years, 1926 and 1930, did her exports show an excess over imports, thus providing funds to meet foreign obligations out of the country's own resources. This healthier condition of affairs would not have come about in 1930 had it not been for the heavy reduction in the cost of most of her imports, owing to the fall in prices of raw materials, and in any case the excess of exports only provided two-thirds of the amount paid out against reparations and commercial debts, in spite of the lowering of the annuity under the Young Plan.

At the end of 1930 the total foreign investments in Germany were valued at RM. 25·5 milliards (£1,275 million), and the total investments abroad at RM. 9·7 milliards (£485 million), leaving a net debt to foreigners of RM. 15·8 milliards (£790 million).

The weakness of this position arose from the fact that whereas RM. 5·3 milliards (£265 million) of the country's investments abroad were on short-term, her short-term indebtedness amounted to at least RM. 10·3 milliards (£515 million), as against RM. 4·1 milliards (£205 million) only four years previously.[2]

It appeared from such figures as were available that the short-term credits of the banks had to a very large extent been used as working capital in the internal economy of Germany,

[1] That is, in 1924, 1925, 1927, and 1928, when she was able to pay for a surplus of exports.
[2] These were the estimated totals as on December 31, 1930.

and therefore could not be readily withdrawn. In other words, short-term money had been used to do the work of long-term money, with corresponding risks to both borrowers and lenders.

During the first six months of 1931, though there was an export surplus, estimated at RM. 1·1 milliards (£55 million), this failed to cover the total foreign obligations, which amounted to RM. 1·3 milliards (£56·5 million), and the position was aggravated by a "very considerable outflow of capital funds." The position at the end of July 1931 was that the short-term indebtedness of Germany amounted to RM. 7·4 milliards (£370 million), as compared with a total of RM. 10·3 milliards (£515 million) at the end of 1930, showing that short-term funds to an extent of RM. 2·9 milliards (£145 millions) were withdrawn in the seven months.[1]

From a persual of these facts it was clear to the Committee that the problem with which they were dealing was in reality in the nature of a vicious circle: Whereas the German financial crisis must be considered as a phase—albeit an acute one—of a problem which had affected all countries of the world, yet Germany plays so important a rôle in the economic life of the world, and, in particular, of Europe, that until the situation in Germany improves there can be no general recovery from the existing state of depression.

It was therefore towards the breaking of this circle that the Committee directed its attention in considering its terms of reference. With regard to the first of these—"The immediate further credit needs of Germany"—two main issues arose:

"1. Whether it was possible to prevent a further withdrawal of capital from Germany and to replace the short-term credits which became due; and

"2. Whether it was necessary to replace from foreign sources all or part of the capital which had already been withdrawn."

The Committee dealt with the first of these points by initiating direct negotiations between creditors and debtors which finally bore fruit in the "Standstill" Agreement of September 1st.[2]

[1] See *Bulletin of International News*, September 10, 1931 (vol. viii, no. 6).
[2] See above, p. 86.

This Agreement, however, did not directly cover certain other classes of Germany's short-term debt, including those of the German Federal States and Municipalities, which amounted to RM. 355 million (£17·75 million), and the Committee recommended that in each case the renewal of such debts should be the subject of direct negotiations between creditor and debtor.

With regard to the second point, it was evident that the internal economy of Germany would continue under a condition of extreme strain until the situation of the Reichsbank had been relieved, and a part at least of the circulating capital which had suddenly been withdrawn from German economy had been replaced.

There were only two ways by which Germany might achieve this without external assistance. The first possibility was that Germany might make further sales of her foreign assets, which amounted at the end of July 1931 to an estimate of RM. 8·15 milliards (£425 million). But the short-term assets of the banks had been reduced since the end of 1930 by 40 per cent., and considerable banking balances abroad were necessary for the normal conduct of foreign trade. In addition, many of the long-term assets, amounting to about RM. 5·0 milliards (£250 million) were not in a readily realizable form, and included enterprises such as branches abroad of German industries. The Committee therefore discarded this method as impracticable.

The second method was for Germany to carry out a policy of acquiring foreign exchange by reducing her imports and stimulating in every possible way her exports. But the Committee rejected this possibility also, by reason of the fact that to make it effective it would be necessary for Germany to export nearly double as much (in value) as she imported, and "to maintain exports, in the highly competitive conditions obtaining at the present time, involves the sale of goods at the very low prices, while the reduction of imports on the scale proposed involves a low level of consumption in Germany. It is therefore a policy of continued impoverishment and high unemployment brought about by restricted credit. Clearly also it will accentuate the world depression by reducing the sales of other countries to Germany, and by creating intense competition for her exports in other markets."

With these two possibilities ruled out, the Committee reached the definite conclusion that it was necessary in the general interest, as well as that of Germany:

"1. That the existing volume of Germany's foreign credit should be maintained; and

"2. That part at all events of the capital which had been withdrawn should be replaced from foreign sources."

This second recommendation presented a further problem, in that, if the additional capital should be supplied in the form of short-term credits, Germany would be faced with a much greater difficulty in six months' time when the obligations became due, and Dr. Melchior particularly asked that no such additional short-term credits should be granted for fear of adding to the embarrassments of Germany.

The Committee therefore were emphatic in recording their opinion that "in order to ensure the financial stability of Germany, any additional credits provided should be in the form of a long-term loan, and such parts of the existing short-term credits as may suitably be treated in this way should be converted into long-term obligations."

Now to investors in long-term loan a satisfactory general economic situation, a favourable balance of trade, and a sound budget situation are essential factors; and, curiously enough, in Germany at that time these factors were all present. The London Conference had itself pointed out that there was nothing basically and fundamentally wrong with Germany's economic situation, a fact that was supported by the rapid recovery of the German export trade in recent years. As regards the balance of trade the statistics placed before the Committee showed that Germany had been able to convert an import surplus into an even balance in 1929, and to create an export surplus in 1930 and the first quarter of 1931.[1] Though the

[1] The actual export surplus for the year 1931 was estimated in January 1932 to be RM. 2·9 milliards (£145 million).

public finances of Germany had frequently been the subject of severe criticism by the Dawes Committee, later in the reports of the Agent-General for Reparation Payments, and more recently still by Dr. Schacht, when President of the Reichsbank,[1] the Brüning Government had given proof of its determination to put the country's finances on a sound basis.

But notwithstanding all these factors in Germany's favour, the Committee could not conceal from itself the fact that the raising of a long-term loan to Germany was impossible without a restoration of international confidence in the financial future of the country. To such a restoration there were two great obstacles, the political risk involved and the external obligations of Germany. Until the relations between Germany and other European Powers had been firmly established on a basis of sympathetic co-operation and mutual confidence, and an important source of internal political difficulty thereby removed from Germany, there could be no assurance of continued and peaceful economic progress, the first and most important condition of credit-worthiness.

In like manner so long as the external obligations of Germany were of a character that involved either a continuous increase of her foreign debt, or, alternatively a disproportion between her imports and exports on such a scale as to threaten the economic prosperity of other countries, the investor was not likely to regard the situation as satisfactory. The Committee were convinced that the London Conference, in recommending the maintenance of the volume of credits then in Germany, did so with the full realization that such a proposal was not a solution of the problem but merely a means of gaining time, during which steps for the re-establishment of the credit of Germany might be taken.

The final paragraphs of the Committee's Report are so pregnant with warning and common sense that no apology is made for reprinting them here, for their message is as appropriate to the position to-day as it was to the situation for which it was written, and the warning, though originally disregarded

[1] See above, p. 28.

with disastrous results, may yet be taken to heart with advantage.[1]

"But time is short. The body of the world's commerce—whose vitality is already low—has suffered a severe shock in one of its chief members. This has resulted in a partial paralysis which can only be cured by restoring the free circulation of money and of goods. We believe that this can be accomplished; but only if the Governments of the world will realize the responsibility that rests upon them and will take prompt measures to re-establish confidence. Their action alone can restore it. We think it essential that before the period of prolongation of credits recommended by the London Conference comes to an end they should give to the world the assurance that international political relations are established on a basis of mutual confidence, which is the *sine qua non* of economic recovery, and that the international payments to be made by Germany will not be such as to imperil the maintenance of her financial stability.

"We wish, however, to recall that, as we said at the outset, the German problem is part of a larger issue which deeply affects many other countries of the world. In this connection we wish to make two observations. The first is that in order to revive the demand and thus to put an end to the continued downward movement of prices—which is enclosing both debtor and creditor countries in a vicious circle of depression—it is essential that the normal process of investment of fresh capital should be resumed with a well-defined economic purpose in view—namely, an increase in the purchasing power of the world.

"Secondly, we would point out that the case of Germany provides the most forcible illustration of the fact that in recent years the world has been endeavouring to pursue two contradictory policies in permitting the development of an international financial system which involves the annual payment of large sums by debtor to creditor countries, while at the same time putting obstacles in the way of the free movement

[1] For text of the Report see *Documents on International Affairs*, 1931, p. 133.

of goods. So long as these obstacles remain, such movements of capital must necessarily throw the world's financial balance out of equilibrium. Financial remedies alone will be powerless to restore the world's economic prosperity until there is a radical change in this policy of obstruction, and international commerce—on which depends the progress of civilization—is allowed to resume its natural development.

"... We wish, however, to add that if a situation were brought about, in which the confidence of the investing public in the future economic and political stability of Germany could be restored, we are satisfied that the consolidation of part of her short-term debt and the provision of the additional working capital needed by her trade would present no serious difficulties. . . .

"*We therefore conclude by urging most earnestly upon all Governments concerned that they lose no time in taking the necessary measures for bringing about such conditions as will allow financial operations to bring to Germany—and thereby to the world—sorely needed assistance.*"

4

The Layton–Wiggin Report,[1] with the Dawes and the Young Plans, and later the Report of the Special Advisory Committee, ranks amongst the four most important documents in the history of reparations. Without any political ends to serve it sets forth clearly and fearlessly certain vital truths deduced from the study of indisputable facts.

Not the least important factor about the Report was its unanimity. At the outset the French member of the Committee had declared his inability to continue to attend the meetings if the question of reparations was to figure in the discussion. What wrestlings of the spirit M. Moreau passed through we shall never know, but eventually his private conscience as an economic expert would seem to have overcome his public

[1] This compound title is necessary in the cause of fairness, for although Mr. Wiggin presided over the meetings of the Committee, the drafting of the Report (as later in the case of the Special Advisory Committee) was in very large measure the work of Sir Walter Layton.

conscience as a nationalist Frenchman, and in face of the facts and the united opinions of his colleagues he signed the Report in the small hours of August 18th.

The Report itself marks a further step on the road towards sanity in the policy of international indebtedness. The Dawes Plan had called for a final settlement of reparation payments, and this the Young Plan had sought to achieve. The Layton–Wiggin Report now called the attention of the world to the futility of pursuing the contradictory policy of expecting "the annual payment of large sums by debtor to creditor countries, while at the same time putting obstacles in the way of the free movement of goods," and demanded an assurance by the creditor Powers that "international payments to be made by Germany will not be such as to imperil the maintenance of her financial stability." Later in the year, the Special Advisory Committee declared that "the adjustment of all inter-Governmental debts (reparations and other war debts) to the existing troubled situation of the world . . . is the only lasting step capable of re-establishing confidence, which is the very condition of economic stability and real peace."

The Committee having finished its work there was some uncertainty as to what should be done with its report. This went first to the Bank for International Settlements, the "parent-body" of the Committee, and was forwarded by the Chairman of the Bank to Mr. MacDonald as President of the London Conference. The uncertainty lay in the exact state of being of the Conference. The German Foreign Office was most anxious that the Report should be the subject of immediate consideration, and its legal experts maintained that like the Hague Conference of 1929, the London Conference had been adjourned until reconvened by its President. British and French official opinion, however, held that the Conference was dead, and that if further discussion was necessary, new machinery, in the shape of a fresh Conference, must be set up.[1]

[1] It should be explained that during this third week of August the Labour Government in Great Britain was passing through its death-pangs, and that British official opinion was completely preoccupied at the moment with the financial crisis in London. See below, p. 99.

For the moment therefore nothing was done. But events did not wait. Even at the moment that the experts signed their report a new phase in the financial crisis was developing. The tentacle of the crisis-octopus had reached to Great Britain, and the inconceivable was happening. British credit was being called in question, and the £ sterling was fighting for its life.

5

The British financial crisis in the summer of 1931 was attributable partly to budgetary policy pursued by the Labour Government and partly to the repercussion of events in Germany. Both these factors brought about the withdrawals of foreign balances in London which forced Great Britain to abandon the gold standard on September 21st.[1]

The warning which Mr. Snowden had uttered on February 11th in the House of Commons[2] had been completely ignored by the British Government, which continued to pursue a totally unsound financial policy. But though Mr. Snowden's Cassandra-like statement was ignored at home, British Socialist budgetary policy had long been viewed with grave anxiety especially in France and in the last month of 1930 and January of 1931, there had been a steady French drain on the gold reserves of London.

A further cause for Continental distrust of the stability of sterling was the fact that it was known that British banks were heavily involved in German credits which, as has already been seen, were considered as "frozen" as from July 17th in order to avoid a financial crash in Germany: "Several leading houses were known to have committed themselves to a particularly great extent, and it was an open secret that the amount of their German credits exceeded their own resources several

[1] It is impossible to deal here with all the complexities of this difficult and controversial subject. An attempt has, however, been made to summarize the immediate causes of the crisis. The full story is told with a wealth of dramatic detail by Dr. Paul Einzig in his book, *The Tragedy of the Pound* (London, Kegan Paul, 1932). See also Professor Toynbee's *Survey of International Affairs*, 1931 (Oxford University Press, 1932).
[2] See above, p. 33.

times over."[1] This gave rise to fears abroad as to the solvency of these acceptances, and the withdrawals from London increased.

An added cause of lack of confidence was the unfortunate moment chosen for the publication of the Report of the Macmillan Committee, according to which London's foreign short-term credits amounted to over £400 million as against her realizable short-term foreign claims. These, after deducting the "frozen" Central European assets, were hardly more than £50 million, thus leaving an uncovered short-term indebtedness of £350 million. This knowledge, given to the world in the midst of the German financial crisis,[2] produced the direst pessimism abroad, and only increased the tendency in France to withdraw balances and credits from London.

Owing to these continued withdrawals the pound on July 15th fell from its par value of 124·21 francs to the rate of 122·50 francs. Between that date and July 27th the losses sustained by the Bank of England amounted to £30 million, and although on the following day Mr. MacDonald in Berlin told foreign journalists that the expression "as safe as the Bank of England" was as true then as ever, it was necessary to resort to foreign credits to make this so. On July 30th the Bank Rate, which had already been raised on July 23rd from 2½ to 3½ per cent., was again raised to 4½ per cent., and on August 1st an arrangement was reached with the Federal Reserve Bank of New York and the Bank of France for the grant of a joint rediscount credit of £50 million to the Bank of England,[3] with which it was hoped to check the outflow of gold which in three weeks reduced the Bank's stock from £165 million to £133 million.[4]

At this moment there occurred an event which made the situation very much more grave and rendered the newly-

[1] Einzig, p. 65.
[2] The Macmillan Report was published on July 13, 1931, the day on which the Danat Bank closed its doors.
[3] In the case of the Bank of France the credit was to stand for three months, the longest period allowed by the Statutes of the Bank.
[4] According to the Cunliffe Report of 1919, the minimum gold requirements of Great Britain was £150 million.

gained credit of £50 million completely inadequate to stem the outrunning tide of gold. On July 31st the Royal Commission on National Expenditure, over which Sir George May had presided, presented its Report, and this sensational document precipitated a further panic abroad.

The May Report threw the searching spot-light of criticism on the economic policy of the Labour Party; it dispersed at one breath the froth of the Government's financial pretences and theories, and exposed the falsity of the original Budget computations, which, far from bringing in the anticipated surplus, would result in a deficit of £120 million.

There followed for the country a week of sickening anxiety, and for the Government of shuddering indecision, before Mr. MacDonald nerved himself for the task of his life and set about taking that swift and adequate action which the gravity of the situation demanded. The Cabinet Committee charged with devising means to bridge the gap between revenue and expenditure was advised that the position was in reality substantially worse than the May Committee had represented it. So grave was the situation considered, and so essential the obviation of all delay in making the necessary measures effective, that the Prime Minister called into conference the leaders of the Conservative and Liberal parties. They pledged their support on one condition—that the Government's measures for balancing the Budget were adequate and in the right proportion of economies and new taxation.

The Cabinet was in daily session during the third week in August, with the Opposition Leaders standing by for consultation.[1] A drastic programme of retrenchment was agreed upon in large measure. In an evil moment this was submitted to the Trades Union Congress (August 21st). This body banned many of the new economies, etc.—especially the proposed cut in the dole payments—and succeeded in intimidating so many Ministers that the Government, after an historic Cabinet meeting, was compelled to resign on August 24th.

[1] This would explain the preoccupation of British official opinion at the moment of the publication of the Layton–Wiggin Report on August 18th. See above, p. 96.

At this juncture His Majesty the King gave an outstanding instance of constitutional wisdom. He directed Mr. MacDonald to form a National Government composed of all parties to meet the financial emergency. The Conservative and Liberal Leaders agreed to serve under Mr. MacDonald, and on August 25th an Emergency Cabinet of ten members was formed, including the former Opposition Leaders and the five members of the former Government, Lord Sankey, Lord Amulree, Mr. Snowden, Mr. Thomas, and Sir William Jowett, who had remained loyal to the Prime Minister. The Marquess of Reading became Secretary of State for Foreign Affairs.

Parliament reassembled on September 8th and gave the National Government a Vote of Confidence by 309 votes to 250, the Labour Party now forming H.M. Opposition. Two days later Mr. Snowden introduced the Emergency Budget which, together with the Economy Bill which followed it, made provision for a balanced Budget in April 1932.

Thus did England meet the national crisis. But, though the drastic measures taken in the form of increased taxation and radical cuts in wages and salaries were wholly justified by the state of emergency, they produced a deplorable psychological effect abroad. The disclosures of the May Report had caused such a flood of withdrawals from London that the £50 million credit secured from the French and American central banks on August 1st was exhausted in little over a fortnight, and further foreign credits were necessary to maintain the stability of sterling.

On August 28th agreement was reached with American and French banks for a further credit of £80 million for the period of a year. In the case of America the arrangement was that a financial group would undertake to take up British Government Dollar Treasury Bills to a total not exceeding $200 million. In the case of France a sum not exceeding 5 milliards of francs would be made available partly in the form of a credit from French banks, and partly by an issue of British franc bills to the French public. In both cases the rate of interest charged was $4\frac{1}{4}$ per cent.

It had been hoped that the formation of a National Government in England might strengthen foreign confidence in the stability of sterling, but to observers, both at home and abroad, the British political situation was too uncertain. The National Government's majority was a very slim one, less than fifty votes, and the outcome of a General Election might, it was thought, very well be the return of the Labour Party to power with a clear majority, in which case the hopes of a stabilized Budget would vanish and the flight of British capital would become accentuated.

So the withdrawals continued almost unabated, and the authorities were using up the balance of their credits to maintain the stability of sterling at an average rate of nearly £20 million a week. By this time it was realized that the battle for stability was a losing one, and that it was really only a matter of time before Great Britain must suspend the gold standard. The final *coup de grâce*, however, came swiftly and unexpectedly.

The reduced rates of pay in the British Navy brought about by the Economy Bill were promulgated on September 12th. Instead of imposing a flat-rate cut from top to bottom an attempt was made to differentiate which imposed quite unnecessary hardships on certain ratings. In addition to this, by an unfortunate series of events these reductions had not been previously discussed with the ratings and came to them as a complete surprise. As a result a mutiny broke out in the Atlantic Fleet at Invergordon and the ships were recalled to their home ports. The "Invergordon Mutiny" was grossly exaggerated in the Continental Press, particularly the French, and also in a section of the British Press. It administered the final blow to the stability of sterling.

By September 18th the British authorities were forced to inform the French and American authorities that they had very nearly exhausted the credits available and fresh attempts were made to continue the defence of the pound. The French banks were prepared to participate in a third credit to the extent of £32 million on condition that the American banks made a similar sum available. The American authorities were, however, unwilling to participate as they duly realized that this third credit would be used up in the same way as the first two.

In view, therefore, of the fact that since July over £200 million had been withdrawn from London (of which £70 million had gone in the third week of September and £43 million between September 16th and 19th), and that no further credits could be obtained, the Bank of England on September 19th warned the central banks in France, Germany, and America that on the following day the Government would announce their decision to abandon the gold standard. The Bill to suspend the operation of the gold standard was passed through all its stages in both Houses of Parliament and received the Royal Assent on September 21st, and on the same day the bank rate was raised to 6 per cent.

Thus Great Britain, after a struggle which had cost her £130 million in additional indebtedness[1] abandoned the gold standard which she had adopted in 1925, and in many quarters in the City of London a sigh of relief went up. Conversely, in many quarters abroad, the news was received with the gravest anxiety.

6

It is necessary to treat the British financial crisis in some detail, partly because it was the outstanding event in Europe in August and September 1931, and partly because of its important repercussions on the reparation problem. The results in France and Germany of the abandonment of the gold standard by

[1] The first Franco-American credit of £50 million was due on October 31st. On this date £20 million (£10 million of each debt) was repaid, the Bank of England selling £15 million to make the repayment, and the balance of £30 million was renewed for a further period of three months. On February 1, 1932, the repayment of the credits of £15 million each to the Bank of France and the Federal Reserve Bank of New York was completed. But on this occasion the repayment did not involve any reduction in the gold reserve of the Bank of England. This fact illustrates the remarkable restoration of confidence in sterling which was brought about by the formation of the second National Government after the General Election of October 27, 1931. The repatriation of funds to London took place on a large scale, despite the difficulties of exchange in some countries.

Great Britain materially affected their policies towards inter-Governmental indebtedness.

France, who, it will be shown later, never for one moment dreamed that Great Britain would take the final step of going off the gold standard,[1] was adversely affected in three different ways. In the first place France had hitched her financial waggon to a golden star, and in 1931 she, together with the United States, held 80 per cent. of the world's gold supply, with her share of which she sought to attain her political ends. Great Britain's example of suspending the gold standard was followed within a few months by a number of other States, amongst them the three Scandinavian countries, Finland, Portugal, Japan, Egypt, Greece, and several South American States. These, together with the British Empire,[2] tended to form a "Sterling Empire," which agreed to accept sterling as its basis of exchange instead of gold.[3] This was a direct and dangerous challenge to the "Gold Empire" of which France, in Europe, was the ruler.

Secondly, the Bank of France, which held some £70 million in sterling balances suffered heavy losses to the amount of £20 million from the depreciation of sterling, the deficit being guaranteed by the State, and other French banks suffered accordingly in proportion to the amount of their holdings.

Thirdly, the depreciation of sterling put a ban on imports and enabled British goods to be placed on the foreign market at very much more favourable terms than before, and this led the French to place a surtax on the importation of goods from England.

It was this third factor which affected Germany so vitally. The competition of British goods at more advantageous rates formed the last straw in the case of numerous German firms which even before the crisis could barely keep their heads above water. In, for example, the matter of coal; British coal

[1] See below, pp. 113–114.
[2] Of the British Dominions, only South Africa remained on the gold standard.
[3] The idea of a "Sterling Empire" is dealt with by Commander Stephen King-Hall in his entertaining if flippant pamphlet, *Britain's Chance*, published by the *New Statesman and Nation*, January 1932.

was obtainable in Germany at 2s. 6d. a ton cheaper than German coal, with the result that the bunkering trade of the ports of Bremen and Hamburg dwindled away to nothing, German ships preferring to take on British coal at Rotterdam.

In addition to this, many firms in Germany carried on their business in terms of sterling, and consequently suffered considerable loss.[1] It is beyond doubt that the abandonment of the gold standard by Great Britain was the direct cause of a large increase in the number of unemployed in Germany, a number which by the end of the year had risen to over 5,900,000, and it contributed materially to the situation which forced Germany to make application for a moratorium on November 19th.[2]

Thus, far from taking action on the advice of the Wise Men of Basle, Europe seemed in the late autumn of 1931 to be heading for economic and financial destruction with increasing rapidity. The steps taken by each individual country to protect itself reacted to the detriment of every other country, and consequently added to the general dangerous condition of all. Yet the time for combined and united action for the betterment of all had not yet come.

[1] This, of course, occurred in many other countries besides Germany, and, indeed, the extent to which sterling was used as an international currency was not fully realized until after the suspension of the gold standard. German machinery was sold to the U.S.S.R. in terms of sterling; similarly grain was exported from Rumania, coal sold by Poland to Scandinavia, and Italian cotton goods sold to China, all in terms of sterling, and the depreciation caused general confusion for a period. See Einzig, pp. 132–133.

[2] The "Abnormal Import Duties" imposed later by the National Government also hit Germany very hard, forcing her to take measures of retaliation, and were a contributing factor to her economic condition at the close of the year.

CHAPTER IV

M. LAVAL IN WONDERLAND

1

ONE of the most important factors in the later phase of the reparation problem was the dominant position occupied by France by reason of the large quantities of her gold stocks and the political ends to which she put them. For France the war did not end with the Armistice and the Treaty of Versailles.[1] The former merely closed the military phase of the hostilities, while the second marked the limit which could be obtained by methods of diplomacy. There remained to France a further field of activity, that of international finance, and, although diplomacy took precedence for some years, the torch which M. Clemenceau and Marshal Foch had lit and carried aloft for France was caught up and handed on by MM. Poincaré, Laval, Tardieu, and Flandin, till, in the summer of 1931, France had achieved the position of financial dictator of Europe and was able seriously to challenge and threaten the supremacy of the United States.

This pinnacle of power was not attained without the circumventing of serious obstacles. From 1920 to 1926 the franc fell steadily in value, and this decline remained unchecked through successive Cabinets, save for the temporarily successful attempt of the first post-war Poincaré Ministry in 1924, which produced a sharp recovery.[2] From 1924 to 1926 the fall of the franc was almost uninterrupted, and touched bottom at 250 to the £ sterling in the August of the latter year, during the

---

[1] As recently as May 1932, M. Poincaré, in a final appeal to the French electorate to support M. Tardieu at the second ballot on May 8th, declared, in a Press interview, "We have not yet finished the war." See *L'Intransigeant*, May 5, 1932.

[2] With the assistance of a credit of £5 million granted by a British banking group headed by Lazard Frères, together with an American credit amounting to $100,000,000, M. Poincaré was enabled to check the fall of the franc and to bring about a temporary recovery. This, however, did not survive the fall of the Government after the May elections of 1924.

distracted efforts of M. Herriot and others to prevent its following the course of the mark and vanishing altogether.

At this moment M. Poincaré reappeared as the saviour of his country and, by means of drastic measures which involved the wiping out of four-fifths of the value of *rentes*, bank deposits, and securities with fixed interest, succeeded in stopping the rot and pegging the franc at 124 to the pound, an action which has been described as "a master-stroke without parallel in financial history," and which marked out its author as "the greatest financial statesman of our generation."[1]

From the moment that M. Poincaré persuaded the people of France, albeit unwillingly enough, to make long overdue fiscal sacrifices, French finances never looked back, and almost at once there began the accumulation of that "fighting fund" which was to play so important a part in the world's history some five years later. The origin of these "sinews of financial warfare" had been in the Spa Agreement of 1921, wherein France was allotted 52 per cent. of German reparation payment,[2] so that a more or less steady flow of gold had been coming into the State coffers even during the worst years of French inflation.[3] From 1927 onwards there were additional sources for accumulation of gold.

The drastic but successful measures taken by M. Poincaré re-established French confidence in France, and much capital which had taken flight abroad between 1919 and 1926 was repatriated. The majority of these exports of capital had been carried out when the franc stood at 50–100 to the pound; repatriations took place when the value was between 124 and 150, so that France repurchased the francs she had sold to

[1] See *Behind the Scenes of International Finance*, by Paul Einzig (London, Macmillan, 1932), pp. 30–31. This book deals in detail with the development and consequences of French post-war financial policy. See also *Le drame financier de 1924–1928*, by Raymond Philippe (Paris, Librairie Gallimard, 1931), pp. 115–148.

[2] By the Paris Financial Agreement of January 1925 the French percentage was increased to 54 per cent.

[3] The Wiesbaden Agreement of 1921, negotiated by Herr Rathenau and M. Loucheur, provided for the reconstruction of French devastated areas by German workmen in part lieu of financial reparation. The Agreement was repudiated by the French Government, who preferred to receive cash payments in gold.

foreigners at about half the price they had paid for them originally. In addition to this, the stabilization of the franc at 124 had wiped out four-fifths of France's external indebtedness in terms of francs, thus freeing her at a stroke from the greater part of her obligations.

On the other hand, the French Debt-Funding Agreements concluded with Great Britain and the United States in 1926 resulted, on account of the pessimistic view generally taken of the then financial position of France, in a considerable measure of scaling down in both cases. The Churchill–Caillaux Agreement of July 12, 1926, cancelled 42 per cent. of the French Debt to Great Britain; while the Mellon–Bérenger Agreement of April 29, 1926, resulted in an even greater reduction of 50 per cent. As a result of the reductions contained in these agreements, the ratifications of which were postponed until 1928 when France had recovered her financial strength, French receipts from reparation payments exceeded the war-debt payments due to Great Britain and America.

Other means were resorted to to swell the gold store of France. France's creditors were paid in francs at the rate of 124 to the pound, while her debtors were expected, and in some cases forced, to pay in gold. For example, the British holders of French War Loans were, in spite of the protests of the British Government, repaid, not at the rate of 31 francs to the pound at which the *rentes* had been bought, but at the value of 124,[1] involving capital depreciation of 75 per cent., and an approximate diminution in interest of 80 per cent.

2

With these and other forces moving in her favour France was enabled in June 1928 to restore the gold standard and to enter into the arena of international finance as an active rival to Great Britain and the United States as a market available for foreign borrowers. By this time too the "fighting fund" had

[1] See British White Paper, Cmd. 3779.

grown sufficiently strong to enable it to be put to its primary use—the realization of French political ambitions.

The first attempt to utilize this new weapon was made during the first Hague Conference of August 1929. The compromise scheme arrived at by the Young Committee had increased the French share of the reparation payments at the expense of the British share, and at the Hague Conference, Mr. Snowden made a stubborn stand against this unjustified reduction in the British proportion.[1] In so doing he made use of certain uncomplimentary phrases at which M. Chéron, French Minister of Finance, took personal offence. French gold withdrawals from London had begun after the victory of the Labour Party in the General Election of May. They now increased heavily in the hope of forcing the British Chancellor of the Exchequer to modify his position. But on this occasion the new weapon of finance proved ineffective, for although some £20 million of gold was withdrawn from the Bank of England, the British position was maintained and the French were forced to agree to the revised scheme of percentages.

Unsuccessful also was the second attempt to influence British foreign policy which occurred in May 1930, during the negotiations for the mobilization of German reparation annuities. Despite heavy gold withdrawals from London, the French authorities had eventually and unwillingly to agree to the proceeds of the London issue of the Young Loan being retained in England, and the London issue not being interchangeable with the rest of the Loan. Nevertheless, French gold withdrawals continued from London throughout the remainder of the year until checked by an agreement reached by British and French Treasury officials in January 1931.

At the same time France made a determined effort to "capture" the Bank for International Settlements. Two initial successes were won at an early date. French influence prevented the seat of the Bank being established in London, preferring Basle as a more suitable site; and French influence secured the appointment as General Manager of the Bank, of M. Pierre

[1] See *Reparations*, pp. 106–123.

Quesnay, one of the most astute and nationalistic of French banking experts.

Having obtained both the seat and the General Manager of the Bank to their liking, the French authorities were anxious to secure the appointment of a number of directors to the Board, which originally consisted of representatives of the Central Banks of the Great Powers. At the board meeting of April 1931, therefore, the French directors proposed the appointment of representatives of the Czechoslovak, Yugoslav, and Polish Central Banks. This project was rejected, and though three new directors were appointed they were representatives of the neutral States of Sweden, Switzerland, and Holland. So that this attempt of the French to gain control of the Board was frustrated.

3

By the spring of 1931 France had attained a position unique in the post-war history of Europe. Her unemployment was negligible, her currency stable, and her armed forces the largest on the Continent with the exception of those of the Soviet Union. Moreover, she had control over nearly a quarter of the gold of the world. It is a matter of interesting speculation as to what would have been the attitude of France at this juncture had no untoward event occurred. French apologists insist that France would unquestionably have pursued a course amicable to all parties and directed towards the general amelioration of the international economic situation had not the whole position been altered by the bombshell of the Austro-German Customs Union, and it is possible, apart from withholding gold supplies from their natural functions, that this is true. On the other hand, with the approach of the Disarmament Conference and the very definite French attitude towards it (disclosed later in the Memorandum of July 21st), it would seem very improbable that France could resist the opportunity to make use of her paramount financial position to obtain the realization of her ambitions.

Nothing, however, can exonerate the German Government from the charge of crass stupidity and lack of judgment in precipitating, at such a moment and in such a manner, a situation which jeopardized the peace of Europe and provided the French Government with an excellent excuse for adopting an aggressive policy both financially and politically. French fears as to the establishment of a German hegemony over Central and South-Eastern Europe were not entirely without foundation. For example, Rumania and Yugoslavia, although close allies of France, were in process of improving their commercial relations with Germany because she offered the best market for their grain and because she could supply them best with agricultural implements. And although it was becoming more and more generally realized that some form of commercial union between Germany and Austria was inevitable sooner or later,[1] no worse time could have been chosen to advance it, and no method more calculated to arouse suspicion and provoke resentment.

Though great blame attaches to Germany for her part in the affair, it is equally difficult to excuse the subsequent policy of France in bringing about an international financial crisis. For France now moved definitely and speedily, directing with military precision three successive financial offensives, the first against Austria and Germany, and subsequently against Great Britain, the second against Italy, and the third against the United States.

The Kreditanstalt crisis, the outline of which has already been given in a previous chapter,[2] provided France with her first opening. The share of the Austrian Government in the deficit of the Bank amounted to some £5 million, and an appeal was made to the financial authorities of the Powers to grant a loan for this amount. A tentative agreement was reached in May whereby French and British authorities, in company with others, would take up the loan, but at noon on June 16th the French authorities presented an ultimatum containing two

[1] The affair of the Kreditanstalt alone gave ample evidence that Austria is economically incapable of maintaining her independent existence.
[2] See above, p. 36.

points : first, that Austria should accept complete financial control by the League of Nations, consenting in advance to abide by any decision arrived at; and, secondly, that Austria should address to the French Government a letter announcing her pledge to the League of Nations and at the same time pledging herself to the French Government that she would not enter into any agreements or affiliations which might impair in any way her sovereignty. This final condition was of course aimed at achieving the abandonment by Austria of the Customs Union project, notwithstanding the fact that this question had been referred to the Permanent Court of International Justice by the Council of the League on May 22nd, and was, therefore, *sub judice*. In return for this undertaking, which had to be agreed to by eight o'clock the same night, France was prepared to grant, not a long-term loan, but a short-term credit of £2,300,000. This attempt at what was nothing less than political blackmail caused considerable indignation in official circles, not only in Germany and Austria, but also in Great Britain and the United States.[1] The Austrian Government refused French assistance on these terms, and its courage was rewarded twenty-four hours later when the Bank of England, through the Bank for International Settlements, advanced a credit of £4,286,000 to the National Bank of Austria.[2]

France was defeated in her first attempt to force Austria to abandon the Customs Union—a defeat which provoked a wave of French indignation against England—but her victory was in reality only postponed. By September the Austrian financial situation had appreciably worsened and she was forced to appeal

[1] It materially influenced President Hoover in adopting the line of action which had been urged on him for some time past by such of his advisers as Mr. Owen D. Young, Mr. Eugene Meyer, Mr. Ogden Mills, and Mr. Mellon. This policy found expression in his offer of June 20th.

[2] At the end of August 1931, the Bank of England, hard pressed in the battle for the defence of sterling, requested the refund of this short-term loan. An agreement was reached that £1 million should be refunded in two instalments (£800,000 on September 1st and the balance on September 16th). On September 17th the League Financial Committee recommended a loan to Austria of £7,100,000, of which £2,700,000 was to be earmarked for the repayment of the British credit. Later, on January 15, 1932, the Bank of England consented to a further prolongation of the loan.

to the League for financial assistance. At that time, with Great Britain, Italy, and Germany eliminated from the international financial arena, there remained only France from whom assistance could come. The Austrian Chancellor could no longer resist French financial pressure. On September 3rd he publicly announced the abandonment by his country of the Customs Union project. Two days later the decision of the Permanent Court on the same question was made public, declaring by eight votes to seven the proposed Union to be legally incompatible with the Protocol of 1922. Though it is believed that the essence of the Court's decision was known in Geneva on September 3rd, Dr. Schober was not allowed to make use of it in making his statement, and was forced to drink the cup of humiliation to the dregs.[1] A fortnight later, on September 17th, the League Financial Committee, with the French representative assenting, agreed to recommend the granting to Austria of a loan of £7,100,000. The French triumph was complete.

In another chapter there is given the record of the similar tactics pursued, unsuccessfully, by France against Germany both during the Franco-American negotiations prior to the Hoover Agreement of July 6th, and, later, during the Paris conversations which preceded the London Conference of July 21st–23rd.[2] In each case Germany, with the support of Great Britain and the United States, was able to reject the French proposals and conditions, but the final advantage went to France, who was able to veto discussion at the London Conference of any question essential to the final solution of the crisis.

In the account of the London financial crisis already given on a previous page[3] no mention is made of individual withdrawals. It is, however, impossible to ignore the part played in the crisis by the big French banks, since during its course they withdrew from London between £40 and £50 million. It would be entirely misleading to attribute the abandonment of the gold standard by Great Britain to French withdrawals

[1] See *Disarmament and Security*, pp. 345–346.
[2] See above, pp. 75–8.   [3] See above, pp. 97–102.

alone, but, on the other hand, it would be equally erroneous to under-estimate the important factor which these withdrawals formed.

There is no evidence to show that either the Bank of France or the authorities of the French Treasury made withdrawals themselves, but it is certain that in the early days of the crisis they took no steps either to check the activities of the French banks or to counteract this movement. It is a well-known fact that banks in France are more susceptible to Governmental influence than in other countries, and it would have been not impossible for the French authorities, had they been so disposed, to take measures to influence the activities of the French banks in favour of sterling.

The withdrawal of French balances from London continued unchecked until the last week of July, at which time the gold reserves of the Bank of England had dwindled to £130 million. It was at this moment that the French authorities became aware of the inevitable disaster ahead and feverishly began to support sterling against a collapse which would endanger their own holdings. The Bank of France began to buy sterling heavily; £15 million was purchased in ten days. At the same time it made offers for a credit for the purpose of supporting sterling, and French banks were requested to refrain from withdrawing further balances.

With the negotiation of the first Franco-American credit of £50 million on August 1st, the French victory seemed complete, for manifestly Great Britain could no longer give financial assistance abroad, and the London market was perforce closed to foreign buyers. But the French had started an avalanche which they could not check. Although French withdrawals declined in volume, those of other countries continued unabated, and a second Franco-American credit of £80 million was necessary if sterling was to be saved. But this too proved ineffectual, and though the French were prepared to participate in a third credit to the extent of £32 million, the American authorities were unwilling.[1] On September 20th the inevitable but incredible

[1] See above, pp. 98–100.

happened and Great Britain, by abandoning the gold standard, wrested from the French the final fruits of the victory. This action "constituted a first-rate victory for Great Britain and a severe defeat for France";[1] for although Great Britain could not give assistance abroad and thus put a spoke in the wheel of France, as in the case of the Kreditanstalt, she had at one stroke placed herself outside the power of France, who was forced to abandon all hopes of influencing British foreign policy. Moreover, the detrimental effect to France of the depreciated pound and the subsequent tariff policy of Great Britain was very considerable.[2]

So considerable were these losses and so detrimental was the new British policy to French interests, that at once a "whispering campaign" was inaugurated to force the pound up again. The Press proclaimed the fervent desire of France to assist Great Britain to stabilize the pound at 100 francs; on numberless occasions the newspapers announced the British intention to do this. On the occasion of Lord Reading's visit to M. Laval early in October it was widely reported that the two statesmen had agreed on this figure, and a few days later there was printed a fictitious interview with one of the directors of the Bank of England in which the rate of 100 francs to the £ sterling was mentioned as stabilization point. But despite all these efforts to the contrary the pound remained at an undesirably low rate of exchange, and French interests continued to suffer accordingly.

In this campaign France had definitely over-reached herself, and the very magnitude of her success recoiled upon her own head and rendered sterile all that had been achieved.

4

The French offensive against Italy was more successful; indeed there were points about it reminiscent of an earlier and better-known Italian campaign. In other works the present author has told the story of the efforts, in the main unsuccessful, made by Italy during the years 1924–1926 to detach the States of the

[1] See *International Finance*, p. 125.   [2] See above, pp. 103–104.

Little Entente from their allegiance to France, and of the much more successful policy pursued by that same country from 1927 to 1930 in forming an anti-Yugoslav *bloc* by means of alliances with Hungary, Bulgaria, and Albania.[1]

By 1930 Italian influence was paramount in South-Eastern Europe, with the exception of Yugoslavia, and Italian diplomacy had succeeded in a large measure in alienating Rumania both from French orientation and from the Little Entente. At the close of 1931 French influence, backed by French gold, was paramount alike amongst the vassal States of France bound to her by ties of alliance and the ex-enemy States which Italy had formerly succeeded in mobilizing against her.[2]

The obvious course open to France was twofold: first, to strengthen the position of her ally Yugoslavia, and, secondly, to obtain control of Italy's allies, Hungary and Bulgaria. Opportunities for this were easily come by in the year 1931. The crisis which had begun in Austria in May had spread east as well as north, and Hungary was soon in as bad a plight as her neighbour. Because of its close connection with the Austrian Kreditanstalt the Hungarian National Credit Bank became heavily involved in the losses of the former, and other Budapest houses were affected. To meet the crisis the National Bank of Hungary in June obtained a credit of £4 million from the Bank for International Settlements, but this amount proved inadequate, and the Government began negotiations for the granting of a credit of £5 million in the form of Hungarian Treasury Bonds, redeemable in eighteen months. It was confidently believed in Budapest that either the Bank of England would repeat its gesture in the case of the Kreditanstalt or that Italy would come to the assistance of her ally with financial aid. But the British authorities were at first too closely occupied with the German crisis and, later, too deeply concerned with the defence of sterling to give help to Hungary; while, however much Signor Mussolini might wish to support her, he wisely, if reluctantly, decided that his first duty was to Italy, and that

---

[1] See *The Problem of Security* (George Allen & Unwin, 1927), pp. 194–195, 198–199; also *Disarmament and Security*, pp. 31–32, 307–312.
[2] See *International Finance*, pp. 108–115.

the financial resources of the country must be conserved against possible attacks on the lira.[1]

With London and Rome eliminated as sources of support, there remained only Paris, and the French authorities were ready and willing to help—but on their own terms. If Hungary wanted French assistance she must abandon her Italian orientation, and cease her campaign for treaty-revision and her aggressive attitude towards the Little Entente. As the summer drew on it became apparent that there was no alternative to acceptance. On August 14th France agreed to participate in the loan to the extent of £2,400,000;[2] £1 million was taken up by Hungarian banks and the remaining £1,600,000 by Italian, Swiss, and Dutch houses. Five days later, on August 19th, Count Bethlen's Government, which had negotiated the Italian alliance, resigned and was replaced (on August 23rd) by a Ministry headed by Count Karl Karolyi, who was credited with pro-French sentiments.[3]

Having established a financial tutelage over both Vienna and Budapest, France began to revive an old dream dear to the heart of the Quai d'Orsay. This was nothing less than the restoration of the Austro-Hungarian Empire under the House of Hapsburg, and it was hoped by this means to destroy for ever all chances of an Austro-German *Anschluss*. There is every reason to believe that this scheme is being held in reserve by the Quai d'Orsay, ready to be brought forward at the appropriate moment.[4]

Such a proposal very naturally aroused the gravest opposition from the Little Entente, which had originally been formed to

[1] The justification of this policy was shown later in the year when, in September and October 1931, the lira was submitted to heavy speculative attacks.

[2] From this amount were deducted certain claims outstanding against the Hungarian banks, so that the amount actually received by Hungary was very small.

[3] In September 1932, when French influence in Central Europe was beginning to diminish, Count Karl Karolyi was replaced in the premiership by the more nationalist General Gömbös, a follower of Count Bethlen.

[4] Italy, too, had been dreaming of a Hapsburg restoration, but along different lines. It was proposed to unite Hungary and Rumania into a dual monarchy with Carol as Emperor, Otto as titular King of Hungary, and Nicholas, if he could be persuaded to forsake his morganatic wife, as Prince of Transylvania.

prevent any form of Hapsburg restoration. But here again France had the whip-hand. On more than one occasion during the summer of 1931 the Central European crisis occasioned runs on the Central Banks of Czechoslovakia, Yugoslavia, and Rumania, which could not have kept their heads above water had it not been for French financial assistance.

In the case of Yugoslavia the fact was demonstrated that even allies must conform to the conditions of France if they desired French assistance. France had never approved the dictatorship which King Alexander had proclaimed in 1929, but hitherto had had little opportunity to mark her disapproval with any other action than diplomatic protest. In the fateful summer of 1931, however, Yugoslavia, in company with other Central and Eastern European States, found herself caught in the toils of the financial crisis. Appeals to Paris for support were met with the implacable reply, "No constitution, no loan." On September 2nd King Alexander bowed before the storm and restored constitutional government to the country. Even then the French authorities were in no hurry to assist the Yugoslav Treasury, and it was not until the middle of October, after it had been necessary to introduce severe restriction on foreign exchange transactions, that the National Bank was able to secure a loan of £2,400,000.[1]

Perhaps the most pathetic was the case of Bulgaria, Italy's second ally. This country was in the autumn of 1931 in desperate straits, and in great need of external assistance. Encouraged by the French authorities to hope for financial help from Paris, the Bulgarian Finance Minister, M. Moloff, stated at Geneva in September that the Government would prefer to forgo the League Loan and to establish direct contact with French banking interests. At the last moment, however, the hopes thus raised were dashed to the ground by the withdrawal of French efforts of assistance and the unfortunate State thus fell between two stools.

---

[1] In April 1932 the Yugoslav Prime Minister, General Zhivkovitch, who had been a strong supporter of the royal dictatorship, resigned, and was replaced by the more francophil M. Marinkovitch.

The defeat of Italy was heavy and complete. The intricate system of alliance which she had so laboriously built up in Central Europe was destroyed owing to the superior financial strength of France. For the moment Italian influence in Vienna, Budapest, Sofia, and Bucharest suffered a complete eclipse, and it was sometime before it was restored. France had gained a substantial victory.

5

The greatest importance was attached by France to her future relations with the United States, upon which the attitude of the United States towards war debts bore so directly. The world looked on with grave anxiety, pondering the issue, for if France could, even temporarily, eliminate America in the same way that she had eliminated Great Britain and Italy, then indeed she had Germany at her mercy and her dream of world-dominion would be realized.

Franco-American relations had not improved during the summer of 1931. The well-laid plans of France, which had received a severe check on June 17th, when the Bank of England had come to the rescue of Austria, suffered a much greater setback three days later, when on June 20th President Hoover made his proposal for a year's moratorium. *Au fond*, public and official opinion in France regarded this step as an unwarranted interference on the part of America and an attempt to cheat France of her rightful and legal due of reparations. French relations with America suffered accordingly.

On the other hand, public opinion in the United States had been deeply shocked at the attitude displayed by France both during the negotiation prior to the Agreement of July 6th, and also during the Paris Conversations and the London Conference of July 18th–23rd, so that in neither country was there any sympathy for the international policy of the other.

Yet despite this antagonism both France and the United States had certain fundamental interests in common which neither could afford to ignore. For example, between them the two countries controlled nearly 80 per cent. of the gold stocks of the world, and hence both were deeply interested in the maintenance of the gold standard, both having been adversely affected by the British abandonment itself.

It was vital to French policy that, at the conclusion of the Hoover Year, the Young Plan should re-enter into force in all its aspects, and should be allowed to continue undisturbed by further philanthropic interruptions. Yet it was known that Mr. Hoover had designs more far-reaching than his June proposals. The exact nature of these plans was uncertain, but it was persistently rumoured that the President would propose an extension of the moratorium for five years, or that he would suggest a drastic scaling down of war debts and reparations in proportion to the lessened capacity to pay of the debtor nations; or again, that he would return to his old thesis of the connection between armaments and indebtedness and propose a cut of 50 per cent. in debt payments in return for a 25 per cent. reduction in armament budgets.

Any of these three courses would run definitely counter to the realization of French ambitions, though they would have proved immensely beneficial to the rest of mankind, and it was well understood in Paris that if any of these proposals were made they would be received with the liveliest enthusiasm by all except France, who would then be completely isolated. The aim of French policy must, therefore, be to nip any such plans in the bud before they could blossom into full-blown proposals. There must on no account be a repetition of the Hoover offer, and it was with this end in view that French diplomacy and French financial influence were mobilized against the United States in the autumn of 1931, when M. Laval determined to negotiate in person with President Hoover.

At a glance it would seem that American Goliath with its enormous gold reserves, more than twice those of its opponent, would be more than a match for the French David. But there were a number of weak spots in the giant's armour. The short-term liabilities of the United States to foreign countries were enormous, and at the end of 1930 the amount of foreign balances held in New York was estimated at three milliard dollars (£600 million). In view of the fact that most of the balances withdrawn from Berlin and London during the crisis were transferred to New York (a direction followed to a great extent by the flight of German and British capital), the figure at the end of September 1931 must have been nearer four and a half milliards (£900 million), and of these balances French banks held a very large number.

Though the amount of American short-term credits in foreign countries was very considerable, it must be remembered that of these the greater part were "frozen" in Germany as a result of the Standstill Agreement, and a further substantial portion in London could not be withdrawn without heavy loss on account of the depreciation in the value of sterling. So that the net amount of New York's short-term liabilities was about two and a half milliard dollars.[1]

An additional short-term liability was to be found in the fact that a large amount of American stocks and bonds was held abroad, and though the immense gold reserves, estimated at 5 milliard dollars, were more than ample to cover the maximum rush from foreign withdrawals, it was feared on Wall Street that heavy withdrawals of gold would cause a panic and might bring about a run on the banks.

The "barrage" of the French financial offensive against America was opened in the last days of September before New York could recover from the first shock of Great Britain's abandonment of the gold standard. France began to buy gold heavily; other countries followed suit. French banks began to repatriate their balances and the dollar exchange moved strongly in favour of France. As a result large shipments of gold began to cross the Atlantic, and that—"The —— arrived at Cherbourg to-day with a consignment of x million worth of gold for France"—became a regular item in the daily newspapers of Europe. It is estimated that by the middle of October over $600 million of gold was shipped from New York, and the Bank of France and the French Treasury became the greatest foreign holders of dollars.

[1] See *International Finance*, p. 132

The effect of these movements justified the fears of Wall Street. In Europe, dollar panics occurred in several countries, the public disposing of their holdings at a discount of from 5 to 6 per cent., and the Federal Reserve Bank was forced to conduct supporting transactions through the Paris Office of the Guaranty Trust Company of New York to maintain the dollar above gold export point. In America all over the country the small and medium-sized banks experienced runs, and an alarming number of bank failures resulted.

Such was the position on the eve of the French visit, and the visit itself, which formed the real offensive, was organized in two "wave attacks." The first was the arrival of M. Farnier, Deputy-Governor of the Bank of France, on October 15th, and the second, the arrival of M. Laval himself on October 22nd. The object of the dual mission was no less than to influence both the external and the domestic banking policy of the United States. In effect, what MM. Laval and Farnier said to President Hoover and Mr. Harrison of the Federal Reserve Bank was this: "Either you stop taking the initiative in the matter of war debts or we will withdraw our $600 million balances from New York. You've seen what we can do, and if you don't do what we want we shan't hesitate to give you extra inconvenience."

It was done more diplomatically than this, of course. France realized the outcry which would occur in every country if it were realized that bargaining was going on in this manner, and for this reason M. Farnier preceded M. Laval to America.

To the American authorities M. Farnier presented a virtual ultimatum. The Bank of France, said he, was anxious to avoid a repetition of its experience with its sterling balances, and unless the par exchange rate of its dollar balances was guaranteed it would be forced to withdraw them. He also asked for a better rate of interest on French official deposits and suggested that, to this end, the New York bank rate should be raised to $4\frac{1}{2}$ per cent. He announced his intention of transferring $200 million of the French official deposits from private banking houses to the Federal Reserve Bank.

The French demand for a higher deposit rate was unanimously rejected, and an agreement was reached that the balances of the Banque de France should remain untouched in New York and held at the disposal of the Federal Reserve Bank. But it was made clear that any final agreement must await the results of M. Laval's negotiations with President Hoover.

No political conference in post-war history has been so shrouded in secrecy as the Hoover–Laval Conversations which took place in Washington from October 22nd–25th. Since neither Statesman spoke the other's language and the discussions had, therefore, to be carried on through interpreters, the conversations lacked the degree of intimacy which played so important a part in the Rapidan Conference between President Hoover and Mr. MacDonald just two years previously, in October 1929, which had so beneficial an effect on Anglo-American relations.[1] The conversations with M. Laval were essentially of a more formal and certainly of a less amicable nature. No intimation of the decisions arrived at was allowed to leak out before the publication of the joint *communiqué* on October 25th.

Reference to war debts was made in the *communiqué* in the following statement:

"So far as inter-Governmental obligations were concerned we recognize that prior to the expiration of the Hoover Year of postponement some agreement regarding them may be necessary, covering the period of business depression, as to the terms and conditions of which the two Governments make all reservations. The initiative in this matter should be taken at an early date by the European Powers principally concerned, within the framework of agreements prior to July 1, 1931."[2]

At first sight this announcement would tend to indicate a complete victory for French policy, by which France recaptured the initiative in the matter of reparations, and the United States agreed that the Young Plan must return into force at the end of the Hoover Year. It was in this light that the *communiqué* was interpreted to the French reading public by

[1] See *Disarmament and Security*, pp. 154–157.
[2] There was also a provision in the *communiqué* that neither State should abandon the gold standard without consulting the other. For full text see *Documents on International Affairs*, 1931, p. 126.

the French Press, and also by M. Laval in his speech to the Chambre on November 26th, when he assured the assembled Deputies that, as a result of his visit to America, France was henceforth amply protected against any such initiative as that of June.

But there were also those who looked more deeply into the position arising in America after M. Laval's departure, and who arrived at a very different conclusion. To these observers it appeared that the joint *communiqué* of October 25th signalized not a defeat but a victory for American diplomacy. There could be no doubt that, by the time of M. Laval's visit, Mr. Hoover had a very good idea of the very considerable opposition with which the ratification of his original Moratorium proposal would meet in Congress, when that body met in six weeks' time. He was also aware of the immediate impossibility of either taking steps to prolong the Moratorium or of doing anything in the direction of scaling down debts and reparations. His political popularity and power were at a low ebb and, all things considered, he was not too reluctant to surrender the initiative to France and to be in the position of being free to accept or reject any proposal which she might make.

France had, in fact, been "left with the baby," and the strength of the American position was clearly demonstrated when, in January 1932, after the report of the Special Advisory Committee, the French Government sounded the United States Government as to the possibility of an American proposal for an extension of the Hoover Moratorium, the reply returned by Washington was that "the initiative must come from the European States."[1]

The final issue had not been reached in the Franco-American affair. In the ensuing months conditions became worse in each country, and in the final analysis the advantage lay with the United States in spite of every effort on the part of France.

---

[1] See below, pp. 182–183.

CHAPTER V

GERMANY'S S.O.S.

1

THE Hoover–Laval Agreement of October 5, 1931, virtually opened a new phase of war-debt problems. From thence the thesis adopted was that reparations, with which inter-allied debts remained linked, were to be dealt with within the framework of the Young Plan, on the initiative of Germany and France, and at once. For France this meant an acknowledgment by the United States of her insistence upon attempting to preserve the distinction between conditional and unconditional annuities, in the hope that she would continue to receive substantial payments. American interpretation of the Agreement was that France and Germany should endeavour to arrive at a reparation settlement so clearly designed to inspire confidence that Congress would feel justified in making a fair counter-contribution by reducing debts.[1]

It therefore behoved M. Laval, on his return to Europe, to take as fleet steps as possible to reach some such agreement with Dr. Brüning, and, indeed, there were other causes which urged him to make his position secure. Even in America there had been tendencies which indicated that, although the United States Government might condone the continuance in force of the Young Plan, there were other powerful influences who thought otherwise. On October 23rd, Senator Borah, Chairman of the Committee on Foreign Relations, had roundly declared in favour of treaty revision as a whole, and specifically of the cancellations of debts and reparations. As if as an echo to this, there came to the French Premier, from across the Atlantic, the report of Signor Mussolini's speech at Naples on

---

[1] The action of Congress in attaching to the resolution ratifying the moratorium a declaration that it is "against the policy of Congress that any of the indebtedness of foreign countries to the United States should be in any way cancelled or reduced" was not anticipated at the time. See below, pp. 166–167.

October 25th, in which he put to his audience this poignant question: "How is it possible to speak of reconstruction unless there is a modification in certain clauses of certain peace treaties which have driven the world to the brink of material disaster and moral despair." Further confirmation of Italy's support for the German case was provided next day (October 26th), when Signor Grandi, then on a visit to Berlin, announced that "the Head of the Italian Government . . . has more than once declared that the reconstruction of Germany must be regarded as one of the most important elements in the reconstruction of Europe and of the whole world."

A further cause of disquietude to M. Laval was the result of the British General Election on October 27th, which brought about the formation of the second National Government (in which Sir John Simon replaced Lord Reading as Foreign Secretary) with a "Doctor's Mandate" and an overwhelming majority behind it. There was very little doubt that the discharge of this mandate would entail the imposition of tariffs which would inevitably prove detrimental to French trade.

Moreover, it was now clear—if it had ever been otherwise—that there was no possibility of Germany resuming payments at the end of the Hoover Year, that is to say, on July 1, 1932. When MM. Laval and Briand had visited Berlin in September 1931, it had been pointed out to them that Germany could not meet both her reparation and her private debts; one or the other would have to be materially reduced. To this the French Ministers had replied that the two liabilities were in no way related and that, whatever her private commitments might be, Germany would be expected to make some effort to resume reparation payments at the expiration of the Moratorium. In the month which followed the economic situation in Germany grew appreciably worse,[1] and by the time M. Laval returned at the beginning of November it was clear that some measures taken in accordance with the provisions of the Young Plan would have to be substituted for the prevailing relief occasioned by the Hoover Moratorium.

[1] See below, p. 128.

Accordingly, on the day following his return to Paris (November 3rd), M. Laval, together with M. Briand, began conversations with the German Ambassador, Herr von Hoesch. The latter, having given a full account of the situation in Germany, reiterated the view of his Government that the existing scale of both political and private debts could not be maintained, and eventually notified M. Laval that the German Government was considering an application to the Bank of International Settlements for the appointment of a consultative committee to investigate the German capacity to pay both reparations and private debts.

This move to link together the two liabilities and thereby to give them some legal connection was anything but acceptable to the French, who would allow no heresies to creep into the newly reconsecrated faiths of the Young Plan. M. Laval insisted upon the strict adherence to the very letter of his bond, and maintained that private debts must continue to be dealt with by direct negotiations between Germany and her creditors.

At the close of more than a fortnight's discussion the French carried their point. Obeisance was made to the Young Plan, and on November 19th Herr Dietrich, the Finance Minister, on behalf of the German Government, addressed a letter to the Bank for International Settlements asking that it should convoke "the Special Advisory Committee for which provision is made in the New Plan of the Hague Agreement of January 20, 1930."[1]

As early as June, Herr Dietrich stated, in explanation of his request, the German Government had decided that they would be unable to continue the payment of the annuities. That decision had been followed on June 21st by the declaration by President Hoover, but the hope that this would bring about a decisive turn in the world crisis had not been realized, and the Hoover Year by itself had proved to be insufficient to banish the danger of collapse. For this reason the British

[1] See above, p. 25. For text of German letter see *Documents on International Affairs*, 1931, p. 160.

Government in July took the initiative of calling the London Conference, the recommendations of which had resulted in the prolongation of the rediscount credit granted to the Reichsbank, in the Basle "Standstill" Agreement, and in the report of the Basle Committee of Experts nominated by the Bank of International Settlements. Important though these measures were, they were merely of a preparatory character. During the subsequent months the deepening of the world depression inevitably *produced* aggravated economic tension in Germany —if such were possible. The Government had, accordingly, decided to take advantage of the provisions of the Young Plan, the application of which was conditional on a declaration to the effect that the Government "had come to the conclusion in good faith that Germany's exchange and economic life might be seriously endangered by the transfer in part or in full of the postponable part of the annuities." In making this declaration the Government felt bound to state that it did not in effect do justice to the actual position, and it considered that the Committee should investigate the problem of Germany's economic situation as a whole, and should particularly consider the fact that the question of her private indebtedness had to be settled in due time, before the end of February, by an agreement to be concluded between the foreign creditors and the German debtors.

For France the sting lay in the tail of this letter, for although the German Government had kept to the agreed thesis that private debts must remain a matter for private negotiation, yet they had taken advantage of declaring this very thesis to draw the attention of the Bank of International Settlements —and therefore the Advisory Committee which it would appoint—to the very real connection which existed between reparations and private debts and the effect which these latter exercised on the economic situation of Germany. It was to this move that M. Laval's speeches in the Chambre on November 26th and 27th, and his Note of December 7th to Great Britain and Italy formed a reply.[1]

[1] See below, pp. 136, 137.

2

The German Government were justified in their statement that the bare declaration demanded of them by the Young Plan did not do justice to the gravity of the situation. Bad though the position in Germany was before September 20th, it grew appreciably and rapidly worse after the depreciation of sterling which followed the abandonment of the gold standard by Great Britain on that date. Germany's British commercial rivals were enabled to compete at a vast advantage, and, in addition, many firms who carried out their transactions in sterling suffered considerably. The depreciation of the pound gave the *coup de grâce* to a number of tottering firms and severely dislocated many others.

There remained no incentive to make profits beyond the actual standard of living, and many industrialists who had looked for some definite action as a result of the Layton–Wiggin Report began in desperation and disappointment to cut both production, staff, and wages. Throughout Germany failures in business and banking were on the increase. In September 1931 alone there were no fewer than 1,341 bankruptcies and 743 forced settlements,[1] as compared with 759 bankruptcies and 508 forced settlements in September 1930. At the same time 530,000 tons of shipping were lying idle in Hamburg basin alone (exclusive of Bremen), an increase of 150,000 tons on the previous month.

The heavy demand for credit accommodation at the end of September taxed the Reichsbank to a grave extent, increasing the rediscount holdings over RM. 3,500 million, note circulation to RM. 4,600 million, coincident with a decline in gold holdings to RM. 1,300 million, and foreign exchange to RM. 130 million.

To meet the situation, the Government, with the approval

---

[1] The total of bankruptcies for 1931 amounted to over 17,000, the highest number known. Notable among the failures of 1931 were the big brewery of Schultheiss-Patzenhofer and the Borsig Engineering Works, and, of course, the Nordwolle. In January 1932 the Junkers Works at Dessau also failed.

of the President, issued, on October 7th, the third Emergency
Decree within the year, "for safeguarding the economic and
financial situation and for combating political excesses." Like
its predecessors, the new Decree cut into private contracts and
acquired rights, and some of its provisions were very drastic.
Much of the Decree was devoted to assisting the financial
position of the States and municipalities. To the latter, weighed
down as they were by the burden of unemployment relief,
RM. 170 million were allotted in addition to the RM. 60 million
of the June Decree. This, it was hoped, would see them through
the approaching winter. The emergency powers already dele-
gated to the States and municipalities for balancing their
budgets were now extended to statutory public bodies, which
could regulate salary lists at discretion. Pensions were reduced
by 5 per cent., and all joint-stock and commodity bodies were
authorized to adjust their capital to altered economic conditions, either by withdrawing shares or writing down their
nominal value; cuts in salaries were also proposed. The general
object being to force down the level of prices to the reduced
purchasing power of the consumer and to diminish the cost
of production.

A special chapter of the Decree was devoted to the short-
term indebtedness of the municipalities, "which, in the interest
of all parties, demands a just settlement." It will be remembered
that the Layton–Wiggin Committee had recommended that
these debts, amounting to some RM. 355 million, should be
the subject of "standstill" agreements between debtors and
creditors.[1] This the Decree proposed to do; it also established
a "Department for Debt Conversion," under whose auspices,
it was hoped, creditors and debtors would arrive at a voluntary
understanding.

In the matter of "controlling public excesses," the Decree
set up "special courts" for summary judgment of terrorist acts
and serious taxation offences. The already existing severe
measures for repressing violent agitation were tightened up
to a great extent. The inviolability of person and domicile

[1] See above, p. 91.

where persons were found in possession of firearms was suspended; and the police were given authority to close cafés, beer-shops, and dwellings used as "barracks" by the extremist organization if disorder could be traced to them.[1]

In addition, the Decree made provision for other various measures: a practical abolition of all Government building operations for the next three years; a proposal to change the Governmental fiscal year to July 1st instead of April 1st; a reduction of 20 per cent. in the building tax; and a regulation making use of 5 per cent. potato flour compulsory in all wheat products. At the same time the motor-highway transport throughout the country was placed under the control of the Ministry of Transport, thereby establishing parity, after their long feud, between railways and road vehicles.

The position was not improved by a further manifestation of national disunity in Germany. On October 11th there was held a mass demonstration of the "National Opposition," including representative delegations from the Nazis, Nationalists, Stalhelm, and the German Peoples' Party[2] at Harzburg. At the same time the leaders of the "National Opposition," Herr Hitler, Dr. Hugenburg, Dr. Schacht, General von Seeckt, and others, held a conference which resulted in the formation of the "United Harzburg Front," pledged to oppose the Brüning Government and "The System" for which it stood.

By far the most important development of the Harzburg Conference, however, was a speech by Dr. Schacht, in which he attacked the financial policy of the Government, accusing them, together with the Reichsbank, of concealing the real financial position of the Reich. This, he insisted, was substantially worse than was generally believed. More particularly he declared that the foreign indebtedness of Germany was

---

[1] In this connection it is of interest to note the increase of political violence in Germany during recent years. In 1928 there were 8 deaths; in 1929, 42; in 1930, 50; and in 1931 a sudden rise to between 90 and 100. For example, there were 15 deaths, 200 serious casualties, and over 1,000 minor casualties in April and May 1931. See *Berliner Tageblatt*, June 1, 1931.

[2] This marked the formal adherence of the German Peoples' Party to the National Opposition, a move which had been anticipated since their support of the Stalhelm Referendum in August 1931.

considerably greater than had been shown in the Layton–
Wiggin Report, and that the Reichsbank was bolstering up
the Government.

This speech created a deep sense of uneasiness both at
home and abroad, and this was barely dispelled when Herr
Dietrich, on the following day (October 12th), in replying
to Dr. Schacht's allegations, declared that the Reichsbank
had not lent the Government a single *pfennig*, but had,
on the contrary, repaid RM. 287 million of floating debt
during the last six months. The weekly statement of the
Reichsbank, he maintained, in no way misrepresented the
position.

Nevertheless, when on October 30th the Reichsbank published its Report on the Foreign Indebtedness of Germany,
it disclosed the fact that Dr. Schacht had been justified in one
respect. The Reichsbank's Report showed that on July 28th
the short-term indebtedness of Germany amounted to
RM. 12,000 million, and her long-term debts to RM. 11,500
million. Now the figures supplied to the Wiggin Committee
—and published as annexes to its Report—had given the
short-term credits at the end of July as RM. 7,400 million
and the long-term credits at RM. 5,000 million. This dis-
crepancy proved Dr. Schacht once more to be a true—if
dangerously true—prophet.

Public and official confidence in the stability of the Brüning
Cabinet was somewhat renewed during the brief session of the
Reichstag (October 13th), in the course of which the Chancellor
scored a series of personal victories over the united efforts of
the Harzburg Front and the Communists, defeating a vote of
no confidence and a motion calling for a dissolution of the
Reichstag and a general election. But fears as to the political
situation in Germany were soon revived. On October 9th,
immediately before the session of the Reichstag, Dr. Brüning
had reconstructed his Cabinet. That is to say, he had dropped
Dr. Curtius and Herr Wirth, taking the portfolio of Foreign
Affairs himself and combining the Ministry of the Interior with
that of Defence under General Groener. In many quarters it

was believed that this was merely a temporary measure
pending the further reconstruction of the Cabinet towards the
Right, and this belief was strengthened during the latter days
of October and the beginning of November, when Herr Hitler
had a series of interviews with President von Hindenburg and
with the Chancellor. Dr. Hugenburg, the leader of the Nationalist Party, was also called into consultation, but eventually
the negotiations were abandoned as no common *modus vivendi*
could be found, Dr. Brüning firmly refusing to agree to the
terms put forward by the Harzburg Front, who demanded
the Ministries of Foreign Affairs, Interior, and Defence as the
price of their co-operation.[1]

It soon became apparent that not even the drastic provisions of the October Decree would suffice to combat the
rapidly worsening situation. Unemployment increased at a
rate which, even when seasonal increase was taken into consideration, proved greatly disquietening, as the following table
shows:[2]

Unemployed	Date	Increase	Since
4,355,000	September 30th	35,000	September 15th
4,484,000	October 16th	129,000	September 30th
4,622,000	October 30th	138,000	October 16th
4,840,000	November 15th	218,000	October 30th
5,057,000	November 30th	217,000	November 15th

The net increase was, therefore, more than three-quarters
of a million in two months. It continued to increase until, in
February 1932, it reached its peak of 6,128,000. At the same
time trade returns began to show a decline. Whereas in September and October a most satisfactory surplus of exports over

[1] A certain uneasiness abroad was also caused when, at the end of October,
it became known that Herr Hitler had had interviews with Lieut.-General
von Schleicher, Chief of Staff, and *chef de cabinet* to General Groener. Of
General Groener's two principal lieutenants, General von Hammerstein (who
succeeded General von Seeckt as General Officer Commanding the Reichswehr)
was known to be implacably opposed to Herr Hitler and the Nazis. General
von Schleicher, on the other hand, was said to entertain Nazi sympathies,
and it was therefore disconcerting to find him receiving the leader of the
party which had been shown at the Leipzig trials in the autumn of 1930 to
have successfully undermined the loyalty to the Reich of certain young
army officers.

[2] Official German figures quoted each fortnight in *The Times.*

imports had been returned,[1] by November a decline of 15 per cent. in exports was shown.

The financial position of Germany, too, during these months once again gave rise to anxiety, partly as a result of the uncertainty as to whether Germany would follow Great Britain's example in abandoning the gold standard. Before the end of September the Reichsbank had discovered certain gaps in the legislation and decrees affecting foreign currency, and also certain flaws in the "Standstill" Agreement of September 1st, which allowed a not inconsiderable amount of that currency to leave the country.[2] This was illustrated by the report of the Reichsbank for September 30th, viz.:[3]

Date	Gold and other Covering	Total Money in Circulation (Million Marks)	Bills
August 31st ..	1,722	5,313	3,101
September 23rd ..	1,672·2	5,123	3,003
September 30th ..	1,440	5,644	3,669

To meet this position, an Emergency Decree of October 2nd reduced the limit of *devisen* holdings without licence from the Reichsbank from 200 marks to 100, and the same limit was made to apply to the export of marks. Despite these restrictions and the great surplus of exports for September, the Reichsbank lost more gold and *devisen* in the first half of October. The covering of the Reichsbank notes amounted on October 15th to only 28·6 per cent., the £30 million of foreign credits being calculated as part of the covering. This unfavourable development of the position of the Reichsbank continued

---

[1] The September foreign trade returns reached a record in surplus of exports over imports. Exports were 835 million marks, imports only 448 million marks. The October returns also showed a surplus of exports amounting to nearly 400 million marks.
[2] In the month of September the Reichsbank had to pay out rather more than 400 million marks in gold and *devisen*, but this was on account of the release of 25 per cent. of the foreign credits.
[3] The *Economist*, October 10, 1931, p. 659.

unchecked, and by the middle of November the gold and
exchange reserve had fallen to something less than RM. 1,200
million, of which RM. 630 million were foreign credits lent
to the Reichsbank for a few months. In the second week of
November alone the Bank lost RM. 72 million worth of cover,
and even after the issue of a further foreign exchange regulation on November 15th the loans for the third week amounted
to RM. 50 million.[1] But for the great excess of exports over
imports the position would have been far worse.

Throughout October and November the economic and
financial position of Germany was considered by the Economic
Advisory Council—an emergency body rather in the nature
of an economic Privy Council, over which Marshal von Hindenburg presided in person—and on December 8th the remedies
which were considered necessary to meet the situation were
promulgated in the form of the fourth major Emergency
Decree, or *Notverordnung*. The severity of these measures was
unequalled save by the stringent emergency legislation during
the war. The Chancellor, in a national broadcast speech of
great dignity and statesmanlike appeal, described the Decree
as cutting deeper into the established notions of legal right
and sanctity than any since "times of great antiquity," and
said that Germany had been forced to take these measures
by the world situation. Under these conditions, he declared,
the payment of reparations must dislocate the economy of the
world, or of Europe, in the moment when Germany was
required to pay from an export surplus instead of from borrowed money, as in the past.

Under the provisions of the Fourth Emergency Decree, all
prices fixed by Cartel Conventions were to be reduced to within
10 per cent. of the level of July 1, 1931, and a corresponding
reduction of other than fixed prices was to be brought about
by means of a price regulation commissioner (*Preiskommissar*)
with far-reaching powers.[2] Railway freight rates were reduced

[1] This made an aggregate loss to the Reichsbank of RM. 550 million gold
and exchange since the coming into force of the "Standstill" Agreement on
September 1st. See *Economist*, November 28, 1931, p. 1008.
[2] Dr. Gördeler, Chief Burgomaster of Leipzig, was appointed to this post.

by from 5 per cent. to 25 per cent. as from December 16th,[1] and a similar reduction was made in postal rates and in the charges for gas, water, and electricity. An all-round reduction of rents was also provided.

At the same time a compulsory reduction of interest rates was ordained. Rates on all fixed interest-bearing securities, long-term Reich and municipal loans, other than loans contracted abroad, mortgages, debentures, etc., were to be reduced from 8 per cent. to 6 per cent.; interest at a higher rate than 8 per cent. to be reduced by from 25 per cent. to 50 per cent. Wages and salaries were cut down to the level prevailing in 1927;[2] pensions, too, were reduced.

Severe measures were outlined for those who placed outside the State the capital which they earned within it in such a way that it was lost to German industry and the German Exchequer. Delinquents were to be liable to a confiscatory tax of a quarter of their property. Arrest and imprisonment were to follow any attempt to evade the tax.

The Decree also included "measures to ensure public safety." It was forbidden to private persons to carry weapons, and both they and private societies were ordered to deliver up all weapons in their possession. The wearing of any uniform or sign that the wearer was a supporter of "any extreme political opinion" was likewise forbidden, and severe punishment was to be meted out to any person convicted of treason against the State. Lastly, a "Christmas Truce" was proclaimed from December 20, 1931, to January 3, 1932, during which no public political meetings or demonstrations might be held.

Such was the Decree of December 8th, which the Special Advisory Committee described in its report as "without parallel in modern legislature," and which illustrated to that body only too clearly the desperate state of the patient for whom it was their duty to prescribe a remedy.

[1] This involved a drop in the Reichsbahn revenue of approximately RM. 300 million.
[2] This measure resulted in the salaries of Civil Servants, workers, and employees of the State being reduced as much as 10 per cent.

3

Before passing to a consideration of the work of the Special
Advisory Committee, some account must be taken of a new
move on the part of France to reaffirm her position as regards
reparations in general and to leave her fellow-creditors of
Germany under no false impression as to her views and intended
policy in regard to private debts.

The first step in this phase was taken on November 26th
and 27th, during the closing scenes of the debate in the
Chambre des Députés on interpellations on the foreign policy
of the Government.[1] M. Laval took the opportunity to review
the events connected with the Hoover Moratorium and with
his recent visit to Washington, and passed therefrom to a
very exact exposition of French policy. As to reparations, he
said, France had the right to be disturbed at the prodigal
expenditure of Germany, whose habit it was to spend her
money and, when the moment came for paying her debts, to
declare herself insolvent. M. Laval confessed that he fully
realized the wretched plight of the German people, but, he
asked, if the position was reversed, what would Germany
think of it? Fresh emphasis was laid on the importance of the
sanctity of treaties, and M. Laval demanded to know how
confidence could be restored as a first step to surmounting
the crisis except on the basis of respect for the written word?[2]
France could not refuse to examine a scheme for a new
arrangement with her debtors, but she could not accept any
such arrangement except for the duration of the economic
depression, and she could only agree to a reduction of what

---

[1] In considering this speech it must be remembered that on the previous
day, November 25th, the Prussian Diet had adopted a resolution urging the
Government of the Reich "immediately to take in hand a revision of the
Young Plan, with the aim of a complete suspension of all 'tribute payments.'"
For text of M. Laval's speech see *Documents on International Affairs*, 1931,
p. 162.
[2] M. Laval apparently ignored the consideration that confidence in German
credit might be more seriously shaken, and the doubts an investor might
feel as to the wisdom of lending money to Germany more seriously affected
by heavy defaults on commercial debts than a failure by the Government
to honour political obligations.

was due to her in proportion to such equivalent reduction as she herself might obtain from her own creditors.

On the matter of private debts, M. Laval was especially emphatic. He would not, he declared, consent to any priority of these obligations over reparation payments. The German memorandum of November 19th to the Bank of International Settlements clearly showed that private debts were to be settled between German debtors and foreign creditors, and while there was a strong *de facto* connection between reparations and inter-Allied debts, there was none between reparations and private debts.

Having made his position clear to his own countrymen,[1] M. Laval proceeded to demonstrate it to the Powers concerned. On December 7th a Note was sent to Great Britain and Italy containing the views of France. The French Government, it stated, was prepared to accept the request of the German Government for an inquiry by the Advisory Committee under the terms of the Young Plan as a straightforward step of a debtor desirous to meet his obligations, but in respect of the inquiry the French Government preserved a free hand, because the terms of the German application, although known in Paris, had not been submitted for its approval. The responsibility for German default could not be blamed alone on the economic depression; an additional and very important cause was the systematic over-spending and over-borrowing on the part of the German Government. While ready to make far-reaching concessions for the relief of the situation, France insisted that the fundamental principle of reparation payments must be upheld for two reasons: (1) because there was absolutely no proof that Germany would remain bankrupt for ever, and (2) because it was imperative to maintain respect for the inviolability of international agreements.

The financial crisis, the Government averred, was not favourable to an inquiry of a final nature into Germany's capacity to pay. The Advisory Committee concerns itself only

[1] The Government secured a vote of confidence by 327 to 151 on November 27th.

with the recommendations of temporary measures for the solution of a temporary state of affairs, and must leave to an international conference to be held later the whole question of capacity to pay. The Committee must, however, take account of the all-important question of German capital invested abroad and the measures needed to bring it back.

The French Government definitely refused to admit the practical value of the demand for the priority of short-term credits, "because the two problems of reparations and private debts are but the elements of the fundamental problem of the capacity to pay and of respect for contractual obligations."

Finally, "any alteration in the principle laid down in the Young Plan is possible only simultaneously with a reduction of inter-Governmental debts. The benefit from such a reduction would have to be passed on to Germany."

Taken in conjunction, the speech of M. Laval and his Note to the Powers were a clear declaration of reparation policy. France refused definitely to consider any question of cancellation, and would only agree to a reduction in proportion to similar reductions granted her by the United States and Great Britain; above all, reparations must take priority over private debts.

The reactions caused by this Note in London and Rome were not favourable to the French point of view. The British Reply, received in Paris on December 17th, reiterated a belief that reparations and war debts formed one of the main causes of the world economic crisis, and that the removal or mitigation of this cause would be the most effective and quickest means of dealing with the crisis, and re-emphasized the point made by the Prime Minister on November 9th[1] that the situation in Germany paved the way to the European crisis.

[1] Speaking at the Lord Mayor's Banquet at the Guildhall on November 9th, Mr. MacDonald said: "The present position of Germany in relation to the rest of the world must be the subject of a complete overhaul in which Germany itself should be a willing co-operator, and financial agreements should be reached which are tolerable and practicable, which do not lead in their working to more and more financial and trade difficulties, and which will not prevent the international exchange of goods and services settling down into normal channels."

The French view on the matter of private debts was not allowed to go unchallenged. The British Government repeated the arguments in favour of the repayment of Germany's short-term loans, and quoted at length the Layton–Wiggin Report on the reasons for which action on this matter was essential and the ways in which the problem might be approached.[1]

The British Note then began to develop a new and hitherto unused argument. Germany, it was pointed out, had, for the last few years, been kept alive and enabled, incidentally, to pay reparations mainly by loans from Great Britain, while the British policy of the open door for imports had enabled Germany to enjoy a favourable commercial balance, especially where her trade with Great Britain was concerned.

Thus Germany might in some senses be regarded as having been living on British sources for years past, and as having paid reparations to France to a great extent out of these sources or out of wealth created by them. France had, therefore, drawn a large part of her receipts on account of reparations indirectly from Great Britain.

In conclusion, the British Government reiterated its insistence on the belief that the problem of war debts and reparations was urgent for the reasons already stated; that a firm and final settlement must now be reached, and that no temporary half-way measures would do.[2]

Further support for the British thesis was found in the Reply of the Italian Government dated December 21st. Signor Mussolini had on many occasions declared that a final settlement of the reparations problem was essential to European economic recovery, and his Note now expressed once more the desire that the solutions to be arrived at should be calculated to bring about a lasting revival of, or a normal basis of, economic and financial activity, both in Europe and outside. Such a result could only be obtained if it was remembered

---

[1] See above, pp. 94–5.

[2] The British Note called forth a reply from M. Laval, who, in a speech in Paris on December 20th, reiterated his insistence on the necessity for refusing to compromise in the matter of cancellation of reparation payments, and repeated that, whatever was done, "the Young Plan must not be torn up."

that there exists a close interdependence in the relations of States, the economic structures of which are separate, and if the interests of the various parties concerned were harmonized with the common interests of all.

This exchange of Notes during the month of December, which was supplemented by visits to London of M. Flandin, French Minister of Finance, and of M. Paul Hymans, Belgian Minister for Foreign Affairs, though it failed to achieve any prospect of united action and agreement on the part of the creditor States, did, however, disclose the fact that France stood isolated and alone in her desire for temporary measures preluding a return to the Young Plan payments. French statesmen realized that if they were to gain their ends very considerable opposition must be overcome by one means or another.

4

The Bank for International Settlements, on receipt of the German Government's Note of November 19th, acted with that same commendable display of energy which it had shown in appointing the Layton–Wiggin Committee in August. The Board of the Bank announced on November 25th that, in accordance with Article 127 of the Young Plan, the Governors of the Central Banks of the seven countries mainly concerned had nominated the seven ordinary members of the Committee, and that the Board, in accordance with Article 45 of its Statutes, had convened the first meeting of the Committee for December 7th.

The original membership of the Committee was as follows:

Professor Alberto Beneduce (Italy).
M. Emile Francqui[1] (Belgium).
Sir Walter T. Layton, C.H., C.B.E.[1] (Great Britain).
Dr. Carl Melchior[1] (Germany).
Mr. Daisuke Nohara (Japan).
Professor Charles Rist (France).
Dr. Walter W. Stewart (U.S.A.).

---

[1] Members of the Wiggin Committee, August 1931.

These members met at Basle on December 7th, and proceeded to the formal duty of electing a chairman. In accordance with the tradition to which reference has clearly been made,[1] Dr. Stewart was asked to take the chair, but on his declining, on grounds that America was too interested a party, Professor Beneduce was elected.[2] Availing themselves of the privilege conferred on them by Article 129 of the Young Plan, the Committee co-opted the following four additional members:

> Dr. R. G. Bindschedler[3] (Switzerland).
> M. H. Colijn (Netherlands).
> Dr. Diouritch[3] (Yugoslavia).
> M. Oskar Rydbek[3] (Sweden).

The full Committee met for the first time on December 8th,[4] and began its labours, as had the Wiggin Committee, with a statement by Dr. Melchior on the economic and financial situation of Germany, supported, as before, by a most valuable array of documentary evidence.

An explanation was first given as to the reconciliation of the figures of Germany's indebtedness given in the Layton–Wiggin Report of August and those of the Reichsbank Report of October. The Layton-Wiggin Report had given the total German indebtedness as RM. 23 milliards, of which RM. 8 milliards were short-term credits. The Reichsbank Report, based on data not available at the moment when the Wiggin Committee was in session, showed the total indebtedness to be

[1] See above, p. 87.
[2] Herein lies a curious commentary on the nature of nomenclature. The Advisory Committee was the first committee of inquiry not to be presided over by an American citizen; equally it is the first not to be known by the name of its chairman. Attempts made in the British and American Press to speak of the "Beneduce Committee" rapidly ceased, partly doubtless due to the mistrust in which all Anglo-Saxons hold everything with a foreign name. It is more than probable that, had Mr. Stewart not stood aside, the Committee would have borne his name, but, as it is, the fact remains that it will go down to history as the "Basle Committee." It should not be lost sight of that Mr. Owen D. Young, in the course of the election primaries in America during the spring and summer of 1932, found the fact that his name had been given to a plan for "the final liquidation of the reparation problem" anything but an asset.
[3] Members of the Wiggin Committee, August 1931.
[4] On December 11th there opened in Berlin negotiations between the German Debtors Committee and the representatives of the eleven creditor countries for an agreement for dealing with Germany's private debts at the termination of the August "Standstill" Agreement.

RM. 29 milliards, of which RM. 12 milliards were short-term credits. This showed the Reichsbank figures to be RM. 6 milliards regarding all foreign investments in Germany and RM. 4 milliards regarding short-term commitments in excess of the figures of the Layton–Wiggin Report.

This difference was attributed to three possible causes:

1. The initial balance for 1924 in respect of Germany's investments abroad and foreign investments in Germany, which the Wiggin Committee had computed to be RM. 2·9 milliards in Germany's favour, was estimated at too favourable a figure. Supposing that at that time the respective investments had balanced, then one-half of the difference would already be explained.

2. The balance of capital movements during 1924–1931 had been estimated at too low a figure. Small errors in the estimates of the balance of payments, which are within the range of normal sources of error in large calculations, could explain the difference. Assuming, for example, that exports were 3 per cent. lower and imports 3 per cent. higher, then the balance would already be less favourable by more than RM. 5 milliards.

3. It was thought that German investments abroad might have exceeded the RM. 8·5 milliards estimated by the Wiggin Committee. The mere fact that in the case of exports surprisingly long credits had been ascertained in some instances suggested that German short-term credits were higher, as a result of the extension of export credits, than was assumed by the Wiggin Committee.

In any case, it was stated there was "absolutely no data available which would permit of an even relatively accurate statistical distribution of the difference under these three possible explanations."

Dr. Melchior went on to explain that the total of short-term credits included, in addition to the money borrowed by the banks, RM. 3,700 million borrowed by industrial, agricultural, and commercial firms and individuals. He also supplied details of the four categories of debts which necessitated external payments either for their service or redemption:

1. Long-term loans issued abroad;
2. Loans not issued publicly abroad, mortgages in favour of foreigners and long-term loans granted to Germany;
3. Bonds and shares issued in Germany and held by foreigners;
4. Short-term debts of all kinds.

In regard to this last category, Dr. Melchior furnished an estimate to the Committee showing that German short-term loans abroad reached their highest aggregate in 1929, when they totalled RM. 5·5 milliards, and by July 1931 had decreased to RM. 3·5 milliards. German holdings of long-term investments abroad had never fallen below RM. 4·4 milliards since 1926, and in July 1931 were estimated at over RM. 5 milliards.

Turning to Germany's foreign trade position, Dr. Melchior showed that the favourable balance during the six months May–November 1931 had averaged RM. 350 million, but despite this the Reichsbank cover had declined from about 30 per cent. to only 12 per cent., after the reduction of the foreign exchange liabilities of the Bank. The Reichsbank estimated that during the past six months about 1 milliard marks had been repaid by Germany in the matter of private debts. It was the firm intention of the Government to maintain the gold standard for the following reasons:

1. Much of Germany's external debt was denominated in dollars or gold;
2. A large part of the internal debt was denominated in gold marks;
3. The Government had given an undertaking that for the purposes of the Hague Agreement and Young Plan, 'the reichsmark shall have and shall retain its convertibility in gold or foreign exchange, as provided in Section 31 of the present Reichsbank Law, and that in all circumstances, for the general purposes of the New (Young) Plan, the reichsmark shall have and shall retain a mint parity of 1·2790 kms. of fine gold, as defined in the German Coinage Law of August 30, 1924.[1]
4. Public opinion in Germany, more than in any other country, feared inflation, having already experienced its hardships in 1923.

---

[1] This undertaking was conveyed in a letter from the then President of the Reichsbank, Dr. Schacht, to Mr. Owen D. Young, Chairman of the Experts Committee, and forms Annex II to the Young Plan. See *Reparations*, p. 217.

The Committee appointed a sub-committee[1] to examine the statistics which Dr. Melchior had submitted, and passed, on December 10th, to a consideration of a statement made by Count von Krosigk, Director of the Budget Department of the German Ministry of Finance. Count von Krösigk dealt with the budgetary situation, the fall in tax yield, the influence of unemployment, and the probable effects of the Emergency Decree of December 8th, which, he assured the Committee, had profoundly impressed the whole population. The Budget revenue for the past three years, 1929–1931, had dropped seriously, and that for 1932 would probably not exceed RM. 7·25 milliards, the receipts showing a fall of RM. 2 milliards as compared with those of 1929. Income-tax had dropped 50 per cent., and the corporation tax by some 80 per cent. He outlined the economies effected since 1929, and said that, after allowing for those resulting from the new Decrees, a saving of RM. 4 milliards would have been effected in three years.

Having appointed a second sub-committee[2] to consider the German Budget, the Committee next dealt with the question of the German State Railways, which were considered one of the principal sources of reparation payments. The Young Plan had assured that in normal circumstances, with an annual gross income of approximately 4 milliards gold marks and a working coefficient of 80 per cent., a net profit of 800 million gold marks could be estimated. In addition to this net profit, a yield of 227 million gold marks from the transport tax was expected, making altogether more than a milliard gold marks, of which 635 million were to be contributed annually to the reparation account for unconditional annuities. As against this, statistics were produced to show that in fact in no year since the coming into force of the Young Plan had the working coefficient reached 80 per cent., and that, on the contrary, in 1930 it was 89 per cent. In the same year the excess of pay-

[1] Consisting of MM. Frère (Belgium); Nordhoff and von der Gablens (Germany); Powell (United Kingdom); Thomas (U.S.A.); Lacour-Goyet (France); Formentini (Italy); Kiwchi (Japan); Bozzola (Swiss).
[2] Consisting of MM. Colijn (Netherlands); Frère (Belgium); Gaillet-Billotteau (France); Rowe-Dutton (U.K.); Schwerin von Krösigk (Germany); Zanchi (Italy).

ments over receipts was RM. 180 million, with a consequent deficit of RM. 312·5 million, which it was only possible to meet by using up the surplus of the previous year and by cancelling RM. 133·6 million of credits of the Reich. For 1931 it was estimated that there would be a deficit of RM. 567·8 million, and when all reserves had been drawn upon it was impossible to reduce this amount to less than RM. 41·8 million. A third sub-committee[1] was appointed to consider this problem.

For the next few days the Committee was in a state of devolution, sitting in a series of sub-committees which finally presented their findings to a plenary session of the full Committee. The first sub-committee dealt with two subjects: the statistics regarding interest and amortization of German foreign indebtedness, and also the question of German assets abroad. In drawing up the first of its reports, it was of course dependent for particulars on figures supplied by the German delegation. The total indebtedness was shown at between RM. 28·5 and 30 milliards (£1,500 million) at July 31, 1931, and the figures were given for the estimated cost of the service of the long-term loans and the short-term debts separately.

The former, which were divided into four groups, were stated to require, for interest and amortization, annual payments totalling 818·4 million marks for those issued abroad, 156 million for debts not issued publicly, 24 million for internal bonds owned by foreigners, and about 150 million for the yield from shares and real estate owned by foreigners. The short-term debt was estimated to call for payments of interest of between 600 and 700 million marks, so that the total figure of interest and amortization payment was put at 1,850 million, as a maximum, for all foreign debts.

In the report dealing with German assets abroad, it was found impossible to obtain reliable statistics, but the total of the long-term investments was placed at 5,000 million. The short-term claims of Germany were even more difficult to assess, but it was certain that the lengthy terms which she

---

[1] Consisting of MM. Rydbeck (Sweden); Leverve (France); Gutt (Belgium): Homburger (Germany); Sir Osborne Mance (U.K.); de Corné (Italy).

had extended in respect of her exports had resulted in the building up of considerable claims abroad. A figure of 8,100 million was put forward as an estimate of the total for all forms of foreign assets, but the sub-committee expressed itself unable to form an opinion as to its accuracy. As to the amount of interest which Germany might be expected to receive during 1932, the sub-committee was unable to be more explicit than to state that this might be put at between 300 and 400 million marks.

The second sub-committee examined the details of the Budget, and its report was the longest of those submitted to the Advisory Committee, since it dealt with the expenditure of the Federal States and municipalities as well as of the Reich. Among the points brought out were the following:

The total expenditure of German public bodies increased between 1926 and 1930 (fiscal years) from 17,200 million to 20,963 million. During the year just passed, however, as a result of emergency Decrees, the increases in salaries made in 1927, which were in a large measure responsible for this rise in expenditure, had been more than cancelled, and salaries were on a lower level than in 1926.

Of the total increase of over 3,700 million, 1,600 million were for account of the Reich and 2,100 million for account of the States and Communes, and with regard to the relation between the Reich and local authorities the Report says the sub-committee felt that

"Some part at least of the increase in the total expenditure of public authorities had arisen from the fact that the financial relations between the Reich, the Federal States, and the Communes permitted the latter in particular to embark upon additional activities which were paid for out of the share of taxes levied by the Reich, but transferred on a percentage basis to the States and Communes. As the yield of these taxes rose in times of prosperity, money flowed into the coffers of the Communes, and part of their present difficulty is due to the fact that their receipts from these sources have now fallen off, while their expenditure cannot be easily or quickly reduced to correspond. The amount of taxes transferred by the Reich in this way to other public authorities rose from 2,620 million marks in 1926 to a maximum of 3,412 million in 1928, and subsequently declined to 3,050 million in 1930 and to

2,321 million in 1931. . . . An improvement has, however, been effected
by the recent emergency Decrees . . . under which the municipalities
have the power, and, in certain circumstances, the obligation, to levy
additional taxes for themselves. These include a poll tax, a local beer
tax, and a tax on beverages, the unpopularity of which acts as a powerful
further stimulant upon the municipal authorities to effect economies
in their budgets."

Reference was made to the development of the public debt,
the total of which, at March 31, 1931, was shown as 24,078·9
million marks. Of this, the Reich accounted for 11,342 million
odd, the Federal States for over 2,802 million, and the Communes over 9,934 million. The aggregate figure had increased
by no less than 9,480 million in the last four years,[1] and of
this more than 2,000 million were in respect of claims in the
debt register for war damages and Polish indemnities and of
reparations loans of the Reich (two-thirds of Young Loan),
which entailed a burden for interest and amortization, but
brought no new capital which could be employed.

The Dawes and Young Loans were shown as accounting
together for 3,400 million (£170 million at par).

Turning to the revenue side of the Budget, the sub-committee
found that the falling off in receipts had lately assumed
"catastrophic proportions." For example, the yield from
income-tax, which in 1929 amounted to 1,440 million, was
not expected to reach 1,000 million in 1931, and in 1932 was
estimated at 700 million, a decline of over 50 per cent. in
two years. The corporation tax, in the same period, showed
a drop of nearly 80 per cent., and the Report stated that

"though the German Government has resorted to a series of emergency
measures to increase taxation, they have been entirely unable to
produce sufficient revenue to meet normal expenditure, which has,
therefore, had to undergo sweeping reductions."

An attempt was also made to analyse the "sketch budget"
for 1932, as a result of which it became clear that there was
serious reason to fear that the estimated revenue might not
in effect be realized, while the possibility of further cutting
down expenditure was open to doubt, unless—what was very

[1] The total on March 31, 1928, was 14,598·6 million.

undesirable—the amounts set aside for debt redemption were further reduced. As to this, the sub-committee "could not but feel, having regard to the alarming increase of the total public debt . . . that it is vital for the German Government to pursue the firmest policy of debt reduction in order that the burden of debt may not become insupportable." With regard to the Budget prospects in general, the sub-committee expressly stated that it had no opinion as to the probability or otherwise of an early reversal of the present downward movement in business activity, not only in Germany, but in the whole world, but took occasion to point out that "unless this movement is reversed, there can be no hope of a recovery in the Budget situation, and even if a speedy reversal should take place, it must be some time before the Budget will benefit therefrom and return once more to a sound basis."

The last report was that of the sub-committee on the Reichsbahn, of which the profits had declined so seriously as to make it impossible for them to furnish the 635 million marks required for the unconditional portion of the reparations annuities. In each of the years 1926, 1927, 1928, and 1929, the margin of receipts over payments was nearer 900 than 800 million, but in 1930 it dropped to 480 million, and in 1931 was about 178 million. The amount due to be paid by the Railway on account of reparations in 1931 was 635 million, so that there would be a deficiency of 457 million. Allowing, further, for the preference share dividend, the service of new debts, and the writing off of the concession, the deficiency was brought up to 567 million marks. As regards 1932, drastic economies in working were expected to bring about a surplus of receipts over payments of 252 million, which was, of course, totally inadequate to meet the calls upon the Railway. The conclusions at which the sub-committee arrived were that in 1931 it would be impossible to balance the Company's budget, while as to the position in 1932 and subsequent years, the sub-committee was not asked to express any opinion, but in any case it would have been unable to find the answer. Nevertheless, the figures available suggested that once Germany and the world at large had recovered their balance the Reichsbahn (fundamentally a sound undertaking) would be able in future years, if managed on a commercial basis, to yield a net operating surplus comparable with that earned by other big foreign railway systems.

With these conclusions before them, the Advisory Committee drew up its Report in four chapters dealing with the elements of the problem as already enumerated.[1] The first of these was far the most detailed, since in it the Committee made reference separately to the various elements going to make up the then existing condition of affairs. After noting that the effects of the crisis were, in Germany and other Eastern European countries, devastating, and that the stringent measures of exchange control—necessitated by the need for protecting the currency—had accentuated the already serious restriction in the volume of economic activity, the Committee described the Emergency Decree of December 8, 1931, as including "measures without parallel in modern legislation." Dealing in turn with the foreign debt, the trade balance, and the balance of payments, the Report called attention to the following points:

The large amount of foreign short-term liabilities made Germany peculiarly susceptible to the credit crisis, and 2,900 million marks of these credits were withdrawn between January and July last.

At the end of July the total of advances repayable at short-term amounted to nearly 12,000 million. The "Standstill" Agreement, signed in September, applied to rather more than half of this total.

The monthly export surplus averaged 160 million marks during the first half of 1931. During August–October it was between 300 and 400 million, but in November dropped to 267 million, and must be expected to continue to decline.

The surplus had not become immediately available to Germany in the form of foreign exchange which could be utilized to repay debts because Germany, while paying cash for her imports, gave extended terms of credit to her buyers,

[1] For text see *Documents on International Affairs*, 1931, p. 164.

especially in the case of Russia, and in addition to this German exporters, in spite of legal restrictions, had been able to keep abroad part of the foreign exchange resulting from exports.

Overhead figures of the balance of payments (export surplus, foreign assets of German banks, rediscount credits and gold reserves, etc., on one side, and reparations and interest and amortization payments on the other) showed that the total of capital withdrawn during 1931 amounted to approximately 4,900 million marks. The export surplus was shown as 3,000 million, and the amount paid in reparations and interest on loans together at 2,300 million. The Report stated that

"The withdrawal of capital . . . forced Germany to have recourse not only to the reserves held against their foreign liabilities by the German private banks, but also to increase such credits as were commercially available by the rediscount of credits granted to the Reichsbank and Golddiskontbank. This did not obviate heavy sales of gold, and the striking feature of this balance sheet is the drain which the withdrawal of capital has placed upon the reserves of the Reichsbank."

In dealing with the position of the Reichsbank, attention was called to the fall in the reserve to 1,161 million marks on December 15th, as compared with 2,576 million at the beginning of June. The percentage cover for the note issue was thus only 25·6 per cent. But even these figures did not allow for the fact that the Bank owed, at July 31, 1931, 630 million in respect of the rediscount credits granted to it by the Bank for International Settlements and the Central Banks and to the Golddiskontbank by the Lee–Higginson group, and if this amount was deducted the note cover was only 11·7 per cent.

Under the heading of Production and Employment it was shown that nearly 25 per cent. of the labour personnel of the country was out of employment, and the index of industrial production had fallen to 66—in other words, one-third of the industrial life of Germany had stopped. Both prices and wages had been reduced by legislative Decree, and the rate of interest for advances to industry had gone up to about 12 per cent., thereby further contributing to the decline in activity. Agriculture was in even more serious difficulty, and could not earn enough to find interest on the debts it contracted when prices were high, so that measures of financial relief, amounting almost to a moratorium, had been taken in order to prevent a general collapse.

As regards the Budget, after citing many of the figures given in the sub-committee's Report, the Committee came to the conclusion that the burden of taxation had become so high that there was no margin for a further increase.

The second and third chapters of the Report were devoted to a short outline of the course of the crisis and of the measures taken to meet it, and in the section dealing with Germany's debt the Report stated that

"Germany's demand for capital to fill the gap left by the war, the aftermath and the inflation, was very great. As a matter of fact, the influx of foreign capital, which began as soon as the mark was stabilized, and which was estimated by the Banker's Committee to be about 18,000 million marks, has been partly offset by the 10,300 million of reparation payments."

A large amount of capital had, however, been invested in both public and private enterprises, and this was forthcoming partly from Germany's own savings, but

"the foreign holding of so large a proportion of her capital wealth makes her peculiarly vulnerable to financial disturbance, particularly to the extent that this capital is withdrawable at short notice. Moreover, a substantial part of these short-term credits have proved to be immobilized in long-term investments. The withdrawal of these credits must, therefore, threaten not only the exchange, but also the liquidity of the banks themselves."

Reverting to the Budget, the Report quoted figures given by the sub-committee, and went on to call attention to the fact that

"The Reich levies taxation of which it retains part only, and of which a proportion fixed by law is automatically handed over to the States and Communes, which only cover their expenditure from their own resources to the extent of 75 per cent. Such a system means that the control of expenditure is divorced from the responsibility of raising the revenue to meet it, and although the system may have been moderated by recent ordinances of the Reich, we think that reform in this matter would have beneficial results."

As a matter of fact, among the measures taken by the Reich with a view to controlling expenditure, new regulations had been made limiting the extent to which savings banks and allied institutions might finance the municipalities in future, and for the time being they were not allowed to grant them new credits, so that the tendency to launch out into schemes of development was curtailed, in one respect at least.

So far the Committee had found little difficulty in drafting its Report, for up till this point it had merely been a matter of registering a series of facts brought out through the deliberations of the sub-committees. Section IV of the Report, however, presented greater difficulty, since it had to contain the conclusions of the Committee.

It had become evident during the discussions that the Young Plan could no longer be operative, and yet the difficulty was to find a formula which would make this clear and at the same time be acceptable to all members of the Committee. The news of this state of affairs caused considerable anxiety amongst the Governments of the Powers. M. Rist declared that France would not allow the Young Plan to be torn up. King Alexander of Yugoslavia paid a hurried visit to Paris *incognito*; two high officials of the Quai d'Orsay arrived on a special mission to Basle; and, finally, the Belgian Minister for War arrived with instructions from his Government for an immediate conference with the Belgian member of the Committee.

The final draft was accepted late on the night of December 22nd, and the Report actually signed in the small hours of December 23rd. The formula reached was as follows: "That Germany would be justified in declaring—in accordance with her rights under the Young Plan—that, in spite of the steps she has taken to maintain the stability of her currency, she will not be able, in the year beginning in July next (1932), to transfer the conditional part of the annuity."

In addition, however, the Committee drew attention to "the unprecedented gravity of the crisis, the magnitude of which undoubtedly exceeds the 'relatively short depression' envisaged in the Young Plan—to meet which the 'measures of safeguard' contained therein were designed."

The Plan had presupposed a steady expansion of trade, "not merely in volume but in value"; in effect the exact opposite had taken place: the trade of the world had shrunk in volume and gold had fallen exceptionally in price. The fundamental economic basis of the Young Plan no longer existed, and it was therefore the duty of the Powers to take fresh steps to meet a new situation, for which no legislation existed.

This, then, was the basis of the Report. The position was extraordinary and demanded extraordinary measures. "In the circumstances the German problem . . . calls for concerted action which the Governments alone can take."

Perhaps for the reason that Sir Walter Layton was its editor, certain paragraphs of Section IV of the Report read almost like a continuation of the Layton–Wiggin Report, to which indeed reference is made, more especially to the "emphatic note of warning" which it sounded. That Report had urged upon the Governments concerned the necessity of taking immediate steps if disasters were to be avoided.

"But," said the Advisory Committee's Report, "events did not wait. The year 1931 has not yet ended, and already the crisis has taken formidable dimensions, shattering the exchanges of many countries one after the other and accumulating difficulties which, if not dealt with, will only prove the forerunner of further catastrophes. Unemployment has increased; Stock Exchanges remain closed; economic activity continues with difficulty at a very low ebb in the face of restricted credit, rigid control of the exchanges and paralysing restrictions on international trade. Slowly the effects of shrinking economic activity are making themselves felt in one country after another."

There followed an appeal to the Governments concerned to recognize the importance of facing economic realities, and of not allowing the treatment of these to be influenced by political considerations. When the Governments came to examine the whole group of questions allied to the subject of the Report, they would have to take account of many matters relevant to these complex problems, which "can only be solved in conformity with economic realities." In this connection there were certain considerations which seemed to the Committee of great importance:

"The first is that transfers from one country to another on a scale so large as to upset the balance of payments can only accentuate the present chaos.

"It should be also borne in mind that the release of a debtor country from a burden of payments which it is unable to bear may merely have the effect of transferring that burden to a creditor country which, in its character as a debtor, it, in its turn, may be unable to bear.

"Again the adjustments of all inter-Governmental debts (reparation and other war debts) to the existing troubled situation of the world—and this adjustment should take place without delay if new disasters are to be avoided—is the only lasting step capable of re-establishing confidence, which is the very condition of economic stability and real peace.[1]

"Finally, although the German Government is energetically defending the stability of its currency, steps are necessary to secure that these measures shall have a permanent effect."

The Report closed with an urgent appeal to the Governments for speed and action "in coming to decisions which will bring an amelioration of this grave crisis which weighs so heavily on all alike."

There were many who, in view of the progressive and courageous note struck by President Hoover's Moratorium proposal, and admirably maintained in the Layton–Wiggin Report and the speech of the Hon. Andrew Mellon on December 17th,[2] thought that the Advisory Committee might produce a report along the same lines and give "a Christmas present to the world." To these the actual conclusions of the Report come as a shock and a disappointment. But it is impossible to dismiss the Report as lacking courage.

It is true that it makes no mention of private debts or the unconditional annuities, but it was prevented from doing so under its original terms of reference. It is true that it remitted

---

[1] It was not a little ironical that almost at the same time that this Report was signed the United States Congress had passed, in both Houses, a resolution virtually preventing the very step thus recommended. See below, pp. 166–8.
[2] In a statement on war debts issued by the Department of the Treasury, Mr. Mellon said: "It is the duty of those in authority to deal with realities, and there is no escaping the fact that some of our debtors cannot meet in full the payments due to us until there has been a substantial measure of economic recovery."

once more to the Governments concerned the problem of Germany's external indebtedness, but so it must have done under these same terms. In point of fact it did more than hand the problem back intact. If there is little new in the Report's objective survey of a situation whose essential features had already been elicited some four months earlier by the Wiggin Committee, it did at least dispel any illusions that might still exist as to Germany's capacity to make reparation payments in the near future, and it also showed clearly that the Committee were unable to make any suggestion which would permit the Young Plan to be revived. Indeed, the Report leaves no doubt as to the opinion of the Committee that the fundamental conditions contemplated by the Young Committee, and upon which its recommendations were based, were no longer in existence—it would almost be true to say that they never had existed—and the Advisory Committee, by including in its Report the statement that "the German problem, which is largely responsible for the growing financial paralysis of the world, calls for concerted action which the Governments alone can take," coupled with their appeal for the "adjustment" of all inter-Governmental war debts, indicated pretty clearly that the Young Plan, measures for whose application they were enjoined to consider, could no longer be integrally applied.

No one of its authors would maintain that the Basle Report was an ideal document, but to those who blame it for its lack of definite and courageous recommendation the following facts are suggested for consideration. It was of the greatest importance that any conclusion arrived at should be signed unanimously. It would have been immeasurably easier to have "agreed to disagree" or to have "played for a show-down." Had this happened, there is little doubt that the majority of the Committee would have supported Dr. Melchior and the German thesis; but this would only have resulted at best in a minority report by the French, Yugoslav, and Belgian delegates, and at worst in their leaving the Committee altogether. In neither case would the object of the Committee have been attained, for the French Chamber, as it was then formed, would, without question, have authorized MM. Laval and Tardieu to go no further than the minority report, and, in the case of a break-up, no progress at all would have been made.

At its worst the Basle Report was an inevitable compromise; at its best it presented an exceptionally clever piece of drafting, and is remarkable for the ease with which it is possible to read between its lines and the amount which can be read there.

CHAPTER VI

CANUTES IN CONGRESS

1

"You cannot say to-day," said Mr. Kellogg on one occasion, "what the United States Senate will do to-morrow," and thereby epitomized in one sentence both the strength and weakness of the American Constitution. Both this strength and this weakness were amply illustrated in the struggle for the ratification of the Hoover Moratorium, which dominated the Congress discussions during December 1931.

These discussions were characterized by a degree of bitterness towards Europe which had not been evinced since the historic debates on the Treaty of Versailles in 1920, and, though from the first it was known that ratification was assured, for, as we have seen, President Hoover had secured the support of the Congress leaders of both parties before making his Proposal on June 20th, there was a general feeling in both the Senate and the House that this experiment in international philanthropy should not be repeated.

What, then, had brought about this change of attitude, which was the more remarkable when one considers the almost universally warm welcome with which Mr. Hoover's original proposal had met in his own country? The reasons were partly psychological and partly material. The events of the six months following the Hoover offer had done much to revive all the old American suspicion of Europe, and it must be confessed that this was not without justification. The American statesmen who had taken part in the negotiations which followed the Hoover Proposal in Paris and London during July had been deeply shocked at the French attitude and policy, which seemed to be at complete variance with the spirit of the Proposal. Subsequent events served only to increase this impression. The French attitude towards disarmament, as disclosed in their Memorandum of July 21st, and the frankly political trend of their financial policy, produced on the other side of the Atlantic a feeling of distrust and suspicion which reached its climax as a result of M. Laval's visit in October.

The blatant attempt of France to influence the policy of the United States succeeded in its purpose all too well for France. Not only did Mr. Hoover relinquish the initiative in the matter of reparation, but subsequent action of Congress virtually prevented his ever attempting to reassume it, and provided him with an admirable reason for returning a negative reply to the French "feeler" put out in the following January.[1] And thus France ruined the renewed good feeling of America towards Europe.

Nor must the material considerations be ignored. By December both the Administration and Congress were aware that they were faced with a deficit of $380,495,000 on the first quarter of the fiscal year 1931–1932, foreshadowing a deficit for the whole year of approximately $1,500 millions.[2] In addition, many of the great municipalities, such as Philadelphia and Chicago—and even, later, New York itself—were in serious financial difficulty; while the unemployment figure was computed conservatively to be ten millions. In no way was this concatenation of circumstances one which might influence America to repeat her gesture to Europe, but led her rather to repent of her original offer, which had deprived her temporarily of some $250 million.

Finally, there was President Hoover's personal unpopularity to be remembered. The President's Proposal in June had resulted in a renewal of his election popularity to a quite remarkable degree; but as the force of the depression deepened in America so was the need for a scapegoat increased and heightened, and Mr. Hoover who during his campaign, had

[1] See below, pp. 182–3.
[2] Actually, the figure of the deficit as estimated in President Hoover's Message to Congress on December 9, 1931, was $1,416,949,488 for the year ending June 30, 1932. Even this proved to be too optimistic a figure, for when the official Budget estimates were published on April 16, 1932, they showed the deficit to be $2,250,000,000.

been misguided enough to imply that national prosperity and
the Republican Party were inseparably linked together,
suffered accordingly in prestige and reputation. By December
this unpopularity had attained such proportions that any
proposal having the President's personal endorsement was
certain of strenuous opposition and very probably of rejection.

It was with these considerations uppermost in their minds
that the Senators and Representatives gathered in Washington
for the seventy-second Congress, but, before turning to a
review of their discussions, it is necessary to take some stock
of the conditions under which the allied debts to the United
States were originally contracted.

In 1917 the first thing that the Allies asked for, after the
severance of relations between the United States and Germany,
was money; and it is very interesting to note that the first
instruction that was conveyed to the Treasury by President
Wilson was that in drafting the loan agreements there should
be no deviation from the form in which any loans in peace-
time would be drafted, without regard to the special circumstances in which these loans were required.[1] Herein lies
the basis of the assertion of successive American Adminis-
trations that allied debts have no direct or legal connection
with reparations.

The United States, having rejected the Treaty of Versailles,
made its own peace with Germany by the Treaty of Berlin
(August 1921),[2] and in February 1922 invited her debtors to
make statements as to the manner in which they intended
to fulfil the obligations which they had incurred during the
war. The form in which the Administration began to approach
the problem was by an intimation to Congress that the
moment had now arrived to tackle this thorny question,
whereupon Congress, by joint resolution dated February 9,
1922,[3] appointed a Foreign War Debt Commission under the

[1] See "America and War Debts—The Political Aspect," by Herr Paul Scheffer,
International Affairs (Journal of the Royal Institute of International Affairs),
July 1932, vol. xi, no. 4.
[2] Ratified November 14, 1921.
[3] For text of Resolution see *Combined Annual Reports of the World War
Foreign Debt Commission* (Washington, 1927), p. 6.

chairmanship of the then Secretary of the Treasury, the
Hon. Andrew W. Mellon. In drawing up the terms of reference
of the Commission, Congress made two stipulations: first, that
the debts should be refunded within twenty-five years and
that 4½ per cent. should be the lowest limit of the rate of
interest; and, secondly, it was laid down, in a very complicated legal form, that no connection with any debts arising
out of the war could possibly be created by the agreements
which were to be concluded between America and her debtors.
This was the first time that official and legal expression was
given to the negation of any interconnection between war
debts and reparations.

One of the earliest and most bitter critics of this attitude
was the then Secretary of State, the Hon. Charles Evan
Hughes, who, in a speech delivered at Newhaven in December
1922, complained that Congress had bound the hands of the
Administration in regard to dealing with war debts in the
light of facts which had developed in the meantime. They
had, he declared, treated the whole question from a purely
legal standpoint, and had limited the power of the Executive
to deal with the question. In this speech lies the beginning
of the conflict between the Administration and Congress on
the question of war debts which has continued to influence
the whole situation so disastrously.

The years 1922–1923 were about as barren of result in the
matter of debt funding as they were in the search for a
solution of the reparation problem. There was, however, one
negative and one positive action taken during this period.
The United States, in common with other Powers, rejected
the offer contained in the Balfour Note of 1922, and the
British Government signed its debt-funding agreement in
1923. In the two subsequent years, however, the formula of
common sense—"capacity to pay"—crept into the discussions on both subjects. In 1924 the Dawes Plan, based upon
this formula, opened up the way of solution in the reparation
problem, and in 1925 the United States War Debt Commission
itself took a step forward in saying that the capacity to pay

should be taken into account in considering the funding of foreign debts.[1]

But capacity to pay meant two different things in Europe and in America. In Europe it meant capacity to pay out of reparation receipts, and in America capacity to pay out of the ordinary budgets, assisted preferably by a cut in armament estimates. For practical purposes the European interpretation predominated, since it was only after the Dawes Plan had temporarily insured regular reparation payments that the Continental Powers began to fund their debts, and this system continued in force until the summer of 1931, when the supply of German reparation threatened to run dry, and President Hoover's proposal brought about a breathing space.

Now, although neither the President, nor his lieutenants who had participated in the negotiations, had forgotten—or could forget—the stubborn resistance of the French Government which completely neutralized the psychological effect of the Hoover Moratorium and thwarted in its usefulness an action which the Washington Administration had intended to be really helpful, there is reason to believe that Mr. Hoover did meditate during the autumn of 1931 some extension of the Moratorium period. But all desire to do this departed in the course of M. Laval's visit, and, as has already been suggested, this explains a certain willingness on Mr. Hoover's part to surrender the initiative in the matter of reparations. To put it brutally, he was sick and tired of Europe, which cried out for assistance and then bit the hand that fed it. The President was still determined to fight the Moratorium through Congress in its general aspects, but his heart was out of the business, and he would not go the least measure beyond the letter of his agreement with M. Laval.

Such, then, was the position at the assembly of Congress in December 1931.

[1] See *Reports of War Debts Commission*, p. 37.

2

In a special Message to Congress, dated December 10, 1931,[1] President Hoover urged the prompt ratification of the Moratorium, quoting a sentence from his original proposal of June 20th: "I am suggesting to the American people that they be wise creditors in their own interests and be good neighbours." He then recapitulated the whole history of the Hoover Offer, emphasizing the point that he had consulted leaders of both parties in both Houses of Congress before taking action.

He then said: "I do not approve, even in any remote sense, of the cancellation of debts to the United States. World confidence would not be enhanced by any such action. Reparations are a wholly European problem with which we have no relations. As the basis of the settlement of debts due to the United States was the capacity of the debtor to pay, we should be consistent with our own policies if we take into account the abnormal situation now existing in the world. . . . While this action has no bearing on the land armaments conference in February, we trust that by this evidence of our desire to assist we shall have contributed to the goodwill which is so necessary for a solution of this major problem. It is highly desirable that a law should be enacted before December 15th, when payments are due to the United States from many countries. It is clear that a number of Governments will be unable to meet further payments to the United States pending the recovery of economic life. Therefore it will be necessary in some cases to make still further temporary adjustments. I recommend the re-creation of the World War Foreign Debt Commission with authority to examine the problems that may arise and report its recommendations to Congress."

As if to add further fuel to the flames, there had arrived only that morning from Paris a formal notification from the French Government that any revision of reparations annuities

[1] For text see *Documents on International Affairs*, 1931, p. 129.

would have to be accompanied by a corresponding scaling
down of war debts, and this in itself—a further reminder of
French tactics a few months before—was enough to antagonize
Congress.

By virtue of the fact that the measure was a financial one,
it had to be discussed by the House as well as the Senate,
and the Speaker at once declared that action could not be
taken before December 15th, since "we certainly will not pass
on such an important piece of legislation before we have some
information on it." Now December 15th was the date on
which the half-yearly payments of the Allied debts suspended
under the Moratorium fell due, but on December 12th the
Under-Secretary of the Treasury informed the debtor Powers
that non-payment on this date on their part "would not be
regarded as irregular."

At the outset it was evident that a wide breach—almost
an unbridgeable chasm—existed between the President and
Congress, and that while the Moratorium itself was certain
of ratification sooner or later, it was almost equally certain
that the proposal to reconstitute the War Debt Commission
was doomed to failure. Throughout the discussion in the
Finance Committee of the Senate and the Ways and Means
Committee of the House—the latter of which made it an
excuse to institute an inquiry into the activities of American
banks and bankers in the foreign securities market—there
developed a deep-seated resentment against Europe and an
implacable opposition to any extension of the Moratorium
period. The viewpoint of nearly every Senator and Congressman could be summed up in ex-President Coolidge's terse
phrase, "We hired them the money, didn't we?"

There was manifested also a bitter animosity against the
President, one Congressman, Mr. Louis T. McFadden, of
Canton, Pennsylvania, going so far as to demand from the
floor of the House of Representatives that the procedure of
impeachment should be opened against Mr. Hoover for having
betrayed America in the interests of the international bankers
who had investments in Germany.

The debate on the Ratification Bill opened simultaneously in the Senate and House Committees on December 15th, and although the case for the Administration was ably defended and expounded by Mr. Stimson and Mr. Ogden Mills, who eloquently explained the necessity and inevitability of the President's action if Europe were to be saved from utter financial chaos and American investments from completely vanishing, it became more and more clear that the joint resolution when it was eventually passed would be loaded with reservations which would block all possibility of similar future action by the Executive branch of the Government.

In vain did Mr. Stimson demonstrate to the Senate that the Moratorium had merely forestalled a general European default, after which it would have been almost impossible to get payments going again. In vain did Mr. Mills remind the House that they could not send gunboats to Europe to collect their money. Congress would have none of it. They had the bit between their teeth and proceeded to bolt.

On December 17th the Ways and Means Committee reported the Ratification Bill back to the House with the following amendment:

"It is hereby expressly declared to be against the policy of Congress that any indebtedness by foreign countries to the United States should be in any manner cancelled or reduced, and nothing in this joint resolution for ratification of the Hoover Moratorium shall be construed as indicating contrary policy, or an implication to give favourable consideration at any time to a change in the policy hereby declared."

This was accompanied by a minority report signed by three members of the Committee, who expressed themselves as being of the opinion, first, that the President had not the constitutional right to make his proposal of June 20th, which should have been first submitted to Congress, if necessary called in special session; and, secondly, that they were not convinced of the necessity of deferring the payments at all.

The House, after a debate which terminated in an historic night sitting, adopted the resolution as amended by the Committee on December 19th, and sent it over for consideration by the Senate. It was the earnest desire of the Administration to get the matter finished one way or the other before the Christmas recess, which began on December 22nd, and every pressure was brought to bear on the Senate to give the resolution immediate consideration. Discussion, however, did not begin until late in the morning of the 21st, and was characterized by as bitter an opposition as that which had voiced itself in the House, an opposition which did not hope ultimately to defeat the measure but to embitter its passage; an opposition whose grasp of the true facts of the position and the state of whose mentality may be gauged by the remarks of Senator Johnson of California. The resolution they were to pass, Mr. Johnson told his fellow Senators, was "upon its face a fraud," and provided in fact for the liquidation of Europe's debts, but more was involved than that. They had seen the liquidation of the statesmanship of the world at Versailles in 1919; they had seen since October 1929 the liquidation of the wisdom and omniscience of America's masters of finance; and the Congress of the United States was now, perhaps, to assist in the liquidation of the old traditional policy of the country it professed to represent—the policy of wise aloofness from the affairs of Europe. "If we can by what we say and do here arouse our people to return to the old path," he declared, "even though the resolution be passed, we shall not have striven in vain."

The debate lasted throughout December 22nd, and in its course a number of amendments were brought forward, partly in a perverted spirit of improvement and partly in an attempt to postpone a vote being taken until after the reassembling of Congress on January 4th. Senator Howell, of Nebraska, proposed to withhold the benefits of the Moratorium from any Goverment "until it shall have effectively assented, in a form and manner satisfactory to the President, to the reformation of the Versailles Treaty, including the return to the German Government of its former colonies."

Senator McKellar, of Tennessee, wished to add to the resolution a clause asserting it to be "the care of Congress that there should be no further moratoriums, no additional debt-funding legislation, and no further cancellation, in whole or in part, of the debts mentioned in the joint resolution." Even more dangerous than this was the proposal of Senator Dill, of Washington, which would have altered the House resolution by the addition of two words, declaring it to be against the policy of Congress that any foreign debt to the United States "should be, in any manner, cancelled, or reduced, *or postponed*."

There was some reason to believe that either the McKellar or the Dill amendment might have been adopted had it not been necessary to refer back to the House for agreement any amendment, however slight, to the resolution it had already passed. There was a general consensus of opinion in the Senate in favour of getting rid of the Moratorium Bill before Christmas and leaving Congress free after the holidays to tackle the pressing domestic problems which called for its attention.

Accordingly at 10 o'clock in the evening of December 22nd, after some fourteen hours of debate, the Senate voted by 69 to 12 to ratify the Moratorium, and the Speaker of the House of Representatives and the Vice-President signed the joint resolution, as amended by the House, and sent it to the President.

The resolution in its final form read as follows:

"RESOLVED by the Senate and House of Representatives of the United States of America, in Congress assembled That in the case of each of the following countries: Austria, Belgium, Czechoslovakia, Estonia, Finland, France, Germany, Great Britain, Greece, Hungary, Italy, Latvia, Lithuania, Poland, Rumania and Yugoslavia, the Secretary of the Treasury, with the approval of the President, is authorized to make, on behalf of the United

States, an agreement with the Government of such country to postpone the payment of any amount payable during the fiscal year beginning July 1931, by such country to the United States in respect of its bonded indebtedness to the United States, except that in the case of Germany the agreement shall relate only to amounts payable by Germany to the United States during such fiscal year in respect of the costs of the Army of Occupation.

2. "Each such agreement on behalf of the United States shall provide for the payment of the postponed amounts, with interest at the rate of 4 per cent. per annum beginning July 1, 1933, in ten equal annuities, the first to be paid during the fiscal year beginning July 1, 1933, and one during each of the nine fiscal years following, each annuity to be payable in one or more instalments.

3. "No such agreement shall be made with the Government of any country unless it appears to the satisfaction of the President that such Government has made, or has given satisfactory assurances of willingness and readiness to make, with the Government of each of the other countries indebted to such country, in respect of war, relief, or reparation debts, an agreement in respect of such debt substantially similar to the agreement authorized by this joint resolution to be made with the Government of such creditor country on behalf of the United States.

4. "Each agreement authorized by this joint resolution shall be made so that payment of annuities under such agreement shall, unless otherwise provided in the agreement, (1) be in accordance with the provisions contained in the agreement made with the Government of such country under which the payment to be postponed is payable, and (2) be subject to the same terms and conditions as payments made under such original agreements.

5. "It is hereby expressly declared to be against the policy of Congress that any of the indebtedness of foreign countries to the United States should be in any manner cancelled or reduced; and nothing in this joint resolution

shall be construed as indicating a contrary policy or as implying that favourable consideration will be given at any time to a change in the policy hereby declared."

It will be seen from section 2 of the joint resolution that the repayments of the postponed annuities should be made at the interest rate of 4 per cent. The London Protocol of August 1931, by which the Hoover Moratorium had been made applicable to the European debts had also provided for repayment in ten years but had fixed the rate of interest at 3 per cent.,[1] so that it appeared that if the European debtors of the United States did not wish to lose 1 per cent. on the deal, which did not seem to be in accordance with the spirit of Mr. Hoover's original proposal, some adjustment must be made between themselves and with Germany.

Mr. Ogden Mills nevertheless explained that 4 per cent. was the rate which long-term bonds of the United States Government would have to carry and that the London Protocol had no necessary bearing on the action of the United States which was not a signatory to it. The United States has therefore insisted on its Congressional bond, and agreements as authorized by the joint resolution were concluded with the various debtor States, and between these latter themselves and with Germany, during the summer of 1932.[2]

Though section 5 of the resolution did not specifically place on record the opposition of Congress to an extension of the Moratorium, it left things very much as they would be if it had. For all practical purposes Congress had hamstrung the President as a negotiator with foreign Governments.

3

The Congressional debate on the Moratorium Bill gave to the world a further proof of the fact that too often the foreign policy of the United States is a sort of Penelope's web, now woven by the President, now unwoven by Congress, a body as

[1] See above, p. 68.   [2] See below, p. 208.

irresponsible as it was unmanageable. A study of the *Congress-*
ional Record covering the debate reveals the fact that the
great majority of members of both Houses of Congress were
without any real understanding of the condition to which
the world has been reduced by the war-debts incubus and
by the crippling of international trade by prohibitive tariffs,
and failed to see that their own troubles are merely the reflection
of that condition. The last thing in the minds of the Senate
and the House was consideration of the effect of their deliberations upon the world outside the United States or on the prestige
of the Administration at Washington which they were so
bitterly subjecting to ridicule and vilification.

What actually happened was that the dollar depreciated
in terms of both pounds and francs and it was not difficult
to find the reason for this. In so far as the views expressed
in Congress represented American public opinion—and it is
true to say that they represented them very fairly—the debate
though uninspiring in character was nevertheless illuminating
to those whose business it was to form a judgment on the likely
tendencies of American business, for it could only mean that
the American position was destined to become worse before it
could possibly become better, an indication which later proved
only too true.

By this negative policy of refusing to recognize their own
limitations and of continuing in their sublime belief that by
passing a strongly worded resolution they could permanently
stem the tide of cancellation and reduction, Congress showed
itself as possessed of an amazingly feeble intelligence, and was
destined before the session was over to give clearer proof of
this.

Even so distinguished a lawyer and experienced a man of
affairs as Senator Reed, of Pennsylvania, dismissed as "silly"
the idea that payment of war debts could present any difficulty
to a country like Great Britain, "owning far-flung colonies,
holding funds all round the circle of the globe, with museums
stuffed with art treasures worth millions and millions." He
was apparently under the delusion that the possession of these

things made it easy to buy American dollars with which to meet payments in the United States unless, as was editorially and sarcastically suggested by *The Times*, the suggestion was made that Great Britain might ship the National Gallery and the British Museum to New York in satisfaction of the claims of the American Treasury.[1]

No speaker during the debate appeared to realize the effect of the tariff, raised in 1930 to prohibitive heights, in making it more difficult for foreign countries to remit payments to the United States; or the necessity imposed on them by their present condition of restricting their purchase of American goods as far as possible, or the influence of this restriction in intensifying the depression in the United States.

By the action of Congress in December 1931 America assumed, with France, a large share of responsibility for the continued failure to arrive at a settlement of the war-debt problem. The attitudes of the two countries towards the problem were, broadly speaking, the same—namely, that their debtors must pay, though both were reluctantly driven to admit that a moratorium was necessary during the economic crisis. By insisting on their political debts which are contributing so materially to the world depression, these two countries have succeeded, involuntarily and to their own detriment, in driving a great part of the world off the gold standard, and until some solution of the problem has been found in an atmosphere of economic realism the restoration of that standard seems a dim prospect—a prospect rendered even more remote after the Congressional debate of December 1931.

The fact is not without irony that almost at the same moment that the Vice-President and the Speaker were signing the joint resolution in Washington, across the Atlantic, in Basle, the members of the Special Advisory Committee were putting their signatures to their Report in which they had arrived at the conclusion, *inter alia*, that

"The adjustment of all inter-Governmental debts (reparations and war debts) to the existing troubled situation
_____
[1] See *The Times*, December 21, 1931.

of the world—and this adjustment should take place without delay if new disasters are to be avoided—is the only lasting step capable of re-establishing confidence, which is the very condition of economic stability and real peace."[1]

[1] See above, p. 154.

CHAPTER VII

IN THE DOLDRUMS

1

"For God's sake let us meet at once!" was Mr. Ramsay Mac-Donald's exclamation of anxiety and alarm on concluding his reading of the Basle Report. Yet, despite this admirable aspiration, despite the appeal of the Report itself for "speed and speed and speed and yet more speed," despite even the fact that before the Special Advisory Committee had ever met it had been agreed in principle that their findings should be considered by a diplomatic conference early in the New Year, the fact remains that this conference did not meet until June 16, 1932, some six months after the Basle Report had been signed.

This delay, though perhaps inevitable, did not come about without an effort being made for more immediate action. The British Government, inspired by the same motive which had prompted Mr. MacDonald's ejaculation, at once issued invitations for a conference to meet at the Hague on January 18, 1932, and these were accepted in principle by all the interested Powers.[1] Meantime in London and Paris conversations were carried on between Treasury officials from Great Britain, France, and Italy for technical consideration of the Basle Report and its fulfilment. Tentative suggestions were also set on foot for a meeting between Mr. MacDonald and M. Laval. Though these conference proposals later proved abortive, they formed for the ensuing few weeks the background against which all the statements and actions of responsible statesmen in Europe were made.

Psychologists hold that no individual is entirely normal when at sea, and it might be said with equal truth that no statesman is entirely normal in the period immediately pre-

---

[1] The French Government first asked for a postponement until January 20th, and, later, until January 25th. Ultimately it was decided that the conference should not meet until June 16th. See below, p. 184.

ceding a great international conference. In considering, therefore, the events of January 1932 it must be remembered that
the European statesmen were acting under the impression that
the conference would meet at the Hague or at Lausanne on
January 16th or 25th.

The Basle Report was received in the French Press with
moderate comment and in the German with guarded optimism.
But it was soon evident that in German political circles it
was accepted as having virtually put an end to reparation payments. Though in his first public statement on the Report,
made to the German Press on Christmas Eve, Dr. Brüning
made no definite declaration to this effect and merely looked
forward to the international conference to make a final settlement of the reparation problem, this moderate tone soon
changed, when it became clear that France was still only
prepared to consider a temporary and provisional solution,
which should precede a return to the measures of the Young
Plan, a view to which the British Government was also believed
to be unfavourably inclined.

In his New Year's message to the nation, broadcast at
midnight on December 31st, President von Hindenburg made
this statement, after thanking the German people for the
self-denial and patience they had shown in the face of grave
crisis and national danger:

"But our great sacrifices justify us in expecting the rest of the world
not to hinder our recovery by requiring of us efforts beyond our strength.
Also, as regards disarmament, Germany's just claims should not be
denied to her. Our right to equality in security is so clear that it cannot
be questioned."

These sentiments, particularly those regarding disarmament,
the President re-emphasized next day in his reply to the speeches
of the Diplomatic Corps at the New Year's Reception.

"All Governments," he said, "must co-operate sympathetically in
finding solutions in which inexorable facts are taken into account,
and which will thus permit of the recovery of the world's trade and
finance. . . . It would be disastrous for the world if the hopes of disarmament should be disappointed once more, and it must not happen. If

confidence, the foundation of all international relations, is to be restored, there must in future be no discrimination in this respect between one nation and another."[1]

On the same morning (January 1, 1932), *Germania*, the official organ of the Chancellor's party, put the German view in very firm terms. The German Government, it said, was not in a position to entertain such conceptions as a proposed moratorium covering only the conditional annuities and providing for the "commercialization" of the unconditional payments as during the Hoover Year.

"Germany's attitude at Lausanne is as simple as can be imagined and is dictated by the force of facts: German payments in any form are out of the question, and the disappearance of the reparation factor is the only means of putting an end to the chronic crisis."[2]

As might have been expected, the French Press did not allow these statements to go unchallenged, and the *Temps* on January 2nd, commenting editorially on President Hindenburg's addresses, warned Germany that she must modify her pretensions or must take the responsibility for a failure, the repercussions of which would be felt throughout the world. Although the majority of the Press, as well as public and official opinion, in France agreed with the attitude adopted by the *Temps*, there were certain signs here and there in the country that some Frenchmen at least were in favour of a change of French policy towards Germany. On January 3rd, the *Dépêche de Toulouse*, the leading provincial newspaper, supporting the policy of the Radical Groups in the Chamber, printed an article from the pen of its political director, M. Arthur Huc, which gave voice to a new point of view

Germany, he declared, did not intend to pay reparations and was no longer afraid to say so. What she demanded was not only a moratorium but a cessation of payments. It also appeared that France would have to give up reparation receipts in practice, if not permanently, at least for an undefined period. But in that case, asked M. Huc, why take so much trouble to keep up appearances? Would it not be much better frankly to abandon reparation payments with the certainty

that such a gesture would have a good effect on German feeling?
In addition, by such a gesture of sacrifice for the common
good France would be in a strong position to face the exigencies
of Washington. But what statesman in France had the courage
to make such a gesture? It would need courage rather than
skill, but the latter was unfortunately the more common
quality.

The Paris Radical Press hailed M. Huc's *démarche* with
delight, strong support being given editorially by the *République*
and the *Populaire*, and even such organs of the Right as
the *Temps* and the *Echo de Paris* were significantly moderate
in their comments. In the January issue of the *Revue des Vivants*,
M. Edouard Dolléans advanced the argument that the adoption
of M. Huc's policy would have the effect of cutting the ground
away from under Herr Hitler's feet, as his followers would
then perceive that Germany's difficulties were not due to
reparations. It would also have the additional advantage of
placing France in the position of insolvent debtor *vis-à-vis* the
United States. He added, "Perhaps America will grumble a
little but she will have nothing to reply." M. Dolléans urged
that France should approach Dr. Brüning, "a man full of
sincerity and moral grandeur . . . with a hand not half closed,
but fully open, ready to give as much as to receive. A gesture
is needed, and this gesture must come before it is too late."
M. Herriot, however, writing in the *Petit Parisien* of January 8th
with an eye to the forthcoming elections, considered that France
must insist on the payment of the unconditional annuities in
some form or another, while believing it to be not impossible
to agree to measures of relief which would save the situation
in Germany.

Meantime, in Germany, Dr. Brüning was endeavouring to
create a united front with which to come to Lausanne and
Geneva. He was anxious if possible to avoid the necessity of
a presidential election, and to prolong for a period of one year
President Hindenburg's period of office which expired in March.
There were many reasons in favour of this policy. It was essential
that the old Marshal should be if possible at the head of the

nation at the time of the Lausanne and the Disarmament Conferences, partly because of the general respect with which he was regarded throughout the world and partly because of his complete reliance and confidence in Dr. Brüning. Such being the case it was desirable that an election should be avoided both on account of the severe physical strain and mental anxiety which it must necessarily occasion the Marshal and because of the emphasized dissensions and party quarrels which it would inevitably bring about.

With this end in view Dr. Brüning summoned the leaders of the Nazi and Nationalist Parties to Berlin and endeavoured to persuade them to agree to support in the Reichstag, which he proposed to convoke in special session on January 12th, a measure to prolong President Hindenburg's period of office for one year.[1] The conversations continued throughout January 7th and 8th with no satisfactory result and finally broke down in the third week of January, Herr Hitler being unwilling to forgo the opportunity for propaganda and the possible chance of success which the election campaign would provide.

Dr. Brüning realized the necessity of demonstrating to the world at large that, despite internal dissensions, Germany was determined and united in her belief that reparation payments could not continue. Simultaneously with his conversation with the leaders of the Right, the Chancellor conferred with the German Ambassadors in London, Paris, and Rome who had been summoned to Berlin, and ultimately he received the British, French, Italian and Belgian Ambassadors who had been directed by their Governments to ascertain definitely the attitude of Germany. It was here that German diplomacy provided once more an example of a lack of appreciation of the situation's requirement. So far as it is possible to see, Germany did not put her case in identical language to all three Powers, she spoke with varying voice in each case,

---

[1] President Hindenburg had agreed to this course provided that all parties, with the exception of the Communists, agreed. According to the Constitution of the Reich, the prolongation of the Presidential term of office requires a two-thirds majority of the Reichstag—that is to say, 385 votes are necessary. This majority could be assured if the 107 Nazis and the 47 Nationalists supported the Government.

although the underlying *motif* was the same—"We cannot pay."

To France, of whom Germany is rather afraid, she said, "I'm very sorry but I can't pay you anything for a year or two." To England, of whom Germany is less afraid, she said, "I can't pay you now, and I don't think I can pay you later on." To Belgium and Italy, of whom Germany is not at all afraid, Germany said: "Not a penny will I ever pay to you or to anyone else."[1]

In any case, these interviews with the Ambassadors were never meant to become public property and were intended only for the private information of the various Foreign Offices concerned. Reuter's Agency, however, acquired a knowledge of what Dr. Brüning had said in Berlin and circulated accordingly: "It is in brief that Germany is unable to pay reparations either now or in the future if the economic life of the world is to be revived, and that the German Delegation at the Lausanne Conference must press for the total abolition of reparations."[2]

The Press of the world carried the Reuter message, and Dr. Brüning had no alternative than to substantiate in a public statement what he had already said to the Ambassadors.

Accordingly, later in the day the Chancellor gave to the German people and to the world, by means of an interview given to the Wolff News Bureau, his now famous statement on reparations. At the forthcoming Conference, he said, Germany would demand the complete cancellation of reparation payments.

"The continuation of political payments is rendered impossible by the situation in which Germany is to-day. It is clear that any attempt to uphold the system of political debt payments would lead not only Germany but the world to disaster. . . . At the coming Conference Germany can only describe the actual situation and appeal to other participating States to take this situation into

[1] See an article by Mr. Wickham Steed in the *Sunday Times* of January 24, 1932.
[2] See a Reuter message dated January 9, 1932.

account and to refrain from seeking compromise solutions for which a basis of reality no longer exists. . . . The test will be finding the courage to put this realization into practice and not allow the political idea again to influence the treatment of economic problems."

To many this statement by Dr. Brüning was a natural corollary to the Layton–Wiggin and the Basle Reports, and even those who least believed in its fundamental principle could scarcely have ignored the probability of its being made. But in France there arose so strident a clamour of protest that for a time it was thought that she might boycott the Lausanne Conference.

" 'Dr. Brüning's declaration,' said M. Flandin, French Minister of Finance, on the evening of January 9th, 'amounts to the annulling of the Versailles Treaty and the Young Plan, and makes the holding of the Lausanne Conference useless. France cannot accept Germany's unilateral denunciation of reparations compacts, freely signed, which means the destruction of France's sacred rights to reparations.' "

The French reaction to Dr. Brüning's statement was the more severe since the statement itself coincided with a Cabinet crisis in Paris. M. Maginot, the Minister for War, had died suddenly on January 7th and M. Briand, for reasons of health, had resigned the portfolio of Foreign Affairs on January 8th. At the moment of Dr. Brüning's declaration, M. Laval was, therefore, in the act of reconstructing his Cabinet and the effect in Paris resulted in a Government more conservative in character than its predecessor, with M. Laval himself at the Quai d'Orsay and M. Tardieu as Minister for War.

No surprise was therefore felt at the terms of the new Ministerial Declaration made before the Chamber on January 19th. M. Laval described the proposals made "in certain quarters" for the wiping out of reparations and debts as the outcome of a state of mind which could only be attributed to the fact that the world, hungry for a formula which promised a cure for its ills, was too ready to welcome quack theories. The French Government, in any case, would not allow their right to reparations to be denied, and in all negotiations for the purpose of adapting the existing debt agreements to the period

of economic depression it would continue to observe strictly
the basic principles which Parliament had always approved.

The British view of the German statement was more reserved
and less hysterical than the French. Mr. MacDonald's statement issued on January 10th showed that it had occasioned
no surprise. Some such declaration of policy was inevitable,
and the fact that it had been made before the Lausanne Conference rendered that Conference all the more necessary. The
Prime Minister was sure that appeasement of the situation
depended upon facing hard facts.

But support for the German thesis came alike from business
men and economists in Great Britain. The Hon. Alexander
Shaw, a Governor of the Bank of England, declared himself
wholeheartedly in approval of cancellation of war debts, for
"if things go on as they are now going the choice is quite
simply between repudiation and chaos." Further qualified
support came from Sir Walter Layton in a speech to the Eighty
Club on January 13th. Unconvinced that Germany could not
pay anything at any time and fully aware that the cancellation
might not prove an unmixed blessing to Great Britain, Sir
Walter Layton said that he considered it "highly desirable if
the slate were wiped clean because of the removing of a long-
drawn-out source of irritation and a sense of war-psychology.
If it were done by agreement it would repay itself a thousand-
fold, and if France wants to make her position really secure the
best thing she can possibly do is to take the lead and either wipe
out the reparation liability or make it a nominal pound a year."[1]

Perhaps the most characteristic reaction was that of Italy.
On January 12th and 14th there appeared two articles in the
Popolo d'Italia, which, though unsigned, bore unmistakable

[1] The first official intimation of the British attitude since the publication of
the Basle Report was contained in the reply of H.B.M. Government to
the Report of the Commission of Enquiry into European Union, published
by the League of Nations on January 15th. The reply stated that it was
"the conviction of His Majesty's Government that a satisfactory settlement
of the question of inter-Governmental debts is an essential condition for the
revival of confidence, and the achievement of such a settlement is the most
important contribution which can be made by the Governments concerned
at the present time towards the restoration of normal prosperity throughout
the world."

marks of the opinions and style of Il Duce. These articles
contained appeals, first to Europe and secondly to America,
calling for a clean slate and were accepted as the official Italian
pronouncement on the situation. There was a ring almost of
the mediaeval Papal Bulls in these articles. The "Epistle to the
Europeans" declared that the civilization of Europe was at the
parting of the ways such as former civilizations had reached,
and at which they often fell. "The Lausanne Conference must
decide to make what by this time is known as a 'stroke of the
sponge'; it must end by cancelling the debts and credits . . .
the tragic bookkeeping of War." This was urged, first, because
the creditor countries, principally the United States and Great
Britain, had already recovered the subsidies paid out on account
of materials supplied to the Allies, by means of a very high
tax on excess war profits, and hence further payments by the
debtor countries were now no more than a forced tribute;
and, secondly, because in consequence of the fall in prices, it
was necessary to repay these creditors by double the labour
and double the quantity of goods in order to pay the same
unchangeable amount of debts. "Better declare a moratorium
of useless conferences bringing only disillusion, if the Lausanne
Conference should not succeed in achieving a final solution."

"The Epistle to the Americans" appeared two days later
(January 14th) and was addressed to the United States, as the
only country owing nothing to anybody—a situation which
"does not complicate, but simplifies, the problem." An appeal
was made to the "idealism and disinterestedness" of the
United States to cancel the European debts, an action by which
she would in reality gain more than she lost. The first step,
it was admitted, must be taken by the European States in
cancelling war debts amongst themselves, and, having done so,
in presenting America with a *fait accompli* which she would
eventually accept, since she could not change it.[1]

Thus, as in the case of the French Note of December 7th,
1931, each new phase of the reparation problem showed more

---

[1] Compare these arguments with the similar reasoning used by M. Dolléans
in the *Revue des Vivants*. See above, p. 175.

clearly than the last the alignment of Europe in the matter. France was isolated in her demands for continued reparations, while Italy definitely and Great Britain more reservedly, supported Germany's thesis of cancellation. Across the Atlantic the Washington Administration still refused to consider the word cancellation, but it was admitted in Wall Street that, even if Europe repudiated her debts to America it might not prove a great hardship. "We might make up our losses many times in the trade boom which would probably be hastened by a settlement," said one authority.

2

Dr. Brüning's statement of January 9th and its consequent repercussions opened a new phase of the situation which, it was clear almost from the first, must end inevitably in the postponement of the Lausanne Conference.

Despite every effort on the part of intermediaries it was impossible to arrange a meeting between Mr. MacDonald and M. Laval. Even the suggestion of an exchange of letters was looked upon unfavourably, M. Laval possibly remembering that a personal correspondence with M. Poincaré in 1924 had been followed by a complete defeat of his Government at the elections.

British and French Treasury experts however continued their consultations and at length a tentative agreement was reached between their Governments as to the action to be taken by the Conference. It was suggested that for the present there should be merely an extension of the Hoover Moratorium for another six or twelve months as far as Germany was concerned with a promise of further consideration of cancellation at the end of this period.[1] At the same time an appeal should be made to the United States to make a similar extension.

In many ways there was much to recommend such a proposal.

[1] It is understood that the British experts were in favour of a complete moratorium on all German payments, including both conditional and unconditional annuities, without any provision for these being repaid with interest at the termination of the period of remission. To this, as may be supposed, the French experts were unalterably opposed. Needless to say, German opinion was also opposed to any form of extension on any terms.

The impending elections in Germany, France and the United States rendered the position unusually precarious and it was hoped that by the end of the extension period the Disarmament Conference, which was to open on February 2nd, might have achieved a sufficiently measurable degree of progress to reassure the United States as to the serious intention of Europe to cut its armament budget. On the other hand, the strong desire in many quarters for a final settlement found expression in very clear opposition to any temporary arrangements which would have no material effect on the revival of trade and confidence.

On January 16th, therefore, M. Laval received the American Ambassador, Mr. Walter Edge, and put before him the French views, asking him to give a definition of the attitude of the United States Government towards its debtors in the event of an extension of the German Moratorium beyond the Hoover Period. As if in presage of the American reply, Senator Reed made on the same day in Washington an important declaration: "It is impossible for the United States," he declared, "to admit, if Germany is, or may be, unable to pay further reparations, that this automatically cancels debts, since these debts have no relation to reparations. When these debts were created no reparations existed. At the time of the funding the amount was estimated on the normal capacity to pay of the various nations, irrespective of reparations."

The official American reply was conveyed to M. Laval in an *aide-memoire* submitted by the Ambassador.[1] In it were repeated the old age-worn arguments that no connection existed between the two categories of war debts, and the attention of France was drawn to the hostility of Congress to cancellation or reduction. The initiative in the reparation question must come from Europe, and the United States would seriously view with disfavour any "united front of debtors to whom it could not give any general undertaking." Finally, the United States

[1] This document also would never have reached the public had it not been for one of those calculated "indiscretions" for which some Foreign Offices are famous. On January 20th the *Figaro* published the text of the American *aide-memoire*, and inquiry at the Quai d'Orsay elicited the information that the text as printed was "substantially correct."

was convinced that Europe could pay her debts if she restored mutual confidence and reduced armament expenditure.[1]

This memorandum was in effect the American reply to the Laval–Hoover declaration of the previous October. M. Laval had insisted that the initiative in the matter of reparations must rest with Europe, that is to say France, and now President Hoover was quite satisfied to let it remain there. The French were at last reaping the fruits of their campaign in the United States in the autumn and winter of 1931, which, though it had secured them the initiative in the matter of reparations, had also very naturally contributed to the attitude of Congress towards inter-Allied debts in general and had thereby provided Mr. Hoover with an admirable excuse to leave France "with the baby."[2]

It was armed with this information that M. Laval met the Chamber on January 19th and made his public comment on Dr. Brüning's statement ten days before. The American reply provided France with the excuse for a further and indefinite postponement of the Lausanne Conference. In the meantime it was hoped that conditions in Germany would have become so bad that it would be no longer possible for her to do anything but accept France's terms. Similar developments, aided by the withdrawal of French balances from New York, were hoped for in the United States.

It may be argued that, as in January France was likely to meet with practically unanimous opposition from the other Powers—both the Italian and British Governments had made it perfectly clear that they were in favour of the cancellation of all war debts—she could not be expected to participate in a conference where she was certain to be isolated. Even from a French point of view it was a grave error to insist upon postponement. In January France was at the pinnacle of her financial power, and in the months which followed this power

---

[1] Commenting editorially on the United States Memorandum, the *Figaro* remarked: "The intransigeant incomprehension of the United States, which in turn intervenes in European affairs to complicate and aggravate them, as by Hoover's proclamation, and then withdraws within itself when things go from bad to worse through its own fault, is nothing new."

[2] See above, pp. 121–123.

began gradually but steadily to decline, partly owing to Great Britain's spectacular financial recovery and partly on account of the deterioration of economic and financial conditions in France itself.

The only point of view from which the postponement of the Lausanne Conference[1] can be explained, if not excused, is from internal political considerations. On the eve of Presidential and Prussian elections in Germany and of a General Election in France, neither country, it was argued, would be willing to make concessions. But, on the other hand, had the electorates in both countries been confronted with a *fait accompli* repudiation would have been difficult. Moreover, it is by no means certain that, had M. Laval agreed at Lausanne in January to a reasonable settlement, this would have meant for him political suicide. Public opinion in France was already beginning to take account of realities—as witness M. Huc in the *Dépêche de Toulouse* and M. Dolléans in the *Revue des Vivants*—and might conceivably have received a reasonable settlement with relief. If, after having agreed to a radical reduction of reparations M. Laval had gone to the country he would have had a fair chance of reaping the reward of his courage and statesmanship. He did not dare, however, to take the risk, and as a result the world remained in a state of anxious uncertainty and the discussion of a reparations settlement was postponed until the third week of the twelfth month of the Hoover Year.[2]

3

The period between the official announcement of the postponement of the Lausanne Conference on February 13, 1932, and its eventual opening on June 16th was undistinguished by any event or happening, either in international or national affairs, which might have enhanced the prospects of its success. Two Presidential ballots in Germany in March and April and

[1] The postponement was announced by the British Foreign Office on February 13th.
[2] See *Finance and Politics*, by Paul Einzig (Macmillan, 1932), pp. 35–36.

a General Election in France in May effectually prevented the period of interval from being utilized for a further exchange of views, and thus the months passed, perforce, without any progress towards a reconciliation of national view-points.

In international affairs the stage was dominated by the opening of the Disarmament Conference on February 2nd to an accompaniment of the bombardment of Chapei, and by the Danubian Customs Union proposal, which found decent burial in the London Conference of April 6th–8th. In the first of these Conferences, French policy as pursued at first by M. Laval and later by M. Tardieu, who succeeded to the premiership on February 21st, was successful. In the second, it received a decided check.

The French policy towards disarmament had been amply illustrated to the world at large in the Memorandum of July 1931, to which reference has already been made.[1] When the Conference itself met there was no change in the French attitude. The French proposals put forward on February 5th were so frankly fantastic that their serious consideration was impossible, and yet by insisting on them as an essential to any form of disarmament on the part of France, the French delegation were able to "stonewall" and block any constructive step being taken by the Conference. This policy, aided by the inevitable obstruction which technical experts of all countries may also be safely calculated to provide, satisfactorily (from the point of view of France) rendered sterile the process of disarmament. The same refusal to consider disarmament before security—as interpreted by France—was assured, caused the failure of the proposals of Mr. Gibson on April 11th and the Five-Power Conversations at the close of the same month.[2]

But the achievement of the Danubian Customs Union was an object in which the interests of France were very closely concerned. As has been shown, France had "bought" Central Europe in the summer of 1931 and, although she had not

[1] See above, p. 80.
[2] For the progress of the Disarmament Conference see *Bulletin of International News*, vol. viii, no. 16 (February 4, 1932), no. 17 (February 18, 1932), no. 21 (April 14, 1932), and no. 23 (May 12, 1932), and vol. ix, nos. 3 and 4.

spent a very vast sum in doing so, she soon found that her purchase was distinctly more of a liability than an asset. Austria and Hungary were, after the negotiations of 1931, completely dependent on French support and the Little Entente States could never have weathered the crisis had it not been for French credits. By the spring of 1932 the European Central situation had become so acute that French financial circles were definitely alarmed.

In Hungary the Government had, on December 23, 1931, been compelled to declare a transfer moratorium for one year with the object of safeguarding the country's gold transfer and exchange reserve. In Austria the position had become so serious that on February 16, 1932, the Chancellor summoned the Ministers of Great Britain, France, Germany and Italy and warned them that his Government would be compelled to take steps to restrict imports as the only means of preventing inflation, but stated that they were ready to enter into negotiations with all nations for an economic *rapprochement*, and hoped that some consideration would be shown to them. The Budget had been balanced at 2,000 million schillings, and the Chancellor stated that the Government would not declare a transfer moratorium for its foreign debts but would maintain its credit by paying the interest on the short-term and the service on the long-term debt, but the unknown factor of the extent to which revenue would probably diminish during the year rendered problematical the degree of success with which the Government could cope with the financial difficulties ahead.

Coupled with the desire to safeguard her financial position in Central Europe, France had the ever-present desire to provide some alternative to the Austro-German *Zollunion*, which it was realized was not dead but sleeping—and without some such union Austria could not economically survive—and to complete, if possible permanently, the weaning of Hungary from her Italian orientation.

With this double end in view, M. Tardieu, on March 2nd, approached the Governments of Great Britain, Italy and Germany with a proposal, not for a definite Danubian Customs

Union, for which it was considered the time was not yet ripe, but for lesser expedients intended to bring about immediate relief, beginning with a consultation between the five Governments concerned (the Little Entente, Austria, and Hungary) with a view to the introduction of preferential measures for the relief of their commercial and industrial exchanges. When the formula for co-operation had been found it would then be the duty of the Great Powers to assist in its practical application —in the granting of credits. The spiritual background of the proposal was pointed by the *Temps*, which declared that "an association of France, Great Britain, Italy, and Germany for the rehabilitation, not of one Danubian State, but of all distressed nations whose interests are so closely linked as to demand mutual aid for their salvation, would be the first experiment in that policy of European solidarity which all good men desire."[1]

The French proposal did not have an enthusiastic reception. The five Danubian Powers were not in the least convinced of the value to them of any kind of Customs Union, though preferential tariffs were, of course, recognized as helpful in specific cases. The establishment of a Customs Union would aid the industrial, but not the agricultural countries, since the latter could not hope to find a sufficiently large market for their surplus production in Austria and Czechoslovakia. According to figures published in Prague, Hungary, Yugoslavia and Rumania have an annual export surplus of 800,000 tons of wheat, 1,300,000 tons of maize, and 1,800,000 tons of barley, but the two other countries require only 550,000 tons of wheat, 250,000 tons of maize, and 70,000 tons of barley. From the point of view of the industrial countries, also, the removal of Customs barriers would not be an unqualified gain. It would not restore to them their pre-war markets, and the industries which have grown up in formerly non-industrial areas in Rumania and Yugoslavia, for example, would continue to compete with them, for they would most probably have administrative protection of some sort to preserve them from disappearance in the national interest. The Governments of those countries could

[1] See *Temps*, March 6, 1932.

hardly be expected to look complacently on while their mineral and fuel resources, the development of which is now well under way, were neglected because they could not as yet compete with the rival productions of other countries. In the case of Austria, in particular, the regaining of some of the former Danubian markets would meet only a part of her present difficulties, because she needs an opportunity for utilizing the trade and financial organization and experience of the city of Vienna. For this the five countries would have to become not only a free-trade but an economically unified territory in a much wider sense with Vienna as the financial centre. In fact, it may be said that Austria would stand to gain more than any of the other five countries by a scheme of economic collaboration of whatever nature. She was confronted with the choice of becoming a part of a larger economic territory or of falling into economic retrogression so serious as to threaten her very existence, and as the attempt to form close economic relations with Germany had been frustrated, participation in some form of commercial collaboration with her neighbours in the south-east would seem to hold out the only hope for the future.

The Great Powers, too, were sceptical. In Great Britian there were many who were disposed to see in the French proposal an attempt to shift the financial responsibility of Central Europe from France to the Great Powers, and of necessity the greater part of the burden would fall on Great Britain. Italy and Germany were only too well aware of the political considerations underlying the proposals. Italy was averse to losing all control over Hungary and could ill-afford to give up trade advantages which she already possessed and which had been consolidated by agreements with Austria and Hungary signed only on March 4 and 7, 1932, respectively. A Customs Union would, moreover, prove a very definite barrier to the policy and conviction of Signor Mussolini that the economic expansion of Italy must be towards the East.

Germany felt as much misgiving at the prospect of a new orientation in Austria as Italy felt at seeing Hungary drawn into the orbit of the Little Entente. The French proposal meant that Austria would be absorbed into a rival industrial and agricultural group to Germany, who felt that in any economic reorganization of Central Europe she should be included. Germany's claim to be included in any preferential tariff system was a very strong one and provided a weak point in France's armour. After the abandonment of the Austro-German *Zollunion* in September 1931, France had produced a "constructive plan" which it communicated to foreign Governments.[1] In this it recognized the necessity of Germany's co-operation in Central Europe so completely that it was incorporated in the economic group which it was proposed to form. In this plan, too, preferential tariffs were suggested not only between the Succession States but also between Germany and Austria. Germany also claimed inclusion for reasons of expediency, since only her co-operation could guarantee the necessary markets for the agrarian products of South-Eastern Europe and, in addition, by her exclusion Czechoslovakia would lose her best customer.[2]

Both Italy and Germany regarded the inclusion of Bulgaria as necessary, and that State made official application for participation on March 16th. This was definitely opposed to French policy, which aimed not only at excluding Germany for political and economic reasons, but also at maintaining within the proposed Union the predominance of power in the hands of the Little Entente. Bulgaria was not only an ex-enemy State but a declared ally of Italy, and for this reason the French Government set itself against her inclusion.

Despite the cool reception which their plan received, MM. Laval and Flandin continued to pursue the line of policy described and set about converting the British Government to the French view, even to the extent of persuading France's

---

[1] For text see *Documents on International Affairs*, 1931, p. 6.
[2] It was estimated by League of Nations authorities that Czechoslovakia imported more from Germany than from the other four Danubian States put together. See League Document E.770, *Chiffres essentiels du commerce exterieur des pays danubiens*.

non-Danubian allies to support her case.[1] In the initial stages
their diplomacy was successful in that they not only persuaded
the British Government to call a Conference of the Four Great
Powers to consider the matter but also arranged for a personal
exchange of views with Mr. MacDonald and his colleagues
before the Conference opened, thereby stealing a march on
their Italian and German colleagues.

A considerable amount of suspicion surrounded the Anglo-
French conversations which took place on April 3rd and 4th.
Mr. MacDonald did not seem to be very easy in his own mind
about them and took the opportunity at the close of each day's
discussions to issue to the Press a complete denial that any
preliminary agreement existed between him and M. Tardieu.
There has seldom been such a desire to affirm so complete a
lack of agreement at an international conversation; conference
bulletins are usually on the other side. "I want to say that
there has never been the slightest justification for that suspicion,"
said the Premier on the afternoon of April 3rd. "The Four-
Power Conference is to sit this week and consider the problems
of the Danube States. There are no agreements beforehand.
There are no draft proposals beforehand." On the following
day Mr. MacDonald again described his conversations with
M. Tardieu as being "a conference for exploration and not an
executive conference of any kind whatever."

When, however, the London Conference met at the Foreign
Office on April 6th, an Anglo-French proposal was submitted,
which showed that possibly Mr. MacDonald had been more
influenced by the result of his exploration than he would have
had the Press believe. It was suggested that in the first place
the plan should refer only to the five States originally mentioned
in the French proposal, amongst whom there should exist a
10 per cent. preferential tariff, and to whom should be made
a £10 million loan raised in the main by France but guaranteed
by Great Britain. It was also proposed that there should be
some form of financial control which should promise real

[1] On April 2nd the Polish Ambassador informed Sir John Simon that his
Government viewed with favour any attempt to relieve the distressed economic
conditions of the Danubian countries.

security and prevent such abuse of the loan as had happened in the past.

This proposition was acceptable neither to Signor Grandi, who proposed a Nine-Power Conference of all parties concerned which might work out a more general method of participation, nor to Dr. von Bülow, who produced an alternative plan by announcing that Germany was prepared to offer, without stipulating for reciprocity, a general preference on all goods, etc. to Austria, and similar preference on agricultural products to Hungary, Rumania, Yugoslavia, and Bulgaria. It was agreed that a second Conference should be held at which the Danubian States should be given an opportunity of discussing the decision of the London Conference, but the problem was, should this Conference consist merely of the Little Entente, Austria and Hungary, as suggested by France, or should it include the Great Powers themselves, a course approved by Great Britain, Germany and Italy, and in any case Bulgaria was to be admitted, a point on which Germany was insistent?

After three days of discussion the Conference concluded on April 7th without having reached any agreement, apart from the issue of a *communiqué* in which the sense of failure was evident. M. Tardieu, by insisting on the French method and the French method only, had forfeited that degree of British support which he had gained earlier in his conversation with Mr. MacDonald.

Central Europe, despite the fact that the Report of the special meeting of the League Financial Committee, which sat from March 3rd to 24th in Paris, called for immediate and drastic action, providing recommendations as to what lines such action should follow, relapsed still further into the Slough of Despond and continued to wallow therein. The only action which the League Council took at its April meeting, called specially to consider the Report of the Financial Committee, was to appoint a further committee of Treasury experts to re-examine the position, a process which resulted in neither decision nor action.

European statesmanship never showed itself in so parlous a state as during this period.

4

In internal affairs the events in Germany, France and America
during the period gave no hint of hope for settlement of the
war-debts problem. In Germany the growing force of National
Socialism was preparing the way for Dr. Brüning's fall. In
France, though M. Tardieu went down to defeat in the General
Election of May, he left behind him a legacy of policy which
his successor found difficult to abandon and the economic
condition of France did not facilitate this. In America, Congress
continued to dance with the inexhaustible and phrenetic vigour
of St. Vitus, a sample of which the world had already seen in
the debate on the Hoover Moratorium.

In Germany the fact that definite action by the European
Powers in the matter of reparations had been postponed materially contributed to Dr. Brüning's defeat, since he had nothing
to offer the German people in return for the continually increasing burden of taxation and economies which he was
compelled to place upon them.[1] These burdens, bringing with
them discontent and despair, together with the complete lack
of success of German foreign policy, provided ample grist for
the Nazi mills. The General Election of 1930 had returned the
Party to the Reichstag with 107 seats; by the close of 1931 it
had nearly a million registered members, and successive State
elections showed that in all classes the reasoning of despair
rather than a belief in the Nazi policy was leading the German
people in an avalanche towards the Right. This was particularly
noticeable in the Presidential Elections in March and April
1932, for though in the first ballot on March 13, Marshal von
Hindenburg only failed of election by half a million votes,
Herr Hitler polled over 11 millions, and in the second ballot
on April 10th his vote had increased by 2 million, showing
that the Nazi Party's voting strength had doubled since the
Reichstag elections.

[1] See "The German Political Situation," by J. W. Wheeler-Bennett, *Inter-
national Affairs*, vol. xi, no. 4 (July 1932); also two articles entitled "The
German Situation," by J. W. Wheeler-Bennett and Hugh Latimer, in the
Bulletin of International News, vol. viii, no. 25 (June 9, 1932), and no. 26
(June 23, 1932).

The elections held in Prussia, Bavaria, Württemberg, and Hamburg on April 24th produced further evidence of this fact. In Prussia the Socialist Government of Dr. Otto Braun had been in power since 1921 and it intended to leave no stone unturned to defeat the Nazis. As a result every obstacle was placed in their way, the use of the Radio was forbidden them as well as other facilities, and, finally, on April 13th, eleven days before the date of polling, the Prussian Minister of Interior, Herr Severing, succeeded in stampeding General Groener into recommending the *Reichskabinet* to dissolve the Storm Troops (*Sturmabteilungen*) and to declare them an illegal organization.

This action was, contrary to expectation, doubly beneficial to Herr Hitler. At one and the same moment it relieved him of the responsibility for a body which was undoubtedly getting beyond his own control and, conversely, it allowed him and his party to appear before the electorate in the guise of political martyrs. The importance of the elections of April 24th can scarcely be exaggerated, since the States concerned covered four-fifths of the area of the whole Reich. In Bavaria the Nazis increased their representation by 34, securing 43 seats in the new Diet, while in Anhalt and Württemberg they made enormous advances. In Prussia they increased the number of seats from 9 to 162, their gains being mostly at the expense of the other Parties of the Reich, including those Splinter Parties which had previously supported the Brüning policy. It seemed clear that the Brüning Government and all that it stood for had lost the confidence of the German people.

At this juncture the Chancellor's opponents were further reinforced. The senior officers of the Reichswehr Ministerium, led by General von Schleicher, the Director of Political Operations,[1] had made no secret of their disapproval of the dissolution of the *Sturmabteilungen* which they regarded as a very valuable asset in the training of the youth of the country and in forming them into a potential trained reserve. These officers, who became known in the Press as the *Generals Kamarilla*, set themselves first to secure the resignation of the

---

[1] Now beginning to be known as the "*Feld-grau Eminenz.*"

Reichswehr Minister, General Groener, and, secondly, to undermine the position of the Chancellor, whose policy they regarded as detrimental to the welfare of the country.

The first of these objects was attained on May 12th, when the *Kamarilla* succeeded in convincing Marshal von Hindenburg that General Groener no longer enjoyed the confidence of the Reichswehr. As a result the General prudently discovered that his health would no longer permit of his holding two portfolios and he agreed to retain only that of the Interior. A further prop had thus been struck from the support of the Brüning Ministry, and the military chiefs found themselves allied with the leaders of commerce and industry in opposing the Chancellor.

The moment had now arrived for Dr. Brüning to take a decision which he had long postponed. The Lausanne Conference was but three weeks away; his position with the Reichstag, though it had recently given him a vote of confidence, was completely negligible, since that body itself had failed to represent the will of the German people, and the German Budget had to be balanced. Dr. Brüning, therefore, determined to ask President von Hindenburg to give him the assurance of his further confidence in him, not only to carry on over Lausanne, but also afterwards; at the same time he submitted for his approval a further batch of Emergency Decrees providing for further reductions in war pensions and unemployment insurance, calculated to bring in some 800,000,000 marks. Provision was also made for the expropriation of certain bankrupt estates in East Prussia.

These estates had already been heavily subsidised, through the organization of the *Osthilfe*, and Dr. Brüning proposed that, in view of the large sums of public money which had been spent in this manner—and in vain—arrangements should be made for settling a number of smallholders on such farms as were so heavily indebted as to remove all hope of their being rescued from insolvency and disuse. There were a number, estimated at about one-sixth of the total, where even the cancellation of half of their floating debt and extensive compulsory reduction

of interest, provided for by the Decree of November 1931, would
not enable them to carry on, and these Dr. Brüning's Government had hoped to take over at a low price, in many cases
only the amount of the first mortgage. The owners of the land,
rather naturally expressed themselves strongly as to the merits
of the scheme. That it might be the only way of working
them profitably or of finding any kind of purchaser was not
an argument likely to appeal to owners in whose family the
land had been for generations, and they told the President
that the whole scheme was nothing better than *Agrar-Bolsche-
vismus*. Their own idea was apparently to get rid of the burden
of debt by curtailing the rights of their creditors to a greater
extent than had already been done by the November Decree,
and, in particular, to secure a conversion of the first mortgages
to 80 per cent. of their value, but they produced no evidence
that, with these concessions, they would be able to work their
land profitably.

The President found himself personally unable to take the
side of his Chancellor against the people of his own caste and
upbringing, and by setting his face definitely against this
part of Dr. Brüning's scheme he was able to make it clear to
the latter that he no longer gave him his full confidence. The
fact that he hoped that Dr. Brüning would consent to serve
as Minister of Foreign Affairs in another Cabinet showed,
however, that he did not interpret correctly the Chancellor's
attitude towards the whole question of the political future of
the country. He was undoubtedly, if not alarmed, at least ill
at ease at what he felt to be socialistic tendencies in certain
of the measures with which the Government was identified,
and he wished for a reconstruction of the Cabinet more to the
Right. He thought it possible to get this without forfeiting
the support and collaboration of the Chancellor.

On May 28th the President and the Chancellor held a long
consultation, in the midst of which came the news that in the
Oldenburg elections the Nazis had secured a complete majority
over all other parties. Convinced that Dr. Brüning no longer
had the confidence of the country, the President pressed him

to remain in a new Ministry as Foreign Minister. But Dr. Brüning speedily undeceived him, and next morning in a final interview which lasted just eight minutes, the Chancellor resigned with his whole Cabinet.

Marshal von Hindenburg, actuated as always by the desire to govern constitutionally, sent for the party leaders in turn. The first to see him was Dr. Breitscheid, the Socialist, who refused to form a Cabinet; the next was Herr Hitler, who declined to take office unless a General Election were held, two years before its appointed time.

Faced with this difficulty—for the Socialists, Nazis, and Catholic Centre are the only three parties with any following of weight or influence—Marshal von Hindenburg is understood to have addressed the Nazi leader in some such terms as these: "As you have refused to take the responsibility of government I shall appoint a Cabinet of my own friends, but I shall not ask them to sacrifice themselves and assume office merely until after the Elections. If, as a result of these, your party is either in a majority or is the largest in the Reichstag I shall require of you an undertaking that three of the key positions in any Ministry that you may form shall be held by members of the Cabinet I am now forming; these offices are those of the Interior, the Reichswehr, and Foreign Affairs." Herr Hitler is believed to have accepted these conditions, though with the stipulation that the Nazis should have the Prussian Government all to themselves.

The President at once set about the task of choosing a Chancellor, with a result which surprised the people of Germany almost as much as it did those of the world in general. The name of von Papen was, in politics, known to few, and to most members of the public he was merely a landowner in the Saar Basin who had been for ten years a member of the Prussian Diet as a representative of the Centre Party and had served as a Military Attaché in the Diplomatic Service abroad. The circumstances in which he left the United States during the war only became known to the German public when the foreign Press came out with headlines reading: "Ex-war spy becomes

German Chancellor," but it was not on this account that the Press of nearly all the parties in the country received his appointment with disapproval. His own party, the Catholic Centre, let him know quite clearly that it did not value the membership of the man who had taken the place of its eminent leader, Dr. Brüning, and the parties of the Left naturally saw in him nothing but the agent of reaction and of vested interests. The Nazi Press was, at first, not impressed; its comments on the whole business were much influenced by the fact that it considered the President's move merely a temporary one, and described the new Cabinet as "obviously transitional." The Nazis had got their way in the matter of new elections, and relied on these to give them a majority in the Reichstag; Prussia, they felt, had already been delivered into their hands.

It may, then, be asked why the President's choice should have fallen upon Herr von Papen. The answer is that he was sufficiently independent of party ties to be the head of a non-party Government, and, in fact, had for some time been actively engaged in promoting understandings between certain of the parties. In particular, he had been attempting to reconcile the Centre Party and the Nazis, and was instrumental in arranging the interviews between the President and Herr Hitler and Dr. Brüning and Herr Hitler. In a wider field his name has also been associated with the idea of a *rapprochement* with France, and he played a prominent part in private movements with a strong Catholic basis for better relations with that country, going so far, it was rumoured, as to include the idea of a military alliance against the U.S.S.R.

The correct light in which to regard Herr von Papen's appearance in so important a position is that of leader of a movement to fight extremism of every kind and, incidentally, to disarm the Nazis. The published programme of Herr Hitler certainly contained proposals sufficiently alarming to make desperate remedies necessary, and the President and his advisers, feeling that it was impossible to suppress the Nazis, decided on an attempt to split the party into its component parts—

Nationalist and Socialist—by coming out with a programme which would enlist the support of the former while irretrievably antagonizing the latter. Those of Hitler's supporters whose sympathies were naturally to the Right would then find themselves in agreement with the policy of the new Government, which, in its turn, would be able to provide them with sound leaders, and those whose sympathies were to the Left would become definitely antagonized and would leave the fold. The issue would be simplified—this has been the tendency in all the recent political developments in Germany—and the major forces in the country would be ranged with the Right or the Left, making it much easier, among other things, to deal with foreign Governments.

Indeed, in the realm of foreign affairs the Papen Government was considerably stronger than its predecessor. The new Foreign Minister, Baron von Neurath, had been a successful and popular Ambassador in Rome and London, and the Finance Minister, Count Schwerin von Krösigk, had revealed himself to his fellow-experts at Basle during the deliberations of the special Advisory Committee, as having a sound knowledge of practical finance.[1] These two personalities in many ways counterbalanced in the eyes of foreign statesmen, the unfortunate war record of the Chancellor and the sinister figure of General von Schleicher, who had become Minister of Defence. Moreover, the Government was not bound by Dr. Brüning's reparations declaration of January 9th; it had no parliamentary responsibility; it had no party executive to keep track of its activities; and, finally, it had the Reichswehr behind it. Any concessions which might be made at Lausanne would, it was believed both by the Government itself and also abroad, be accepted by the Nationalist feeling in Germany, as no concession, however small, could have been accepted if made by Dr. Brüning. Externally, at least, the change might be said to be for the better.

But internally the situation was less fortunate. Between the Government and the Nazis there existed some alliance, one of

---

[1] Count Schwerin von Krösigk is a former Rhodes scholar.

the main terms of which was the immediate lifting of the ban on the *Sturmabteilungen*. Bitter resentment towards this was felt in Southern Germany, where the Governments of Bavaria, Baden, and Württemberg, supported in a lesser degree by Saxony, were entirely opposed to the restitution to the Nazis of their old privileges.

In addition to this, the threat of the Reich Minister of Interior, Baron von Gayl, to appoint a *Reichskommisar* in Prussia, to replace the Business Government which had carried on the Government since the elections, aroused grave misgivings in Bavaria, where a Business Government had governed the country for two years and where the further encroachment of the Central Government was dreaded and resented. The raising of the ban on the Storm Troops on June 15th brought matters to a head, and on June 25th the Bavarian Government determined to defy the Reich and continue to impose the prohibition on uniforms.

This grave threat to the federal structure of Germany was not overlooked in Paris, nor were its potential repercussions underestimated. Ever since the Peace Conference France had aimed at the political dissolution of Germany and had pursued to this end as doubtfully honest a policy as can be found in post-war history. Separatism had been encouraged in the Rhineland both during the Peace Conference and the Occupation of the Ruhr, and when that failed the latest step taken by the Quai d'Orsay was the appointment of a separate diplomatic representative, Comte Lefèvre d'Ormesson, to Munich in January 1932. France was therefore unlikely to disapprove of a German Government which might bring about from within what she had failed to achieve from without, and this accounted for the fact that while the English-speaking Press of three continents attacked the appointment of von Papen as an insult and blunder, the French Press held its hand and gave only a qualified and not unfriendly criticism. They, too, may have thought it a blunder, but not for France.

Thus Germany came to the Lausanne Conference with a new team, rather better equipped with weapons than its predecessor and more able to achieve the end that both were aiming at.

5

In France there were changes too. A defeat in the Chamber on his Electoral Bill caused M. Laval to resign on February 16th, to be followed in office by M. Tardieu on February 21st. This in reality was no more than a ministerial reshuffle, for M. Laval remained in the Ministry, and M. Tardieu, when he met the Chamber on February 23rd, declared in his Ministerial Statement that he intended to maintain the Laval policy regarding reparations—a formula of adjustment of contracts freely negotiated, but no repudiation of signatures.

But the tide was already turning against the Laval–Tardieu *régime*, and the first evidence of this occurred during the debate for the vote of confidence. M. Leon Blum, leader of the Socialists, struck at the very root of French disarmament policy by declaring that a great reduction of armaments was possible without further guarantees of security, and, although assailed by the Right as an advocate of Germany, received considerable support from the Left. The Government secured its vote by only 50 votes, and the mutterings of the storm were clearly heard.

Now, too, began to be felt the effects of the economic depression which France had up till that time been able to resist. By reason of her well-equipped industries, the stabilization of the franc at a low level, and considerable reinforcement of protective measures, France had been able to hold her own with remarkable vigour in adverse circumstances and to maintain a comparatively high degree of prosperity. The proportion of unemployed to total industrial labour was lower in France than in practically any other country, and the fact that she possessed a large and prosperous agricultural population enabled her to absorb a high percentage of her own manufactures.

But by the close of 1931 and the beginning of 1932, despite all these favourable factors, the effects of the crisis began to make themselves felt, more especially in the industrial North, and unemployment grew rapidly. Home trade also suffered a sharp decline in spite of all the protective measures taken. Perhaps the most severe blow to France was the decline of the tourist traffic. Owing to political tension the number of German visitors to France fell off considerably. The "Stay in Britain" movement, together with the depreciation of the pound, kept at home hundreds of thousands of English people who usually visited France during the winter. The growing anti-French feeling in the United States was responsible for diverting many American visitors who could still afford to go abroad into other European countries.

A severe banking crisis ensued. A number of fairly important banks in Paris and the provinces closed their doors and the Banque Nationale de Crédit, the fourth largest commercial bank in France, was only saved from sharing the same fate by official support on the part of the Government, who were put to some considerable sacrifice. By extending its rediscount facilities with the Bank of France and by reason of actual assistance given by the French Treasury, the Banque Nationale was able to meet the run by its depositors. Eventually the Government thought it necessary to guarantee the liabilities of the bank, and compelled other French banks to establish a special guarantee fund out of which its loans could be covered.[1] The bank was subsequently reconstructed under a different name and became the Banque Nationale pour le Commerce et l'Industrie.

The budgetary situation in France was affected very seriously by the development of the crisis. When the Report on the Budget Estimates was published on March 22, 1932, it showed that the Budget for 1930–1931 closed with a deficit of 2 milliard francs (some £16 million). The Budget for the year April 1, 1931, to March 31, 1932, was estimated to show a final deficit of between $2\frac{1}{2}$ and 3 milliards, but the fact that it included the Young Plan annuity as a source of revenue makes these estimates altogether unreliable. The actual deficit was much nearer 4 milliards. The Budget as finally adopted by the Senate and

[1] See *Finance and Politics*, p. 86.

the Chamber on April 1st showed a paper surplus of some 3 million francs, but in reality French financial experts estimated it to close with a deficit of nearly 5 milliards.[1] As the Budget was passed on the eve of the General Election, it was politically impossible for the Government to risk additional unpopularity by increasing taxation or enforcing economies. But despite this, M. Tardieu had to withstand a very trenchant attack on the whole financial record of both his and M. Laval's Governments. In reply he retorted that the *régime* had to its credit the completion of the financial recovery of France, the return to the convertibility of the currency, the success of monetary stabilization, the repayment of 21 milliard francs of debt, and the remission of 6 milliards of taxation. Yet despite this record the fact remains that while M. Poincaré had left the Budget well balanced and the Treasury with a huge surplus, his successors have had to struggle with the problem of finding means to counteract the deterioration in the state of public finances.

The Elections of May 1932, though they recorded a decisive defeat of MM. Laval and Tardieu, did not result in an equally decisive victory for the parties of the Opposition, who, though they gained numerically, were greatly weakened by their own divisions. The Right were in the main united though defeated, whereas there was little love lost between the two principal leaders of the Left, M. Herriot and M. Blum. The actual results gave M. Herriot's Radical-Socialists 157 seats and M. Blum and the Socialists 129, while M. Tardieu's parties had considerable losses. Foreign affairs played little part in the campaign, but it is probable that had not the Prussian Elections of April 24th resulted in such large Nazi gains the swing to the Left might have been even greater.

In view of his defeat M. Tardieu decided not to wait until the Chamber met on June 1st to resign but to place the *demissions* of himself and his colleagues in the hands of President Lebrun

---

[1] On November 7, 1932, it was announced that, though the deficit had had to be made good at about 8 milliard francs, the Budget had nevertheless been balanced.

immediately after the latter's election by the National Assembly on May 10th.[1] The fact that he led the largest party in the new Chamber naturally singled out M. Herriot as the next Premier, but he refused to accept the duty of forming a Cabinet or, indeed, of making any statement at all until after the meeting of the Executive Committee of the Radical Socialist Party on May 22nd. M. Tardieu was therefore requested to continue to transact the business of government, a system which resulted in further postponement of any preliminary discussions before the Lausanne Conference opened. M. Tardieu interpreted his mission literally. He carried on the business of government with perfunctory correctitude, but no more. He issued no instructions to diplomatic representatives abroad and received none in Paris, except in so far as the business of the hour was concerned. This attitude, though strictly correct, was most unfortunate in its necessity.

M. Herriot, having rejected the conditions on which M. Blum and the Socialists were prepared to enter a Government,[2] formed on June 4th a Ministry of the Left-Centre with himself at the Quai d'Orsay and M. Germain Martin as Minister of Finance.

The Ministerial Declaration with which M. Herriot presented the Chamber on June 7th, was, perhaps intentionally, vague. It said nothing of the Polish alliances, etc., the maintenance of the European *status quo*, or of the impossibility of revising the Peace Treaties, but merely stated that the Government's policy was based on "the urgent necessity of building up peace

[1] President Doumer was mortally wounded by a Russian assassin on May 6th, and died on the following day. M. Lebrun, President of the Senate, was elected as his successor on May 10th.
[2] The conditions, transmitted to M. Herriot on May 31st, after the Congress of the Socialist Party, were eight in number: (1) The organization of peace by understanding between nations and compulsory arbitration, reduction of military expenditure to the level of 1928 in at least the next two Budgets; (2) the appointment of a committee of experts to ascertain the exact sum paid by Germany in reparations since 1921; (3) prohibition of trade in arms and control and nationalization of arms factories; (4) the Budget to be balanced by other means than reduction in expenditure; (5) protection of small investors and control of banks; (6) nationalization of the railways and of the insurance system; (7) a legal forty-hour week; and (8) a general political amnesty.

on a general organization of Europe and the world." As to reparations, France would not allow her rights to be contested, but, at the same time, the Government would discuss "any proposal that would bring about by way of compensation greater stability in the world generally or *bona-fide* movements towards conciliation in the cause of peace."

Thus in France, as in Germany, new actors had appeared on the scene. In general it was believed that though M. Herriot might conceivably be more conciliatory in the matter of reparations than his predecessor, in the field of disarmament there would be little change. M. Herriot had, after all, been joint author with Mr. MacDonald of the Geneva Protocol of 1924, and this instrument had become the keystone of the French disarmament policy. It would be difficult for one of its progenitors to declare it a foundling.

6

And in Washington Congress continued to dance; to dance and alternatively to fiddle, while about it the remnants of American prosperity were reduced to ruins. At a time when, to quote Mr. Justice Brandeis of the U.S. Supreme Court, the people of the United States are confronted with an emergency more serious than war." When misery was widespread, in a time not of scarcity but of superabundance, democracy, as a system of government, showed itself to be a failure, and Mr. Ogden Mills, in a speech before the Harvard Club of New York, showed how difficult it was to get any measure of reform and economy through the House of Representatives and the Senate and at the same time receive any serious assistance from the country in its present condition.[1]

Faced with an enormous deficit Congress displayed no vestige of statesmanlike grasp of the situation, but showed rather a

[1] The speech, which was given at a dinner in honour of Mr. Gordon Selfridge, was quoted by him at a luncheon given by the American Chamber of Commerce in London on June 21st. See *The Times*, June 22, 1932.

puerile wrangling over party prejudices and personal dislikes. On two occasions only the intervention of high officials with the most drastic warnings brought Congressmen temporarily to their senses. On March 29th the Speaker of the House, descending to the floor, reminded the Representatives that as soon as the outside world had heard that there was some doubt as to whether the United States could balance its Budget, money had left the country, the dollar had dropped more than it had done at any time during the past twelve years and U.S. securities had fallen sharply. He warned the House that if Congress refused to pass the Tax Bill there would not be a bank in the United States which within 60 days could meet its depositors.[1]

Somewhat frightened by this pronouncement the House hysterically passed taxation proposals calculated to bring in $1,243 million, but, once the initial alarm had worn off, Congress relapsed into its former state of Bedlam. From this they were not aroused again until May 5th, when the President, in a special Message to Congress, declared that "fear and alarm prevail in the country" on account of the failure to balance the Budget and the attempts at inflation.[2] He demanded the prompt passage of the Tax Bill and of adequate economy legislation. This appeal was reinforced on May 23rd by a group of eleven prominent citizens, numbering amongst them President Nicholas Murray Butler, ex-Governor Alfred Smith, Mr. Alanson B. Houghton, and Governor Ritchie, who urged Congress "to lay aside every form of partisanship . . . and quickly to unite to adopt a balanced Federal Budget for the coming fiscal year."

[1] Speaking at Des Moines, Iowa, on October 5th, in the course of the election campaign, President Hoover disclosed the fact that at this time the Secretary of the Treasury had informed him that if drastic measures were not taken the United States could not hold to the gold standard for longer than a fortnight because of her inability to meet the demands of foreigners and of her own citizens for gold.

[2] This latter reference was to the Goldsborough–Fletcher Bill, passed by the House of Representatives on May 2nd, directing the Federal Reserve Board to stabilize the dollar on the basis of its value in 1926. The Bill also authorized the issue of paper money to the amount of $2,500 million required for the cashing of Bonus Certificates. On the following day the House passed the Economy Bill after cutting its provisions for saving from $200 million to $42 million.

All plans were fruitless and Congress continued to fritter away its time in idle recriminations and attempts at "pork-barrel legislation." Meanwhile the veterans of the American Legion were gathering in their thousands to march on Washington to enforce the passage of the Veterans' Bonus Bill. The dollar continued to fall.

On May 31st President Hoover made a dramatic appearance before the Senate, the first to be made since the days when President Wilson read in person his messages to Congress, and made a personal appeal for action to be taken to balance the Budget.

"An emergency has developed in the last few days," declared Mr. Hoover, "which is characterized by an entirely unjustified run on the American dollar from foreign countries, so that to-day despite our national wealth and resources and unparalleled gold reserves, our dollar stands at a discount in the markets of the world." He went on to explain that the long delays in the passage of legislation providing for such reduction in expenses and such additions to revenue as would balance the Budget, together with the proposals of projects which would greatly increase Governmental expenditure had given rise to doubt as to their ability to meet their responsibilities, and these doubts had been "foolishly exaggerated in foreign countries." But "confusion in the public mind and the rising feeling of doubt and fear" were not confined to countries abroad— "It reflects itself directly in diminished economic activity and increased unemployment within our own borders and among our own citizens," causing further stress upon the already diminished and strained economic life of the country. He appealed finally for the immediate passage of the Tax and Economy Bills.

The Senate eventually passed the Tax Bill on June 6th and the Economy Bill two days later. But events had gone too far for these measures to bridge themselves the yawning gap between revenue and expenditure. On June 11th the President called an emergency conference of the Joint Congressional Committee and informed them that "even the enactment of all the proposals now under consideration by Congress would not balance the Budget," and that further economies totalling about $200 million would be needed.[1]

Never could it have been said more truly of Vienna that "*Le Congrès danse, mais il ne marche pas.*"

Such a state of chaos in domestic finance was not likely to bring about anything but a similar attitude towards international affairs. Yet during the early summer there were incidents to indicate that in certain quarters at least there was an awareness of the necessity for American co-operation in the economics of the world.

For example, on April 13th, at the Jefferson Day Dinner in Washington, Mr. Al Smith, a potential Democrat Candidate for the Presidency, proposed that European debtors should be given a twenty-year moratorium and that in the meantime the United States should cancel each year an amount of war debts equalling 25 per cent. of the purchases of American goods made by each country during each year.

Stripped of non-essentials Mr. Smith's proposal amounted to asking the Americans to substitute for their hopelessly rigid attitude of negation one of reasonable accommodation if they expected to make or contribute to progress towards a better economic world condition, and though it must to a certain extent be discounted as a piece of election propaganda, its immediate value, as the *New York Times* pointed out, was that "we have been dealing with this question of international debts in a way bad for ourselves as well as for the rest of the world." At the same time the *Tribune* admitted that neither the British nor the French Governments could live a moment if they attempted to pay America.

Further support for this view was received from a somewhat unexpected quarter when a Delegation of Railway Labour Representatives called upon President Hoover at the White House on May 13th and presented a resolution urging

---

[1] It was announced on June 12 that the Budget had been balanced on paper, but this was not substantiated by subsequent figures.

a twenty-five year moratorium on war debts with the understanding that the funds thus diverted would be used in the purchase of American products. They further submitted to the President a draft resolution which would authorize him to appoint a Commission of five members to be known as "the International Trade and War Debts Commission" which would be instructed to confer with the foreign Governments and determine and institute the most practical measures to stimulate international trade and exports from the United States.

But however much unofficial opinion might turn in this direction there was little or no change in the official attitude and certainly none in that of Congress which remained solidly opposed to any reduction or cancellation or extension of the moratorium. In furtherance of this attitude official notification was sent early in April to the fourteen debtor countries requesting their official signature to the war debt payments suspended in the Hoover Moratorium and which had now to be repaid over a period of ten years with interest at 4 per cent. Agreements to this effect were signed by the Powers during the months of May, June, and July.[1]

When the Republican and Democrat Party Conventions met in Chicago during June 1932, almost the one point which they held in common was on the matter of war debts, and while the Republican Party avoided any mention of the subject at all, the Democrats formulated a plank registering their opposition to any cancellation.

The only step which could be regarded as being in the direction of progress during this period was the official statement that the United States Government would be prepared to take part in a World Economic Conference to be held in London after the Lausanne Conference, but this participation

---

[1] As a result of this policy of the United States, a new agreement was hastily concluded with the von Papen Government on June 6th, known as the Berlin Protocol, by which the interest rate on the repayment of the sum postponed under the Hoover Moratorium was raised from 3 per cent. as recommended by the London Protocol of August 11, 1931, to 4 per cent., in conformity with the new debt agreements concluded between Germany's creditors and the United States.

was made on the condition that the subject of war debts was excluded from the agenda.

The position, therefore, before the Lausanne Conference met showed no change in the official American attitude from that adopted by the Congressional Resolution of December 23, 1931.

CHAPTER VIII

THE LAUSANNE CONFERENCE[1]

1

THE respective positions of the chief European States at the opening of the Lausanne Conference, *vis-à-vis* the reparations problem, had in theory undergone no change since the previous January, but though the intervening months had been characterized by no event or series of events which might justify more than the slightest hopes for the success of the Conference, there was, nevertheless, the world over an increasing tendency to look facts in the face, and to realize that, in effect, the world was faced with a *fait accompli*. Reparations, it was realized, would not or could not be paid, and the Young Plan was dead, dead as from June 20th, 1931, when Mr. Hoover made his famous proposal. The problem then was to discover some formula which would at the same time save the face of France and regularize the existing position.

On the Conference stage new actors had appeared perhaps better qualified to make a success of their parts than had been their predecessors. For example, the Ministerial Declaration of the Papen Government, issued in Berlin on June 4th, though it proclaimed the intention of the Government to attain "full equality of rights and political freedom," did not include an unqualified reaffirmation of Dr. Brüning's reparations statement of January 9th. Similarly in Paris, M. Herriot told the Chamber on June 7th that his Government would not allow the rights of France to be contested, but he added that they would discuss "any proposal that would bring about by way of compensation greater stability in the world generally," and he avoided repeating his predecessor's pledge to maintain the sanctity of the Young Plan.

[1] Reprinted from articles in the *Bulletin of International News*, vol. ix, no. 1 (July 7, 1932), and no. 2 (July 21, 1932).

In Great Britain and Italy there was no change of policy, since these States had for months past stood for the "clean slate" policy. America pointed with a certain guilty pride to the joint resolution of Congress on December 23, 1931, declaring against the cancellation of war debts. But in the main the world was swinging back to sanity.

It is a matter of deep regret that the principal European statesmen who were to meet at Lausanne had no opportunity to discuss matters between themselves before the opening of the Conference. The rapidity with which events moved in Berlin during the first week of June; the fact that a virtual interregnum existed in France between the resignation of M. Tardieu on May 10th and the formation of the Herriot Cabinet on June 4th, taken in conjunction with Mr. MacDonald's eye-affection, Mr. Neville Chamberlain's gout, and Sir John Simon's preoccupation at Geneva, combined to defeat any preliminary form of discussion. In fact, apart from Baron von Neurath's hurried visit to London, when on June 7th he presented to the Foreign Office a memorandum laying forth the reason why Germany could not pay, and Mr. MacDonald's conversations with M. Herriot in Paris and Geneva on June 11th–14th, there was no preparatory consultation at all.

2

The Conference opened on June 16th in the hall of the Beau Rivage Hotel with Mr. MacDonald in the chair. In his presidential address Mr. MacDonald struck a note which at once lifted the whole discussion on to a higher plane than that on which the reparation problem had previously been discussed. The question was no longer one of policies but of world catastrophe, and in this failure there was "no France, no Germany, no America, no Great Britain apart from the rest of the nations of the world. There is nothing smaller than a world, there is nothing less than a system, which is crumbling under our feet." He surveyed the position as reviewed by the Basle Report and emphasized that an agreement reached quickly would have a far greater effect than "one painfully and imperfectly secured at the last moment of exhaustion after long-drawn-out, irritating, and pettifogging discussions." But one principle must be kept very definitely before them: "engagements solemnly entered into cannot be set aside by unilateral repudiation," this, however, had its corollary, that, if default was to be avoided, engagements which had been proved incapable of fulfilment should be revised by agreement.

On the following day the Conference reached its first concrete result. A declaration was issued signed by the heads of the delegations of Great Britain, France, Italy, Belgium and Japan, to the effect that the five Governments were of opinion that, without prejudice to the solution which might ultimately be reached, the execution of the payments due to the Powers participating in the Conference in respect of reparations and war debts should be reserved during the period of the Conference, which the Governments intended should complete its work in the shortest possible time. The Governments declared that they were prepared to act on that understanding and invited the other creditor Governments to adopt the same course.

Having thus indefinitely prolonged the Hoover Moratorium (which expired on June 30th) as far as Europe was concerned, and having thus given itself a breathing space, the Conference proceeded to statements of national policy. Herr von Papen, in a very moderate speech made in faultless French, admitted frankly the legality of the Hague Agreements and of the Young Plan, but submitted that it was not for the Conference to deal with the legal aspect. The economic crisis was accompanied by a credit crisis unparalleled in history, the most important causes of which were international and uneconomic political payments. Only when these special causes had been removed and radically reviewed could the credit crisis be overcome and the depression relieved. The time of small remedies, half-measures and adjournments was over, a final settlement was the only thing now practicable.

That was all very well, said M. Herriot following, they all

knew that Germany could not pay at the moment, but the
Basle Report had said that Germany would recover one day
and had created an economic workshop on a grand scale.
Moreover, cancellation of reparations was not merely a question
of principle but one of hard cash. France's receipts under the
Young Plan were about 360 million marks a year more than
her debts, and other countries would also lose balances on which
they rested. France was convinced that improved security was
a necessary preliminary for a return to stability. "There can
be no political peace without economic peace, but there can
be no economic peace without political peace."

After this somewhat Delphic remark, Mr. Neville Chamberlain
placed on record the willingness of Great Britain to take her
share in a general wiping of the slate. Great Britain originally
had been owed in all £2,000 million in war debts and reparations
and had lost £200 million from the delay in funding their
debts from Continental countries. The British Government was
nevertheless convinced that "the real problem we have to
consider is not the capacity of one country or another to
make these payments, but rather whether the making of such
payments or even the uncertainty about the future created
by a liability to make them, does not constitute a standing
menace to the maintenance of financial stability and the freedom
of international trade."

When the opening speeches, which were generally and rightly
regarded as admirable in that national cases were stated
emphatically but without provocative declarations of unalter-
able policy, had closed the first stage of the proceedings, the
Conference resolved itself into a series of discussions *à deux*
between Mr. MacDonald and M. Herriot. In these conversations the British Premier was fighting Germany's case for her
—not in the guise of an honest broker, but as a proponent of the
policy of the "clean slate," a clear and definite policy to the
furtherance of which he was prepared to employ any means
within his power. The position of Great Britain as Germany's
advocate was a strong one, for she was freer than was her
principal from political *arrière-pensées* and could put forward

the general economic case for cancellation with a far greater power of conviction than Germany, who would inevitably be suspected of using it as a disguise for selfish financial and political motives.

As an alternative to the British policy, M. Herriot advanced that of the idea of a German recognition of indebtedness, a kind of I.O.U. to be redeemed after, say, five years' suspension, if Germany became sufficiently prosperous again. To this the British replied that, first, the "clean slate" policy was the only one on which Europe could hope for liberal treatment from America and on which Europe could—as some suggest— refuse to pay her; and, secondly, that Great Britain as France's creditor—in the event of continued French harping on Germany's future capacity to pay—would be forced to adapt her claims on France to her actual and future capacity to pay.

This placed M. Herriot in a very difficult position. He looked to both the Right and the Left for support in the Chamber. The Right parties were campaigning against any relaxation of French claims, and already the Press were attacking Mr. MacDonald for trying to engineer the Conference for the benefit of Great Britain. "Mr. MacDonald plans to wipe out reparations and then launch a vast plan for restoring European stability with France paying the cost by redistributing her gold," declared Pertinax in the *Echo de Paris*. M. Herriot was constrained to hold fast to his policy of compensation.

But at this point the question of disarmament was projected into the reparations discussions with dramatic suddenness. Before coming to Lausanne, Mr. MacDonald and M. Herriot had visited Geneva, and had found there a Disarmament Conference apparently as moribund as the Young Plan, which seemed mainly concerned with fixing the date of its adjournment. All practical results had been nullified by the endless discussions of the expert committees, which had outdone the learned mediæval philosophers of Bologna, who passed their days in disputing as to how many angels could stand on the point of a needle and kindred important subjects. The experts had very nearly reduced the Disarmament Conference to a *chose à rire*, more especially at the moment when a certain delegate, in answer to the question, when is a battleship a defensive weapon? replied: "When it is flying the British or American flag."

Both Mr. MacDonald and M. Herriot had revisited Geneva on June 19th, and while the latter had taken the step of withdrawing M. Tardieu's proposal for an international army, the former had lunched with Mr. Hugh Gibson, the leader of the American delegation. The sequel was swift and dramatic. On the night of June 20th Mr. Gibson and M. Herriot, each with a lieutenant, met at the village inn of Morges, on Lac Léman, midway between Geneva and Lausanne. Mr. Gibson there laid down the position of the United States with regard to disarmament and war debts, pointing out America's anxiety to see something real accomplished at the Disarmament Conference, and saying that this should be done by means of reducing effectives. M. Herriot replied that any form of quantitative reduction was inacceptable to France, whereupon Mr. Gibson frankly told him that if, as a result of the Lausanne Conference, an appeal was made to the United States to make a sacrifice in the reduction of debts, public opinion would be unalterably opposed to the granting of any such appeal if Europe continued to spend on armaments enough money to pay the services of those debts.

The next move came simultaneously from Geneva and Washington. The General Commission of the Disarmament Conference was hastily convoked on the afternoon of June 22nd to hear a statement by Mr. Gibson, while at the White House President Hoover issued a manifesto to the same effect. Mr. Hoover made the following proposals, basing his argument on the fact that all nations of the world, by signing the Kellogg Pact, had agreed to use their arms solely for defence; that reduction of armaments should be carried out not only by means of broad general units, "but by increasing the comparative power of defence through decreases in the power of the attack"; that as armaments had grown up in mutual relation to each other, such relativity should, generally speaking, be preserved in their reduction; that reduction must be real and positive, effecting economic relief, and that in considering the question of reduction all three branches of armaments, land, sea, and air, were interconnected and could not be dissociated one from the other:

"1. The reduction of all world armaments by a third.
"2. The abolition of tanks, chemical warfare, and large mobile guns.
"3. The abolition of all bombing air-machines, and the total prohibition of all bombardment from the air.
"4. The reduction of one-third in the strength of all land armies."[1]

It was proposed to take the figure to which Germany had been limited by the Treaty of Verasilles—one hundred thousand men for 65 million people—as the ratio for "a basic police component of soldiers and that reduction of one-third should be made in the strength of all armies over and above the police component." As regards naval armaments a reduction of one-third was asked in the Treaty number and tonnage of all battleships; a reduction in the Treaty number and tonnage of all aircraft-carriers, cruisers, and destroyers by a fourth and of submarines by one-third. No nation should have more than 35,000 tons of submarine craft.

These proposals were accepted in their entirety by Italy, were received with guarded approval by Great Britain and with guarded disapproval by France, and were declared to be inacceptable to Japan.

Meantime little progress had been made at the other end of the Lake. The Anglo-French conversations, though they had resulted in an agreement as to Germany's inability to pay either now or during the period of recovery, had reached a deadlock on the word "finality." Both sides found themselves in favour of a finality of settlement, that is to say of ending the existing uncertainty regarding the future and of providing against the disturbance of ordinary commercial relations by any future payments. But whereas the British, Italians, and Germans interpreted "finality" as meaning a "clean slate," the French still clung to the idea of a "final" payment of some kind.

The attempt of British mediation having failed to achieve the desired result, the second stage of the Lausanne Conference closed. The third opened on June 24th, when for the first time Herr von Papen and M. Herriot met for a personal interview which was followed by two full meetings of the French and German delegations.[1] At these meetings the German delegation restated its case along now very familiar lines as to why Germany could not pay now and why she could not commit herself to pay in the future. The French replied that though they could not renounce the claim to a future payment by Germany, they were prepared to consider any means by which it could be done, thereby leaving open the door for concrete German proposals. The two delegations parted cordially, and M. Herriot showed that if Herr von Papen could talk French, he could at least quote German—-or misquote it—since to the assembled journalists he announced, *"Die Luft ist kühl, aber es dunkelt nicht,"* forgetting perhaps that the Lorelei song begins *"Ich weiss nicht, was soll es bedeuten."*

Negotiations were now interrupted for the week-end to enable the German Chancellor and the French Premier to return to Berlin and Paris respectively to consult their ministerial colleagues. Before leaving Lausanne, however, Herr von Papen gave an interview to the representative of the *Matin* which was destined to influence the whole course of the Conference. "I am," Herr von Papen told the *Matin*, "the first to acknowledge France's right to compensation for the renunciation of reparations. France has a guarantee that Germany will endorse any German-French agreement that I sign. In contrast to my predecessor I represent all the national forces of Germany." He added that "if France and Germany can agree to put the European house in order, the United States cannot possibly refuse to make an honourable contribution to European reconstruction."

On arrival in Berlin on the morning of Saturday, June 25th, the Chancellor found that he had roused a storm of obloquy

[1] This phase was jocularly referred to as the German intervention between England and France.

which brought down on him even more scathing comments than had been passed on Dr. Brüning. The Nationalist Press flatly contradicted his claim to speak for them. The *Deutsche Allgemeine Zeitung* declared that he had laid the onus of making proposals on Germany, and had thus put his country in an unfavourable tactical position which all efforts had been exerted to avoid. He had further put Germany in the united front against the United States, a thing German policy had also always sought to avoid. "The Chancellor is wrong in saying that all Germany would endorse his signature. Germany would not follow him on this path." The *Tageszeitung* remarked acidly that Herr von Papen's references to reparations "are not what national Germany expects from a national Chancellor."

Not all the Chancellor's protestations and explanations served to appease the Press and the general forces of German Nationalism, and although the Cabinet approved the attitude of the Delegation at Lausanne and its future intentions as put forward by the Chancellor, the Chancellor himself received a severe "wigging" for his untoward utterances, and this was partly responsible for the stiffened attitude of the whole delegation on its return on Sunday to Lausanne.

On the other hand, the Chancellor's attitude towards "compensation" had earned him considerable merit in France. No German statesman—not even Dr. Stresemann—enjoyed a better Press than did Herr von Papen, and the only fear expressed was that he might not survive the Reichstag elections of July 31st. As a result the Nationalists' attacks on the Chancellor in the Berlin Press were received with a certain anxiety in France, where even the *Temps* had begun to realize the idleness of insisting on the resumption of German payments. "The principle of reparation payments must be maintained," it stated on June 27th, "but far be it from us to say that we look upon the 'net balance' from a selfish point of view. The word 'compensation' has been uttered in certain responsible German quarters. Could this 'compensation' take the form of certain commercial agreements or of an agreement which would be the starting-point of real economic co-operation?"[1]

With the return of the Chancellor and M. Herriot to Lausanne, the Franco-German negotiations were resumed on June 27th, but M. Herriot complained that he found the German Ministers less cordial than before their week-end in Berlin. Some slight progress was made in that, after the inevitable repetition by Count von Krösigk, as to why Germany could not resume payments, or even admit the possibility of a final payment, he went on to outline very generally the suggestion for the "first measures for the restoration of Europe" in which Germany was prepared to take part, "as her economic situation permitted." Germany was, he declared, prepared "to make direct contribution within the limit of her modest means, to a general pool for the reconstruction of Europe, especially of the Danubian countries and other States of Central and South-Eastern Europe. She was also ready to enter into negotiations with France for the elaboration of a really practical trade treaty, and to take any steps compatible with her other trade treaties to stimulate and facilitate trade exports and imports. Although she was unable to make reparation payments Germany was ready to make considerable sacrifices in the interests of constructive international co-operation.

M. Herriot still stuck to his guns in the matter of a final payment and the maintenance of the principle of reparations, and waited in vain for the magic word "compensation" to escape Herr von Papen's lips. But the Chancellor, recollecting the Berlin Press and his more Nationalist colleagues, had apparently expunged it from his vocabulary. The meeting broke up after four hours of fruitless discussion, and both Herr von Papen and M. Herriot hurried off to lay their cases separately before Mr. MacDonald.

The position had therefore reached a deadlock as Germany would not pay further "tribute payments" but was prepared to make a "contribution to a general pool." The difference is

[1] This statement on the part of the *Temps* is particularly significant not because it is Nationalist and anti-German in character, but because it represents in a large degree the interests of the French heavy industries.

clear. The first was an act under compulsion, the second one of volition. To the French it savoured of chicanery; if she can pay in one form, why not in another? they asked with pardonable logic. The Conference had reached a very acute stage of crisis.

At this moment of real danger of failure Mr. MacDonald exerted every possible effort to save the Conference. On the Tuesday (June 28th) he held a three-party Conference with Herr von Papen and M. Herriot, and when he had failed to bring about a compromise in their conflicting theses, he summoned the help of the Belgian, Italian and Japanese delegations in a further attempt to reach an agreement, and a Six-Power Conference was called for Wednesday afternoon.

But before this meeting an event occurred which might well have wrecked the Conference altogether. On the morning of Wednesday, June 29th, the German delegation issued a *communiqué* which, had it been final, must have resulted in the collapse of the Conference. The statement declared it to be the Chancellor's considered opinion that "confidence cannot be re-established in the world unless the victorious Powers make up their mind to remove the discrimination of the Treaty of Versailles." When they had restored Germany's right to equality and security the Chancellor could conceive of the possibility that "Germany could make a contribution to the common effort to rehabilitate the economic structure of the world. That contribution would depend on the complete restoration of economic equilibrium in Germany and the world."

Had the German delegation set out with the explicit intention of torpedoing the Conference they could not have gone about it in a more masterful manner than by delivering an ultimatum at such a moment. As it was, this was far from their intention. There is no doubt that Herr von Papen had expressed himself in these terms during the Anglo-Franco-German discussions of June 28th, but it is quite unknown why he allowed them to be made public within a few hours of his appointment to meet M. Herriot. The kindest explanation is

that he did not realize the repercussions which such an announcement would have and that he wished to assure the Nationalist
Press that he was no longer talking of "compensation" and
"concessions." A less kind interpretation, but one in great
circulation, is that he had been stampeded by Nazi pressure
from Berlin. Whatever the cause, the effect was to render any
further direct discussion between the French and German
delegations impossible for the moment and their meeting on
Wednesday morning was of the briefest.

The delegates of the six Powers met in the Hotel du Château
at 4 o'clock in no very optimistic frame of mind. But the result
was better than might have been expected. Mr. MacDonald
made a reassuring speech in which he reviewed the course of
the negotiations to date, explaining all the points of agreement
and tactfully glossing over the gravity of the points of difference. Having failed to secure a compromise, he appeared intent
on forcing a solution by speeding up the Conference. It was
therefore agreed to set up a Bureau consisting of one representative of each of the six Powers "to examine the present position
of reparations in the light of the preliminary exploration that
has already been carried out," and to make recommendations
to the six Powers as soon as possible. An Economic Committee
was also set up consisting of the six Ministers of Commerce,
charged with the consideration of "the measures necessary to
solve the other economic and financial difficulties which are
responsible for and may prolong the present world crisis."
The report of this body was to serve as a preparation for the
World Economic Conference to be held later in the year.

Thus by jockeying the Conference into the committee stage
Mr. MacDonald saved its life, for he had drawn its attention
away from its more general political aspects to the more
detailed and technical side. The Press of the world paid tribute
to the almost superhuman efforts of Mr. MacDonald. The
French themselves were strong in admiration. "At the last
moment," wrote the *Petit Parisien*, "those responsible for the
deadlock hesitated and Mr. MacDonald seized the opportunity
provided by this hesitation in a remarkable way. But it is

impossible to guess whether he will succeed at the eleventh hour in refloating the sinking ship."

But the ship was refloated. The Bureau worked throughout June 30th, and, although no compromise was reached, the gap had grown no wider, and the fact that the negotiations had reached the point where actual figures were discussed was in itself a mark of progress.

The day was marked by varying vicissitudes. It began well with a German offer of a final "composition" payment on condition that the word "reparation" did not figure in the agreement. To this the French at first objected, but later agreed, though they considered the sum mentioned as inadequate. The French then introduced a further complication in the form of a stipulation for a safeguarding clause in the agreement concerning war debts, for which Germany would be made liable if America refused cancellation. With this proposal Great Britain associated herself, but Germany protested that this was at variance with the principle of a final settlement.

On the evening of June 30th, when the Bureau rose at 11.30 p.m., the position stood as follows:

1. Germany had offered a contribution of 2,000 million marks (£100,000,000 at par) to be paid into a central pool, known as the 'European Assurance Fund,' which fund would be administered by the Bank for International Settlements.

2. France had demanded at least RM.7,000 million (£350 million), of which two-thirds should be set aside to meet Europe's debt to America should the United States refuse cancellation, and the remaining third devoted to European reconstruction.

3. Great Britain, France and Italy had insisted that, in the event of no debt settlement being reached with America, further payments must be made by Germany.

4. Germany had retorted, using the American argument, that there was no relation between war debts and reparations; that it was impossible to have this threat hanging over her, and that in any case it violated the principle of a final settlement.

5. It had been agreed that Germany was unable at present to pay anything, and it had been proposed by the creditor Powers that the amount finally agreed upon should be covered by the issue of bonds, which would be met as and when Germany was able to pay, her ability to pay being measured by some form of index.

July 1st was spent in deep and constructive deliberations

which resulted in some approximation towards agreement.
There was manifested in the meetings of the Bureau and in
the private conversations outside the conference room, a sincere
will to agree, for it was keenly realized that, in the words of
Sir Robert Horne, "civilization is resting on a knife edge and
the shock of failure at Lausanne might finally upset the financial
structure." M. Herriot had returned to Paris, where he announced that complete agreement now existed between the
French and British delegations, but at the Conference it was
felt that, in relation to the safeguarding clause, perhaps too
much stress had been laid on the relation between reparations
and war debts, since this would scarcely be a good recommendation to American public opinion in the event of forthcoming
approaches in the name of fair play and might jeopardize
the chances of American co-operation in the World Economic
Conference.

A series of meetings of the Bureau during July 2nd resulted
in an agreement being reached by the five creditor Powers as
to the proposals to be put before Germany. These were as
follows:

1. A complete moratorium of three years, to be then prolonged until
such time as the Bank for International Settlements, acting by a majority
of its Board, should determine Germany's ability to pay.

2. When German payments began, Bonds, which should have already
been issued, would be made liable to interest at the rate of 5 per cent.,
and to redemption spread over a number of years.

3. The Bonds by which the plan was to be financed were to be
handed over to the Bank for International Settlements, which was to
determine when they were to be issued and how payments were to
be effected.

4. The total sum to be represented by the Bond issue was to
be RM. 4,000,000,000 (£200,000,000), inclusive of a year's arrears
under the Hoover Moratorium, but exclusive of the services of the
Dawes and Young Plan Loans, of the American Mixed Claims Payments, of the payments on account of the costs of the American Army
of Occupation and of the Belgian Marks Agreement. The Bonds
would be issued on the security of the German Government, not
specifically on the railways, but on German national property as
a whole.

5. The total sum when it was eventually paid would go into a com-

mon fund for European economic reconstruction, although it might be 'utilized in other directions.'[1]

It will be remarked that the word "reparations" did not appear, that the figure £200 million was a compromise between the £100 million offered by Germany and the £350 million demanded by France, and that the question of war debts was carefully camouflaged under the provision that the German contribution might be "utilized in other directions." It was also stated in the proposal that the agreement should be "realized in the framework of a general settlement," using the words of the declaration of June 17th.

It may also be observed that the British had abandoned their "clean slate" policy in exchange for the French proposal of a "final payment," or, alternatively, for the German plan of a "contribution." This may be attributed to the discovery during the Conference from the tactics of the Germans themselves, ·that they were, in effect, able to pay something. The Germans, who began by saying they could pay nothing, had admitted that they could manage to squeeze out something, if only it was not "tribute" but in the nature of a "contribution," and that they could perhaps manage to squeeze out a little more if the "war-guilt" clause of the Treaty of Versailles were removed. There was in addition the argument presented by M. Germain-Martin, French Minister of Finance, that America herself might prefer that, when the question of the cancellation of war debts came up, her European debtors should be able to present some monetary credit upon which to base their argument and not arrive with entirely empty hands.[2]

[1] The idea of a bond issue to meet a final payment on the part of Germany was originally the suggestion of Dr. Carl Bergmann, and had been proposed by him in a slightly different form in 1927, in the final chapter of his book, *The History of Reparations* (see pp. 317–327). It was later reproduced in a form revised to meet the present situation.

The plan for a common pool for European economic reconstruction to which debtors and creditors should pay alike, originated with Herr Paul Scheffer, the well-known correspondent of the *Berliner Tageblatt*, who had for sometime preached this doctrine of common contribution. Mr. Avenol, Deputy Secretary-General of the League of Nations, had also advocated a similar plan.

[2] Writing in the *Revue de Paris* (July, 1932) on "The Results of Lausanne," M. Henri Bérenger, Chairman of the Foreign Affairs Committee of the Senate, dated Mr. MacDonald's *volte-face* as June 23rd, and attributed it to the

The outline of the Creditors' terms, when published in Berlin, caused some perturbation in the Nationalist Press, which, with one important exception, urged the Chancellor to stand firm and to make no concessions. The exception, curiously enough, was the same *Deutsche Allgemeine Zeitung* which had previously attacked the Chancellor so fiercely for his *Matin* interview. In an appeal to the German Delegation it said: "Do not be misled by considerations of home policy and refuse seriously meant negotiations. With a solution bearable for Germany, and which brings life into business, the Government will create for itself a platform on which it can stand with safety."[1]

The Creditors' terms were handed to the German Delegation on Sunday morning (July 3rd), and by the same evening the German reply was in the hands of the Bureau and the period of bargaining began. The reply, while not amounting to a definite rejection of the terms proposed, contained some very serious objections. In the first place, as might have been expected, it was maintained that the sum of RM. 4,000 million was too large; and, secondly, it was desired that the required vote of the Board of the Bank for International Settlements should be unanimous and not by a majority. Immediate ratification of the agreement was urged which would give Germany a further assurance that reparation cancellation would not be linked up with the settlement of war debts; and, finally, it was requested that no fresh issue of bonds should be made if previous blocks of bonds had fallen on the market below a given figure.

The German counter-proposals contained suggestions that the amount of RM. 4,000 million should be halved, and that payment should be in some form of annuity instead of bond

---

Hoover disarmament proposals of June 22nd. "In face of this diplomatic *coup à l'américaine*," writes Senator Bérenger, "Mr. MacDonald turned without hesitation towards France, and thus a Franco-British *rapprochement* was achieved. It had been in the air, of course, for months, and in logic for years; but, all the same, let us be thankful for the 'unilaterality' of the Hoover message which gave us the MacDonald–Herriot 'bilaterality.'"

[1] This change of face is more easily understood when it is remembered that the *Deutsche Allgemeine Zeitung* is representative of the great industrialists of Western Germany, who are anxious to get their works started again.

issue. In addition, they raised the question of "war-guilt," all reference of which it was desired should be deleted from the Treaty of Versailles.[1]

The reception of the German terms was not cordial. The French Press ridiculed them as "ridiculous" and "a bad joke." M. Germain-Martin called on Mr. MacDonald early on Monday morning (July 4th) and informed him that the French Delegation could not even discuss the counter-proposals and urged him not to withdraw from the position taken up by the five creditor Powers. Herr von Papen also called on the President of the Conference, and told him that as M. Herriot, who had gone to Paris to deal with pressing matters of domestic financial importance, did not propose to return until Wednesday, there seemed no need for him to remain either, and he proposed leaving for Berlin. An urgent message was therefore sent by the French delegation to M. Herriot, asking him to return to Lausanne at once in view of the grave situation which developed in the negotiations, and in reply he fixed an appointment with Mr. MacDonald early on Tuesday morning. Mr. Mac-Donald himself, in a last attempt to break the deadlock, announced that he must take the night train on Thursday (July 7th).[2]

A further complication now arose in connection with war debts. The Italian delegation, notwithstanding the fact that its representative had taken part in the daily discussions of the Bureau, announced that the agreement should include the

[1] Article 231 of the Treaty of Versailles, which is the first article of Part VIII, that dealing with reparations, reads: "The Allied and Associated Governments affirm, and Germany accepts, the responsibility of Germany and her allies for causing all the loss and damage to which the Allied and Associated Governments and their nationals have been subjected as a consequence of the war imposed upon them by the aggression of Germany and her allies."

[2] It should be remembered that at every international Conference of major importance there is inevitably a moment of great crisis shortly before agreement is reached. It has become part of the technique of this phase of crisis that someone of the principal figures at the Conference gives notice that he cannot remain beyond a certain date. Lord Beaconsfield perfected this technique at the Congress of Berlin when he ordered his special train to be prepared for departure, and President Wilson effectively reminded his colleagues on critical occasions during the Peace Conference of Paris that the *George Washington* was waiting with steam up at Brest. The saying has been attributed to Mr. Lloyd George, "Anyone can produce a crisis; the thing is to produce it at the right moment."

cancellation of European debts, which in effect meant the cancellation of the French and Italian debts to Great Britain. In view of the fact that the "clean slate" policy had not been adopted in drafting the final agreement, this was clearly in-acceptable to the British, but the Italians insisted that some satisfaction must be given on this point.

July 5th passed in a series of fateful interviews between Mr. MacDonald and Herr von Papen and M. Herriot, and in determined haggling on both sides. Eventually the German delegation agreed to increase its offer to RM. 2,600 million, but with two political conditions: first, the deletion of the war-guilt clause from the Treaty of Versailles, and, secondly, the granting of equality in armaments—proposals which M. Herriot declared he could not consider. It was on this point that the deadlock occurred and a proposal to refer the dispute to the arbitration either of the President of the United States or the Permanent Court of International Justice was rejected by both Herr von Papen and M. Herriot. It seemed as though only a miracle could save the Conference.

But the miracle did indeed occur and it was in a large measure due to the indomitable pertinacity of Mr. MacDonald himself. Throughout July 6th he toiled with almost superhuman energy to keep the Conference from shipwreck. On the one hand he maintained contact between the French and German delegations, and on the other he kept the experts at work full time hammering out the last possible details of the final convention so that, when the essential provisions had been agreed upon, there should be no time wasted in fitting them into the general framework.

As the result of his labours the points at issue began to narrow down. The French accepted the German figure but continued to haggle over political conditions. Equality of disarmament they rejected as out of court, the question being in a sense *sub judice* at Geneva, but they were prepared to consider the war-guilt clause. The Germans wanted a definite statement of abrogation, the French would only agree to a tacit deletion. They had their own political conditions also. They revived the old proposal of a "political truce"—aimed at obtaining a temporary cessation of German propaganda in the matter of the Polish frontier and the Corridor, and this the Germans were prepared to discuss under the title of a "consultative pact."

In the hope that it might appeal to the French view, the British delegation put forward a draft declaration of good intentions, followed by an agreement for a wide and friendly exchange of views, either periodically or whenever the prospect of disturbing disputes rendered it desirable. To the Germans this proposal was more acceptable than that of a "political truce" in that it provided opportunities of raising grievances instead of imposing a fine or ten years' silence, which would, in their view, strengthen the basis of the *status quo* which Germany has never accepted and has only agreed, under the Eastern Locarno Pact, not to upset by force of arms.[1] The whole idea was, however, dropped at the instigation of the French themselves and was considered to have disappeared into the limber of "historical might-have-beens" until its sudden resurrection in a new form on July 13th.[2]

July 7th passed in desultory bargaining and disputation, but though no agreement was reached, Mr. MacDonald considered the negotiations to be in a sufficiently delicate condition for him to cancel his departure. Suddenly, in the late evening, events began to move with dramatic rapidity. M. Herriot and M. Germain-Martin dined with Mr. Neville Chamberlain and Mr. Runciman, and by the time the French delegates left, about midnight, a new proposal had been submitted to the Chancellor and Baron von Neurath, who arrived almost at once. Feverish negotiations—aided by the consumption of sandwiches and beer which have come to be an integral part of the technique of modern conferences—continued throughout the early hours of July 8th between Mr. Chamberlain and the Germans on the one hand, and Sir John Simon and the French on the other. By three o'clock a sufficient degree of agreement had been reached to justify the negotiators in going to bed. The

---

[1] See *Disarmament and Security*, pp. 36–42.   [2] See below, p. 240.

conversations were renewed in the morning and agreement was reached at a plenary meeting of the Conference the same night.

3

The agreement itself, which was signed in the Beau Rivage Hotel on July 9th and will be known to history as the Lausanne Convention,[1] is in the form of a Final Act with five annexed instruments. The first is an Agreement with Germany. By this reparations are cancelled and Germany—of her own volition—undertakes to make an eventual contribution by means of a bond issue to the amount of RM. 3,000 million (£150 million), but only after the termination of a three-year moratorium. The proceeds of the bonds issued are to be placed to a special account, "the allocation of which shall be settled by a further agreement in due course between the Governments, other than Germany, signatory to the present Agreement." The bonds are to be deposited with the Bank for International Settlements at once, but during the moratorium period they will bear no interest. At the expiration of this period the issue of bonds is to be made at the discretion of the Bank, and only if the operations can be carried out without disturbing normal economic relations or endangering Germany's credit. In any case the issue cannot take place until German Government securities are on a 5 per cent. basis or better. The issue price of the bonds must not be less than 90, and they will bear interest at 5 per cent. and 1 per cent. amortization, thereby extinguishing the obligation in 37 years after the date of issue. The whole of the issue operation will cease in twelve years from the date of issue, and any bonds unissued at that date will be destroyed.

Annex II prolongs, in respect of German payments, the declaration of the six Powers made on June 16th, and subsequently adhered to by all parties to the Conference, suspending payments during the duration of the Conference. This prolongation is made for the transitional period which must elapse between signature and ratification or until one of the six Powers

---

[1] For text of the Convention, see Appendix I, pp. 259–71.

notifies the other signatory States that it has decided not to ratify. The second article provides for the initiation of negotiations between the German Government and the Bank for International Settlements regarding the necessary adaptation of machinery governing the discharge by the German Government of its obligations in respect of the Dawes and Young Loans. The third article sets up a Committee of representatives of the German Government and other Governments concerned to draw up proposals regarding the execution, by means of deliveries in kind, of contracts and works of construction.

There follows, as Annex III, a Resolution on non-German Reparations, recommending that a committee of experts be set up to consider this and cognate questions, and providing that, in order that the committee may be able to carry on its work thoroughly and undisturbed, the payments involved shall be reserved until December 15, 1932, failing a settlement before that date.

By Annex IV it is agreed, with a view to achieving the financial and economic reconstruction of Central and Eastern Europe, to appoint a Committee which shall submit proposals to the Commission of Enquiry for European Union as to those measures which it may consider advisable for meeting difficulties of transfer and arising out of exchange control, and stimulating trade activity with special reference to the low price of cereals.[1]

The fifth and final Annex refers to the summoning of a World Economic Conference. It will be remembered that the terms of reference of the Lausanne Conference included not only the consideration of the reparation problem in the light of the Basle Report, but also of "the measures necessary to solve the other economic and financial difficulties which are responsible for and may prolong the present world crisis." The Conference, however, decided to concentrate all its efforts on achieving a solution of the first problem and to shelve

[1] The Committee was to consist of two representatives each appointed by the Governments of Austria, Belgium, Bulgaria, Czechoslovakia, France, Germany, Great Britain, Greece, Hungary, Netherlands, Poland, Rumania, Switzerland, and Yugoslavia.

consideration of the second until it could be referred to an Economic Conference. The Annex embodies the results of the discussions of the Ministers of Commerce present at Lausanne. It gives expression to the decision to invite the League of Nations to convoke a world conference on monetary and economic problems and recommends, in the meantime, an examination of the problems by a committee of experts (which will doubtless divide into two sub-committees on monetary and general economic questions), to consist of two representatives of each of the six inviting Powers, three financial and three economic members nominated by the League Council, two financial members appointed by the Bank for International Settlements, and representatives of the United States, if that country accepts the invitation to appoint members.

The Agreement with Germany is preceded by a General Declaration in which the Powers recognize at the same time the legal validity of the Hague Agreement and the complete cancellation of reparations. No mention is made of war-guilt, but the signatories aver that there will transpire from the deliberations of Lausanne "a new order" permitting the establishment and development of confidence between nations in a mutual spirit of reconciliation, collaboration, and justice. The Declaration concludes with the statement that this "new effort in the cause of real peace . . . can only be complete if it is applied in both the economic and in the political sphere" and if all possibility of resort to arms and violence is rejected. The signatory Powers also undertake to make every effort to resolve the problems which exist at the moment or may arise subsequently "in the spirit which has inspired the present Agreement."

It will be realized that in the final text of the Agreement there is no mention of Germany's contribution to a general pool and that the disposal of the fund is left to the creditor Powers. Whether this omission was intentional or whether in the excitement and hurry of getting out the final draft it was merely overlooked, the effect of its absence was viewed with a critical eye in Germany.

At the opening of the final session of the Conference, Mr. MacDonald read an important declaration submitted to the Conference by Sir John Simon, M. Germain-Martin and Signor Mosconi, to the effect that the temporary prolongation of a moratorium on inter-allied debts contained in the declaration of June 16th (which the Lausanne Convention prolongs in the case of reparations) would be extended until the ratification of the present Agreement.[1] The signing of the Convention then followed, the delegates using the seal of the City of Lausanne, first used in 1525.

In his valedictory speech Mr. MacDonald declared that "our work has put a new page in history, not the end of a chapter, but the beginning of a new book." "We have opened a new book. There are no more reparations. Those great payments of sums which represented no transfer of goods have not been a punishment to one nation, but an affliction to all." The burden imposed on Germany had had disturbing effects on world trade. Lands as far-flung as New Zealand and Australia had been disturbed, and a nation as self-contained as the United States was as hard hit as ourselves. "Europe cannot exist alone. The agreements signed here must have a response elsewhere," the last remark being interpreted as a hint to the United States.

And indeed it was this unknown—or possibly this too well-known—attitude of the United States which had overshadowed the Conference and made its only practical achievement an indefinite prolongation of the Hoover Moratorium as far as Europe is concerned. As it stood, the Lausanne Convention meant for Great Britain the loss of some £19,000,000 a year on account of reparations and a similar sum on account of war-debts payments which have been suspended. At the same time payment of some £38 million is due to the United States.

---

[1] This decision was embodied in an exchange of Notes between Great Britain, France and Italy, in which the former regretted the impossibility, in actual circumstances, of cancelling or modifying the war-debt settlements. While the moratorium is extended until the ratification of the Lausanne Agreement, in the event of its non-ratification the legal position would revert to that which existed under the Hague Agreements and the War-Debt Funding Settlements, in which case the British, French, and Italian Governments "would have to examine together the de facto situation thus created." See Appendix II, p. 272

In the case of France the amounts involved were equally great as a previous annual surplus of £16 million became a potential deficit of £12 million—the amount of the payment due from her to America. The creditor Powers could never afford to forget that they themselves were debtors to America, who was due to receive on December 15, 1932, $91,950,000 from Great Britain, $30,000,000 from France, and $7,395,500 from Italy, and to these sums had to be added the amount of the first instalments for the repayment at the rate of 4 per cent. of the annuities suspended under the Hoover Moratorium.

4

Having refused to adopt the policy of the "clean slate" towards Germany, the European Powers could not expect America to adopt it in their own cases. Moreover, there had been a strong tendency in the United States towards the attitude that if any "scaling down" of European war debts were effected it should be done in accordance with the capacity to pay of each individual debtor, a policy which would be more detrimental to France than to this country. Of the danger of this policy the French themselves were only too keenly aware and were also determined that Great Britain should not break up the United European Front to America as she had done on two previous occasions.[1] It was for this reason that a second agreement, a secret "Gentlemen's Agreement," was signed at Lausanne on July 2nd—a full week, be it noted, before the final agreement was reached with Germany on the 9th— whereby the European creditor Powers sought to protect themselves against any untoward developments across the Atlantic. The pith of the agreement, which was not communicated officially to Herr von Papen until after the terms of the Lausanne Convention had been accepted, is contained in the following paragraphs:[2]

[1] These two occasions were in 1923, when Great Britain, without previously consulting France, had signed her debt-funding Agreement with America, and, secondly, in June 1932, when Great Britain had agreed, contrary to the wishes of France, to repay the postponed Hoover annuity at 4 per cent. instead of 3 per cent., and had signed an agreement thereto.
[2] For full text, see Appendix II, pp. 272-75.

"The Lausanne Agreement will not come into final effect until after ratification as provided for in the Agreement. So far as the creditor Governments on whose behalf this *Procès-verbal* is initialled are concerned, ratification will not be effected until a satisfactory settlement has been reached between them and their own creditors. It will be open to them to explain the position to their respective Parliaments, but no specific reference to it will appear in the text of the agreement with Germany. Subsequently, if a satisfactory settlement about their own debts is reached, the aforesaid creditor Governments will ratify and the agreement with Germany will come into full effect. But if no such settlement can be obtained, the agreement with Germany will not be ratified; a new situation will have arisen and the Governments interested will have to consult together as to what should be done. In that event, the legal position, as between all the Governments, would revert to that which existed before the Hoover Moratorium."

Confronted by a *fait accompli*, Herr von Papen had no option but to acknowledge the Agreement when informed of it, but in order that the position should be quite clearly defined in the minutes of the Conference itself, the Chancellor put a question to Mr. MacDonald at the plenary session of July 8th, as to what procedure it was proposed to follow in the event, which he recognized to be improbable, of one of the six Powers concerned not ratifying the Convention. To this Mr. MacDonald replied:

"I am happy to be able to put this on record. It would be most inadvisable, and very difficult, to embody it in the Annex, but the declaration I am now making on behalf of the Inviting Powers will, I think, be sufficient. It is that in the event of any inability to fulfil this Agreement and its Annexes, a further Conference will be held."

Now whether M. Herriot did not fully appreciate the meaning of the term "Gentlemen's Agreement," or whether it was not sufficiently binding in its secret state for his taste, one cannot say, but the fact remains that at the moment when Mr. MacDonald was being received with enthusiastic cheers at Victoria Station, the French Press was disclosing the existence of the agreement. Apart from a guarded reference in *The Times* of Saturday, July 10th, there was no hint of the existence of this instrument in the British Press. On the same evening, however, the *Temps*, and on the following day the *Matin*, *Journal*, and *Petit Parisien* gave substantially the text of the

Agreement.[1] "The Gentlemen's Agreement," said the *Matin*, "is a link which has been not only clearly established, but openly avowed between Lausanne and the adjustment of the American Debt; it is the expressed condition of the ratification of the Agreement by the Parliaments, and if there is no settlement of the American Debt the Lausanne Treaty will be considered null and void. Further, if there is no settlement the Young Plan would be legally the only system of fixing the actual payments of Germany."

Subsequently the English Press began to be concerned. On Monday two papers of such antagonistic political standing as the *Morning Post* and the *Daily Herald* found themselves in agreement in outlining and condemning this secret understanding.

The Lausanne Debate in the House of Commons was fixed for the night of July 12th, but on the previous evening Mr. Churchill launched an attack on the work of the Conference which he declared had been nullified by the secret agreement, and had merely become a restatement of the Balfour Declaration of 1922.

When Mr. MacDonald met the House on July 12th he found that much of the enthusiastic reception with which he had been met on his return to London on Sunday had evaporated and had given place to a degree of uncertainty and even suspicion.

The House was only too anxious to applaud the work done by the Conference in connection with the termination of reparations, on which there was very little clash of opinion save that many regarded the abandonment by the British Government of their policy of the "clean slate" as regrettable. But there is inherent in the British character a dislike and distrust of secret diplomacy which found its last outlet in a protest against the circumstances in which the Anglo-French Naval Compromise of 1928 was arrived at.

Mr. MacDonald ably defended the actual Lausanne Convention; he was less convincing, however, when dealing with

[1] The *Manchester Guardian*, commenting editorially on the "Gentlemen's Agreement" on July 13th, stated that "statesmen should have realized by now that secret diplomacy is not only pernicious, but is, in view of the relations between the French Government and the Press, impracticable."

the "Gentlemen's Agreement." He drew attention to his statement to the German Chancellor at the close of the final Plenary
Session and declared that the Agreement went no further than
that, and that failing a settlement with the United States there
would be no ratification and there must be another Conference.

Mr. Lloyd George made a trenchant attack upon the Convention in general and the "Gentlemen's Agreement" in particular,
and demanded that it, as well as the text of the Convention,
should be laid before the House, to which Sir John Simon
replied that H.M. Government had already asked the other
Governments to assent to its publication[1] and reaffirmed that
it merely interpreted the fact that since German Reparations
had been a global payment the ratification of the releasing
creditors must be in common, and that the German Delegation
had expressly declared that they thoroughly understood the
reasons for this Agreement.

The position was not improved by the statement by Mr.
Neville Chamberlain that there had been conversations with
representatives of the United States and that there was reason
to believe that a favourable agreement would be concluded.
The effect upon the United States was not a happy one. As
early as June 21st, the circulation of rumours concerning the
visits to Lausanne of the American delegates to the Disarmament Conference forced the Secretary of State to make a formal
declaration that there was "no truth whatever in the statements
from London; that the American Government or its representatives had had no negotiations and made no suggestions as
to Debt questions at Lausanne or Geneva . . . the American
representatives at the Geneva Conference were dealing solely
with the question of Disarmament." But these rumours had
increased and had had the effect of re-emphasizing the suspicion
of Europe in the minds of Congress, and of reaffirming their
opposition to any debt reduction.

On July 9th Senator McKellar of Tenessee introduced a
resolution declaring that Congress alone was empowered to
modify Debt Agreements and that it was the will of Congress

---

[1] Publication was actually made on July 14th.

that such modification should not be made. The rumours of the "Gentlemen's Agreement" merely had the effect of stiffening this attitude, and again the State Department, on July 7th, had to repeat that the official attitude of the United States Government had undergone no alteration from that announced by Mr. Hoover in his Moratorium statement of June 20, 1931, which declared that he did not approve in any remote sense of the cancellation of debts. But Mr. Chamberlain's mention of conversations with American representatives revived all the old suspicions, and Senator McKellar introduced a further resolution calling upon the President to make a statement as to whether there had been negotiations or not regarding the question of war debts.[1]

With a view to clarifying the position President Hoover addressed to Senator Borah a letter, made public on July 14th, in which he said:—

"I wish to make it absolutely clear that the United States have not been consulted regarding any agreements reported by the Press to have been concluded recently at Lausanne, and that, of course, it is not a party to, nor in any way committed to any such agreement.

"While I do not assume it to be the purpose of any of these agreements to affect the combined action of our debtors, if it shall be so interpreted, then I do not propose that the American people shall be pressed into any line of action or that our policy shall in any way be influenced by such a combination, whether open or implied."

The official attitude of the Administration was one of embarrassment. Some other method of procedure would obviously have been preferred, and in any case it was regretted that the "Gentlemen's Agreement" was not immediately and publicly made known. Such a course of action would have done much to allay suspicion in Congress and the Press in the United States, where any formation of a "united front" on the part of America's debtors has always been viewed with disfavour.

[1] An official statement was issued by the British Treasury on July 14th to the effect that by his remarks in the House of Commons Mr. Chamberlain "did not suggest, and of course had no intention of suggesting, that representatives of the United States had approved, either tacitly or explicitly, what was done at Lausanne. The proceedings there were throughout on the basis that the right course was to seek a European solution of reparations without involving the United States in the discussion."

The result of the disclosure of the "Gentlemen's Agreement" was to intensify the intractable mood already obtaining in Congress, which adjourned, on July 16th, in the same antagonistic spirit towards reductions of war debts in which it met in December. Rather than facilitating the situation, the effect of the Lausanne Conference had been further to complicate it. In any case, nothing could be done until after the presidential elections of November, but it was optimistically hoped in some quarters that, with Congress in recess, it might be possible for the statesmen of America to approach the problem of the reduction of war debts in a less distracted and more constructive frame of mind.

5

To Germany the Lausanne Convention was intended to be beneficial both psychologically and materially. The psychological gain was to be the end of reparations and the material gain the reduction of her capital liability of £1,770 million under the Young Plan to £150 million under the new Agreement. But since Dr. Brüning's statement of January 9th Germany had lived under the belief that reparations were at an end not only in name but in fact, and that, in effect, no more payments *of any kind* were to be made. The financial gain, therefore, had been completely discounted in Germany, to whom the Lausanne Agreement came as a great disappointment, more particularly as it brought no political gains or concessions.

It was in an effort to palliate this that Herr von Papen issued his *communiqué* on July 8th. "The final abolition of reparations," he said, "completely restores our economic and financial independence, and complete abolition of all restrictions which have so far existed under the Young Plan . . . and the complete restoration of our internal sovereignty has been brought about. . . . The result of Lausanne and the deliverance from the fetters of reparations open a new era between the nations. The negotiations have been closely connected with the discussion of political questions concerning Germany's equality of right which the Treaty of Versailles denied her. Though there is no mention of these problems in the Agreement, they have been further advanced toward their solution and they will be brought up again in the future."

But this was cold comfort to a people who had expected complete emancipation, both political and financial, from their state of Treaty inequality, and the Lausanne Agreement was received with frank hostility in Berlin. "The result of the Lausanne Agreement, as far as we know," wrote the *Tageszeitung* on July 8th, "cannot be welcomed by us. It means the continuation of political payments without economic returns and without a political condition which on the German side had rightly been formulated as necessary." Next day it bluntly stated that "Germany cannot fulfil the obligations which Herr von Papen has shouldered." The *Börsen Zeitung* declared that "it is for us incomprehensible what could have induced the German delegation to abandon its point of view that the condition for final German payment must be the settlement of the political question." Alone among the Nationalist Press the *Deutsche Allgemeine Zeitung* welcomed the Agreement which it felt no doubt "paves the way for the world's economic reconstruction." The *Germania*, the organ of the Centre Party, argued that Herr von Papen had assumed obligations which Dr. Brüning had declared to be impossible and characterized the term "reconstruction fund" as a mere fiction. The *Kölnische Zeitung* demanded "what Reichstag does von Papen expect to force to ratify this pact?" and Dr. Hugenberg's *Lokalanzeiger* declared "we pay nothing more, absolutely nothing."

The most important reaction, of course, was that of the Nazis, and that one of deep hostility. The *Völkischer Beobachter* appeared on Saturday, July 9th, with a headline, "The Versailles spirit triumphed," and a parade on the same afternoon of one hundred thousand Nazis in front of the Berlin Schloss, though ostensibly organized as an election meeting, rapidly became transformed into a demonstration against the Lausanne Agreement. In addressing the meeting Count Helldorf, the Berlin Storm Troopleader, declared that the confidence which many Germans had given to the Papen Government had been misplaced. "Revealing incomprehensible weakness, Herr von Papen at Lausanne has approved proposals that we liberty-loving Germans never endorsed," and Dr. Goebells stated that the National Socialist Party did not consider itself bound by the Agreement, since Herr von Papen had no authority to sign it. Finally, Herr Hitler announced on Sunday, July 10th, that "in three weeks' time the Lausanne Agreement will not be worth three marks."

There was ample evidence that the attitude of benevolent neutrality which the Nazis had assumed towards the Papen Government in its earlier days was rapidly changing into defiance and hostility, and suspicions of European intentions towards Germany were not greatly allayed by the next move on the political chess-board, which was made on July 13th.

6

The story of Lausanne is like a *feuilleton* of which one is never sure one has reached the last instalment. Hardly had the public become accustomed, though not reconciled, to the fact of the "Gentlemen's Agreement," and before the text of that document had become public, Sir John Simon on the afternoon of July 13th, on the last day of the session, informed the House of Commons that there had that morning been signed in Paris by M. Herriot and Lord Tyrell another accord, "having," he assured the House, "no organic connection with the Lausanne Convention or with the Gentlemen's Agreement" . . . but being an attempt "to formulate the expression of the new political spirit which was illustrated at Lausanne, and which will be so valuable if it can be preserved in the future."

The text of the Accord was as follows:

"In the declaration which forms part of the Final Act of the Lausanne Conference the signatory Powers express the hope that the task there accomplished will be followed by fresh achievements. They affirm that further success will be more readily won if nations will rally to a new effort in the cause of peace, which can only be complete if it is applied both in the economic and political sphere. In the same document the signatory Powers declare their intention to make every effort to resolve the problems which exist at the present moment or may arise subsequently in the spirit which has inspired the Lausanne Agreement.

"In that spirit His Majesty's Government in the United Kingdom and the French Government decided themselves to give the lead in making an immediate and mutual contribution to that end on the following lines:

"1. In accordance with the spirit of the Covenant of the League of Nations they intend to exchange views with one another with complete candour concerning, and to keep each other mutually informed of, any questions coming to their notice similar in origin to that now so happily settled at Lausanne which may affect the European *régime*. It is their hope that other Governments will join them in adopting this procedure.

"2. They intend to work together and with other Delegations at Geneva to find a solution of the Disarmament question which will be beneficial and equitable for all the Powers concerned.

"3. They will co-operate with each other and other interested Governments in the careful and practical preparation of the World Economic Conference.

"4. Pending the negotiation at a later date of a new commercial treaty between their two countries they will avoid any action of the nature of discrimination by the one country against the interests of the other."

There was evidently more than a little perturbation in the mind of the Foreign Secretary in making his announcement, for he was at considerable pains to explain the inoffensiveness of the new pact, and indeed it was the object on all sides of such fervent apologies that one is tempted to wonder why it was ever negotiated at all. "Indeed it is no substantive agreement at all," said Sir John, "but we hope all the leading European Powers will respond." It was in no sense—apart from the fourth paragraph—special or exclusive, and in the case of the first three paragraphs the invitation was general to the other countries in Europe "to declare their adhesion to the rule that they will endeavour to promote political appeasement in Europe by open and friendly discussion on all grounds of difference by seeking a solution at the Disarmament Conference that shall be *beneficial* and *equitable*"—Sir John Simon laid special stress on thes two words[1]—"and by co-operating in the

[1] In drafting the wording of the new accord considerable difficulty occurred over the word *equitable*, which the British insisted on including as a gesture towards Germany and which the French wished to omit as binding their future decision at Geneva.

preparation for the all-important World Economic Conference . . . in connection with which we hope to have the advantage also of American assistance." It was strongly emphasized that in no sense was there an intention of forming, on the one hand, an Anglo-French *bloc* against Germany, or, on the other, of creating a united European front towards America.

In order to clear up any misapprehension that might remain an official statement was issued from 10, Downing Street on July 14th, pointing out that other Governments had been invited to adhere to the Declaration and that there was "no truth in any statement that it is applicable to the question of British debts to the United States. The use in the Declaration of the words 'European *régime*' expressly excludes from its purview any questions affecting non-European countries."[1]

That such a statement was necessary may well be judged from the fact that the Accord was to be subject to a somewhat different interpretation on the other side of the Channel. M. Herriot's remarks before the Foreign Affairs and Finance Committees of the French Chamber were significant. Describing it as a revival of the "Entente Cordiale," and as the opening of a new era in Franco-British relations, he said that in future no problem affecting the interests of the two countries would be treated separately. Its immediate consequence would be that Great Britain could not, as in 1923, undertake in future to make payments to the United States for the settlement of debts without previously consulting the French Government. A certainty, he added, of a concerted attitude was henceforth an acquired fact, which would facilitate success in the negotiations with Washington. While, in the course of a communication to Sir John Simon, referred to by the latter on July 14th, M. Herriot stated that he did not regard the initiative as a contribution towards an Anglo-French Pact, but purely as a plan of European procedure, his first statement above may be taken as a significant indication of the manner in which French policy would like the Accord to be interpreted.

[1] This reassurance was emphasized by the British Ambassador, Sir Ronald Lindsay, in a personal call at the State Department in Washington.

While the Belgian and Italian Governments immediately gave their adherence to the Accord—the latter noting, without laying undue stress upon, the divergences of interpretation—and the Polish Government adhered on July 18th, the German Government was more critical. A clear interpretation of the aims of the "consultative pact"—as Germany prefers to call it—was considered essential, as also was an assurance that it would not be exploited for the formation of a "united front" against either the United States or Soviet Russia and would not in any way limit Germany's freedom of action or the raising by her of political issues and the questions ventilated at Lausanne. Inquiries in this sense were made at the Foreign Office on July 19th.

The German Government was naturally surprised and annoyed to find a plan, which they themselves had proposed and which had been discussed and rejected in the course of the Lausanne negotiations, suddenly revived as an Anglo-French proposal without previous reference to Germany herself. Moreover, Germany was sceptical of the wording of that part of the Accord which referred to disarmament, and scented in it an Anglo-French agreement not to disarm. Their suspicions received confirmation when Sir John Simon's resolution was introduced into the Disarmament Conference on July 21st. The German delegate, Herr Nadolny, vehemently opposed the resolution as making no concession towards Germany's claim to equality, and finally voted against it when the Conference adjourned on July 23rd. A further cause of German dissatisfaction was the multilateral nature of the new Accord. The German proposal had been for a Four-Power Pact of Consultation, or at most a Pact including the Locarno Powers. Since the main object of the Accord was to provide a method of discussing Germany's difficulties with her neighbours, it seemed unnecessary that all Europe should be included.

Nevertheless, Germany adhered on July 26th. Had it been possible to produce a Four-Power Pact immediately, the effect would have been better in every way and would at once have reassured the fears of Germany and Italy that they were being excluded. Such a proposition was rendered impossible by reason of the new British orientation towards France which resulted from the MacDonald–Herriot *rapprochement* at Lausanne, a change of policy which had its repercussions in various European capitals.

The first immediate effect was in Italy, where, on July 20th, Signor Grandi, Minister for Foreign Affairs, resigned from the Cabinet. Ever since he succeeded the Duce at the Palazzo Chigi in 1929, Signor Grandi had based his foreign policy on co-operation with the League of Nations and friendship with England. The failure of the Disarmament Conference to reach any decisive degree of agreement completed the process of disillusionment, or alternatively of cynical disbelief, of Italy towards the League, and within the Fascist Party there had for some time been considerable dissatisfaction at Signor Grandi's continued belief.[1]

The abandonment by Great Britain at Lausanne of the policy of the "clean slate" which she shared with Italy, and the consequent resuscitation of the Entente Cordiale, dealt a heavy blow at the Anglo-Italian friendship which Sir Austen Chamberlain had been at such pains to build up, though he himself damaged it severely in excluding Italy from the Anglo-French negotiations regarding the Naval Compromise of 1928. Now a similar situation had arisen. Italy felt that she should have been consulted in the first place in regard to the new consultative Pact, and her susceptibilities were hurt through being left out in the cold. Hence, though she adhered to the Pact on July 14th, Signor Grandi considered that his policy had failed, and that he had lost the confidence of his colleagues and his party. He therefore resigned after three years of office and was succeeded by Signor Mussolini in person.[2]

It is difficult to see what good can be served by this new

[1] At its session in April 1932, the Fascist Grand Council announced that, at its next session in October 1932, it would examine "the problem of Fascist Italy in the League of Nations." Signor Mussolini announced in his speech at Torino on October 23rd that Italy intended to remain within the League.
[2] Signor Grandi was appointed Ambassador in London on July 21st, in succession to the late Signor Bordonaro. The appointment gave general satisfaction in England, where Signor Grandi had made himself deservedly popular during the London Conference of 1930.

Accord or Pact which roused suspicions in Germany and the United States, and cost Italy one of her, and Europe's, ablest statesmen. Why was this new product of the united sentiment-ality of Mr. MacDonald and M. Herriot, the same combination which produced the Geneva Protocol of 1924, necessary, since it was expressly stated that it was neither to supplement nor supplant any existing agreement? In the Covenant of the League of Nations, the Locarno Treaties, and the Pact of Paris, the world has ample opportunity and machinery for the discussion of its problems if the will to discuss is there, and if it is not there no amount of consultative pacts will create it. A change of heart and not a multiplication of treaties is what is needed to-day.

7

Not the least of the French successes, or of the German defeats, at Lausanne was the measure of relief to be accorded to Austria.[1] The experts at the Conference drew up and the Council of the League of Nations on July 15th adopted an instrument known as the Protocol of Lausanne, providing for a loan to Austria of 300 million schillings (£8 million).[2] The Protocol was signed by representatives of Great Britain, France, Italy and Belgium, acting as Guarantor States, and Austria, and the conditions of the Loan were to be approved by a Committee of the four guaranteeing Powers. The amounts undertaken by the various participating Governments were as follows:[3]

Great Britain				100,000,000 Sch.
Italy				30,000,000 Sch.
France				100,000,000 Sch.
Belgium				5,000,000 Sch.

But it was clearly stipulated that there would be no joint

[1] Reprinted from *Bulletin of International News*, vol. ix, no. 5 (September 1, 1932).
[2] For text of Protocol, see Appendix IV, pp. 277–83.
[3] The British contribution represents a transfer of the short-term credit granted in June 1931, and will therefore not involve this country in any further obligation.
 The remaining 65 million schillings of the Loan was covered by Holland, Czechoslovakia, and Switzerland.

guarantee and that each Government would be responsible solely for the share in the total operation which it was to provide. No guaranteeing Government would be liable for the service or the repayment of a bond of the Loan not included in the portion guaranteed by it. The various national issues, however, were to form part of a single Loan, and no discrimination might be made by the Austrian Government in carrying out its obligations as regards these different issues.

Austria on her side undertook to take the necessary measures to re-establish and maintain budgetary equilibrium and to carry out a programme of budgetary and financial reforms, the text of which was annexed to the Protocol. The execution of this programme and the general supervision of Austrian finances were to be put in the charge of a League of Nations representative and an adviser to the Austrian National Bank, who, for the period of the Loan, that is to say, 20 years, would be virtually the economic and financial dictators of the country, since the Protocol declared that not even private persons or firms might borrow more than 1,000,000 schillings abroad without their consent and approval.

There was, however, a further and indeed a fundamental condition. The assistance given to Austria by the guaranteeing Powers was stipulated to be on the basis of Protocol No. I, signed at Geneva on October 24, 1922, and of all the undertakings resulting therefrom. It was this provision around which the political importance of the Protocol centred. The principal stipulation of the 1922 Protocol under which Austria secured a Loan of 650,000,000 crowns provides that Austria shall undertake:

" . . . in accordance with the terms of Article 88 of the Treaty of St. Germain,[1] not to alienate its independence; it will abstain from any

---

[1] Article 88 of the Treaty of St. Germain reads as follows:

"The independence of Austria is inalienable otherwise than with the consent of the Council of the League of Nations. Consequently, Austria undertakes in the absence of the consent of the said Council to abstain from any act which might directly or indirectly, or by any means whatever, compromise her independence, particularly, and until her admission to membership of the League of Nations, by participation in the affairs of another Power."

negotiations or from any economic or financial engagement calculated directly or indirectly to compromise this independence."

It was on this point that the Permanent Court of International Justice declared by a majority of one the proposed Austro-German *Zollunion* to be illegal, and though in September 1931 the German Foreign Minister and the Austrian Chancellor had perforce to renounce the *Zollunion*, both of them vehemently resisted the pressure that was brought to bear to give an undertaking not to reopen the question at a later date.

Acceptance of the Lausanne Protocol would pledge Austria to refrain for twenty years from any attempt to form any union with Germany in any form, and the general conditions of the Loan closely resembled those which France had sought to impose upon Austria just a year before (June 16, 1931), and which had caused such an outcry in Great Britain and America.[1] On that occasion Austria had been saved by that last act of glorious bluff which the Bank of England had made before abandoning the gold standard; but now almost the same conditions appear under League auspices with Great Britain as one of the signatory parties, and the only protests forthcoming were from Germany and from certain of the political parties in Austria itself, who were opposed to this further postponement of the inevitable and who preferred, if bankrupty were unavoidable, to default for a smaller rather than for a greater sum.

The opposition to the Protocol within the country itself was very strong and found vent in the debates on ratification in Parliament. The Social-Democrat and Nationalist Parties led by Herr Bauer and Dr. Schober, an ex-Chancellor, together with the Pan-Germans, with a combined voting strength of 82, declared their intention of opposing the Ratification Bill and ranged themselves against the Parties of the Government *bloc*, chiefly Christian-Socialists, numbering 83. The Parties of the Government Coalition themselves had some difficulty in reaching a common platform concerning ratification, and in view of the fact that their nominal majority only numbered one the

[1] See above, pp. 110–11.

gravest consideration had to be given to this agreed method of approach.

The Bill was formally submitted to Parliament on July 20th, and the first reading was postponed until the 28th, when the Bill passed automatically into the Committee stage. Only by a threat of personal resignation was the Chancellor, Dr. Dolfuss, able to persuade his Government to refrain from postponing the final discussion until the autumn session of Parliament, and he at length succeeded in inducing them to face a vote of no confidence which was moved by the Opposition on August 3rd. This motion was lost by a tied vote, 81 Deputies voting for each side, and by this narrowest of conceivable margins the Bill scraped through its second reading.

The debate was not without its dramatic touches. How close the issue was may be judged from the fact that the Opposition, confident of success as a result of the illness of two of the Government supporters, were at the last moment deprived of it by the sudden death of Mgr. Seipel, the leader of the Christian-Socialist Party. He died early on the morning of August 3rd, and the Chancellor was able to exercise his right of nominating and swearing-in a substitute deputy before the opening of the afternoon session. Even then the Chancellor was only able to achieve the stalemate which gave him success by issuing an urgent whip to all his supporters to appear sick or well in the House that afternoon. The scene in the Chamber during the debate resembled the Pool of Bethesda rather than a House of Parliament and testified to the loyalty of the Chancellor's supporters, some of whom arrived carried by friends or supported on crutches, rising from sick beds or having barely recovered from serious operations.

Finally, on August 4th, the chief Committee of the Federal Council passed the Bill by 82 votes to 80.

The final debate was once more postponed until August 17th in order to give the Chancellor time to win over enough support from the Opposition to ensure the eventual safe passage of the Bill, but when the last stages were reached this majority was not assured. Once again the scene was a dramatic one, in the

early stages of the debate it was remarked that a group of
Government supporters were absent and it was found that
they had been stranded at a wayside railway station, wherefrom
they were rescued by a special train and arrived in the nick of
time to bring the Government forces up to full strength. This
reinforcement made the parties equal, but the gods seemed to
be fighting on the side of the Chancellor. Herr Vinzl, a member
of the National Economic Party, one of the Opposition *bloc*,
had voted for the Bill on August 8th, and had subsequently
been submitted to so fierce an attack by his party executive
that his health became affected and heart failure ensued. It
was this fact that gave the Government its final victory when
the Bill for Ratification was at last carried by 81 votes to 80.

Even then the Bill was not out of the wood, for the Federal
Council defeated it by 27 votes to 23 on August 19th. The Bill
was, therefore, returned to the National Assembly, who reaffirmed their previous decision by 82 votes to 80 on August 23rd.
The Opposition had in the meantime lost its chief leader, for
Dr. Schober, the Leader of the Nationalist Party, died on
August 19th. His party, however, made a final effort to defeat
the Bill by moving a proposal for a plebiscite on the subject,
but this motion was rejected by the Government's majority of 2.

Austria was, therefore, once more forced to pledge herself
not to attempt an *Anschluss* or a *Zollunion* with Germany, and
in return she received some £8,500,000. The principle of attaching political conditions to the granting of financial assistance
is a questionable one from an ethical point of view, and it may
be questioned why France, who is not the only guarantor of
the Loan, should have the privilege of exacting her own terms.
In any case, the wisdom of a loan at all is open to question.
What does it profit a bankrupt to add to his debts, and Austria
is already finding difficulty in meeting the services of the
guaranteed and unguaranteed Loans granted her in 1922 and
1930. Unless the Loan is accompanied by a considerable lessen-
ing of tariff restrictions by Austria's neighbours it will merely
be a case of throwing good money after bad, and in any case
300,000,000 schillings cannot go far when already one-third of

it has been earmarked to cover part of the year's deficit of 364,000,000 schillings. Either the Loan should be larger, or there should be no Loan at all, and more and more one is driven back to the wisdom of allowing Austria to consummate in marriage that spiritual union with the German Reich which has existed for the last fourteen years, or, in other words, to make an honest woman of her.

8

What then should be said of Lausanne in retrospect? Is it a great achievement and a step towards economic restoration? Frankly the answer must be that no one can say at the present time what the Lausanne Agreement really means. For the moment it merely means that for an indefinite period no inter-Governmental war debt will be paid in Europe; it means this and no more, for the European creditor Powers under the "Gentlemen's Agreement" have pledged themselves not to ratify until each of them has achieved a satisfactory agreement with the United States. Until the ratification of the Lausanne Convention takes place reparations have not been terminated, and theoretically and legally the Young Plan remains in force. These are important facts to keep in mind. There are then three alternative courses open in the future.

1. The European creditor Powers may reach mutually satisfactory agreements with the United States in respect of war debts, in which case the Lausanne Convention will be ratified and the three-year moratorium for Germany will begin, at the end of which the bond issue will be made by the Bank for International Settlements subject to the conditions provided for in the Convention.

2. The European creditor Powers may fail to reach agreement with the United States, in which case the Lausanne Convention goes by the board and a new conference meets to consider the situation afresh.

3. Germany may refuse to ratify the Convention. This eventuality would seem to have been somewhat neglected in the estimation of the work of the Lausanne Conference, but should it occur, presumably, in view of Mr. MacDonald's reply to Herr von Papen's question on July 8th, a new conference will be called.

Meantime there was an interval of at least four months before the next direct move could be taken, for nothing could be done until after the American presidential elections in the first week of November. But in this period at least part of the Lausanne Convention was put into operation. The Committees which were set up under its terms began to function, and they are four in number:

1. A Committee of representatives of the German and credito Governments to draw up proposals regarding the execution, by means of deliveries in kind, of contracts and works of construction.

2. A Committee of Experts to consider non-German Reparations.[1]

3. A Committee to report to the Commission of Enquiry for European Union concerning measures dealing with the difficulties of transfer and arising out of exchange control, and stimulating trade activity.[2]

4. A Committee of Experts to make a preliminary survey of the problems to be considered by the World Economic Conference.[3] This Committee will have two Sub-Committees:

> (a) to deal with monetary, and
> (b) with general economic questions.

Thus the period of waiting was not wasted, but it must be emphasized that in the main the Lausanne Agreement is provisional; either the settlement agreed upon will prove satisfactory and will become definite or it will not, in which

[1] This Committee met in London on November 14th.

[2] This Committee sat at Stresa from September 5th to 20th. It adopted a draft Convention providing for the establishment of all, "or nearly all," the European States would contribute and from which 75 million gold francs would be paid annually to the agrarian States, who would then gradually withdraw their restrictions on imports from industrial States. In addition, the Economic Sub-Committee recommended the conclusion of commercial agreements, the abolition of restrictions on currency and trade, concerted efforts to organize the cereal and timber trades, improvements in transport organization, the adoption of a programme of public works, and the creation of an international agricultural credit and mortgage institution, and of an international bank for short-term credits.

The Financial Sub-Committee recommended that strict attention should be given to the balancing of budgets, that a strict credit policy should be followed by the Central Banks, and that, as regards both long- and short-term credits, attempts should be made for settlement by direct contacts between creditors and debtors.

As regards the Convention, reservations were made by the delegates of Great Britain, Belgium, Czechoslovakia, Germany, and the Netherlands. The British delegate drew attention to the position of those countries which did not impose heavy import duties on cereals and said they must make reservations in regard to participation in proposals involving financial contributions or guarantees.

See League Document C.666, M.321, 1932, vii.

[3] This Committee held its first meeting at Geneva on October 31, 1932, and elected Dr. Trip (Holland) as its president.

case the Young Plan comes into force again, under the safe-guarding clause of which the creditor Powers have the right to have the amount of the debt fixed by an arbitral tribunal. Beyond this one cannot go, except to repeat again the deep regret that Mr. MacDonald allowed himself to be persuaded into abandoning the "clean slate" policy which would have been the more honest course to pursue.

For France the results of the Lausanne Conference constituted a first-class diplomatic victory. Completely isolated at the outset and faced with a British-Italian-German *bloc* in favour of a "clean slate," M. Herriot not only succeeded in detaching Mr. MacDonald from the opposite camp, but, by the "Gentlemen's Agreement," deprived Great Britain of that initiative in the matter of war debts which she had previously held, while the Agreement of Mutual Confidence bound Great Britain still more closely to France. Well might M. Herriot demand and receive the congratulations of the Chamber. In the space of less than a month he had "out-smarted" Great Britain, rebuffed Italy, broken up the "clean slate" *bloc*, maintained the principle of a final payment on the part of Germany, secured the temporary continuation of the Young Plan (though in a state of suspended animation), achieved something dangerously near a "united front" towards America, and generally assumed the lead in Europe. Truly a record to be proud of.

For Great Britain, Italy, and Germany the Conference spelt failure in varying degrees. Mr. MacDonald, as has been shown, had allowed himself to be drawn once more within the French orbit, and by so doing had doomed to disappointment the hopes of many who had looked to the Lausanne Conference to bring about a complete cancellation of war debts and reparations, at any rate in so far as Europe was concerned. Italy's loss was mainly in prestige, for she felt that she had been cold-shouldered in the Anglo-French Convention, and she too had based her policy on wiping the slate clean.

Germany had achieved little save an empty declaration that reparations were at an end, a fact which most Germans had known for some time past, and even this had only been won by conceding the principle of a final payment, whether as "tribute" or whether as "contribution."[1] In addition, the much-hoped-for political concessions, in the matters of "War Guilt" and disarmament, had not been achieved. For although the Chancellor informed the German Press on July 11th that the "War Guilt" Clause had been erased from the Treaty of Versailles with the lapsing of Part VIII, this was but a unilateral statement and found no echo either in the Lausanne Convention itself or in the other European capitals; and the final Resolution which closed the labour of the first session of the Disarmament Conference on July 23rd, gave no satisfaction to the claims of Germany to equality of status.

If and when the Lausanne Convention is ratified it will mark the end of the war period, though in effect it is chiefly the official acceptance of a situation which already existed. Its signature coincided with the first upward trend of public feeling towards optimism, a feeling which tended to diminish as it became realized that ratification was far distant. For the moment, however, one must agree with the inexorable wisdom of Pope Pius XI's comment, *"C'est peu, mais c'est toujours quelquechose."*

[1] It is, however, extremely unlikely that the final payment will ever be made. The safeguards surrounding it are of so complex and far-reaching a nature that it is improbable that the conditions which are prerequisite for the final bond issue will ever be achieved. Herein lies the wisdom of the Bergmann Plan.

NOTE

THE whole fate of the Lausanne Agreement rests precariously on the razor edge of uncertainty. Immediately after it was known that the result of the American Presidential Election would bring Mr. Roosevelt to the White House in March 1933 the British and French Governments drew the attention of the United States to the undesirability of the results of insistence on payment of the December War Debts instalment and requested postponement. The American Government, however, supported with no uncertain voice by Congress, refused the request, and required that payment should be made on December 15th in accordance with the Funding Agreements.

The fundamental principle of the Lausanne Agreement was, therefore, called in question and earnest conversations took place between the British and French Premiers as to the course to be pursued. It was agreed between Mr. MacDonald and M. Herriot on December 8th that the united European front should remain unchanged for the moment pending further negotiations with President Roosevelt in the coming year.

Payment was, therefore, made on December 15th by Great Britain, Italy, Czechoslovakia, Finland, Latvia and Lithuania, the British payment being made in accordance with the statement of the Government that it formed part of a capital payment for a final settlement. When, however, M. Herriot appealed to the Chamber for authority to make payment he was defeated by an overwhelming majority and, as a result, resigned on December 14th. The Chamber recorded its opposition to any further payment which was not preceded by negotiations for revision. On December 15th, therefore, France defaulted, and her example was followed by Belgium, Estonia, Hungary and Poland.

The ultimate effect of this new situation upon the Lausanne Agreement remains to be seen. But one thing alone is certain —the Wreck of Reparations is complete.

December, 1932.

CONCLUSION

RETROSPECT AND PROSPECT

So we have reached the end of reparations, the wreck is completed, and the story is a gloomy one. It has taken the statesmen of the world a fatal thirteen years and thirty-five conferences to discover the truth which Professor Keynes preached in 1919, and this discovery has only been brought about by a process of *reductio ad absurdum*. The history of reparations is a story of a prolonged series of economic experiments with Germany as a subject, a species of economic vivisection. The first experiment was so drastic that it all but destroyed Germany and reduced her to chaos and bankruptcy. The second, the Dawes Plan, was more restrained, but that also was found to be too exacting. Finally, the third experiment, the Young Plan, failed as signally as its predecessors, and the politico-scientists have been forced to abandon their researches as useless and futile.

From the first it was inevitable that reparations on the scale originally conceived would result in economic chaos, but realization has been slow, and adjustment slower. Micawber politics have been the order of the day. Something was sure to turn up to improve matters, it was declared, and the tragedy was played on. At long last it has been seen that this road led to disaster, but only when both feet are over the precipice have we clutched desperately at the shelving brink. To-day we are struggling to maintain that fingerhold which we have managed to keep, and to drag ourselves inch by inch, with infinite labour, back to safety.

On June 6, 1932, it was announced that Germany had made, in all, reparation payments of some £1,029,000,000 (RM. 20,598,000,000). This sum has been extracted and paid only with the most extreme difficulties, and at a cost of £100,000,000 lent to Germany under the Dawes and Young Loans, to say nothing of the private debts now "frozen." One is tempted to think that it might have been better to have accepted the German offer of one hundred milliard marks which Count Brockdorff-Rantzau made in May 1919, as a final capital payment. Had Germany been able to reckon with a fixed sum and a specified time by which to pay it, it would have been possible for her to adjust her capacity accordingly, and the world at large would have been spared considerable distress, and also the spectacle of much bankrupt statesmanship.

So reparations are finished. No more payments will be made by Germany in any form, for it is highly improbable that the bond issue provided for under the Lausanne Agreement will ever be made. But Germany has derived little benefit therefrom. The psychological effect—the only effect which could really improve the Germany position—of Lausanne was to a great extent nullified by the indefinite nature of the Agreement, and, although in practice and in fact reparations are at an end, the average German had assumed that fact immediately the Hoover Moratorium came into force. Hence the Lausanne Agreement, which brought nothing else but an official recognition of the position, came as something of an anti-climax and had already been discounted.

The work and value of Lausanne can only be measured by its results, and so far there has been little improvement in the economic situation of Germany. The gold cover of the Reichsbank reached the record low figure of 22 per cent. at the end of July but has since made a slight recovery. The trade surplus has continued its steady decline from the beginning of the year.

It is upon this surplus, and upon other foreign earnings, that Germany's capacity to pay the services of the Dawes and Young Loans and the foreign short-term credits depend, and a further decline may have the most disastrous effect upon her commitments.

So much for the past and present. What of the future? There remains the outstanding problem of European debts to America, a problem as yet unsolved and looming like a spectre.

Both President Hoover and President Roosevelt have told the world that they are opposed to the policy of cancellation, so that at best revision is all that can be hoped for.

In the United States debts have become linked with disarmament, and it has been a salient argument of Mr. Hoover's that the European States could meet their American obligations out of their ordinary budgets if they made a sufficient reduction in their military estimates. Mr. Hoover omitted, however, to explain in what way this proposal solved the far more difficult problem of transfer, which is the essential core of the matter.

Nevertheless, there is a close connection in principle between the two questions, and it is, therefore, the more regrettable that the Disarmament Conference adjourned on July 26th without giving any but the most cursory consideration to the Hoover proposal of June 22nd.

The Conference has, however, been given a new lease of life by the Five-Power Agreement of December 11th, whereby the claim of Germany to equality of status was recognized and the way prepared for her return to the Conference. It is now not too much to hope that that body may achieve some degree of agreement which will give to our creditors across the Atlantic an assurance that any sums released under a future debt settlement will not be used to increase national armaments.

The flagging hopes and expectations of the world are centred on the Economic Conference which will open in London in the spring of 1933. To a great extent we have lost faith in conferences—there has been a plethora of them since the war; but this should be above the common run by reason of the fact that so much hangs upon its decision. It may be the last upward effort that brings the world from the brink of disaster on to firm ground; it may be the last despairing struggle before the final plunge.

By the date of the opening of the Conference, President Roosevelt will have been inaugurated, and the world will know whether or not he will use the reduction of war debts to bargain for the reduction of tariffs. But whether debt reduction comes this way or not, come it must, in some form or another. For

sooner or later it will be borne in, even upon the Middle
Western minds, that the collection of political debts is economically detrimental to both creditor and debtor, and that the
system of huge political debt payments can be made to work
just so long, and only so long, as the ultimate creditor is willing
to lend his debtors the money.

The revision of debt payments to America upon a generous
scale, while it would not serve as a panacea for the multitude
of ills from which the world now suffers, would unquestionably
mark very considerable progress towards the restoration and
maintenance of world prosperity.

The readjustment called for by the Basle experts is in the
interests of creditor and debtor alike, and the world looks to
President Roosevelt for a lead in statesmanship which has been
long and sadly lacking.

FINAL ACT OF THE LAUSANNE CONFERENCE [1]

THE Lausanne Conference was convoked on the invitation of the Governments of Germany, Belgium, France, the United Kingdom of Great Britain and Northern Ireland, Italy and Japan. In accordance with the announcement made at Geneva on February 13, 1932, on behalf of those Governments, the object of the Conference was as follows:

". . . to agree to a lasting settlement of the questions raised in the Report of the Basle Experts and on the measures necessary to solve the other economic and financial difficulties which are responsible for, and may prolong, the present world crisis.

"This decision has been reached by the above Governments in the hope that it will ease the international situation."

The Conference was opened at Lausanne on June 16, 1932, by His Excellency M. Giuseppe Motta, President of the Swiss Confederation, M. Jules Dufour, President of the Government of the Canton of Vaud, and M. Gaillard, Mayor of Lausanne, being also present. In addition to the inviting Governments mentioned above, the Governments of the following countries were represented: the Commonwealth of Australia, Canada, Greece, India, New Zealand, Poland, Portugal, Rumania, Czechoslovakia, the Union of South Africa and Yugoslavia. The Governments of Bulgaria and Hungary were subsequently represented at the Conference. The Conference elected as its President the Right Honourable James Ramsay MacDonald, Prime Minister of the United Kingdom, and as Secretary-General, Sir Maurice Hankey, G.C.B., G.C.M.G.

The labours of the Conference were inspired by the principles laid down in the report, signed at Basle on December 23, 1931,[2] of the Special Advisory Committee convoked by the Bank for International Settlements in accordance with the request of the German Government made under paragraph 119 of the Experts' Plan of June 1929.

On June 16, 1932, the representatives of the Governments of the United Kingdom and Northern Ireland, France, Italy, Belgium and Japan signed the following Declaration:

"Deeply impressed with the increasing gravity of the economic and financial perils which overhang the world and with the urgency of the problems which the Lausanne Conference has met to consider;

"Firmly convinced that these problems require a final and definite solution directed to the improvement of European condi-

---

[1] British White Paper, Cmd. 4126.   [2] Cmd. 3995.

tions and that this solution must be pursued henceforward without delay or interruption, with a view to its realization in the framework of a general settlement;

"Noting that certain payments of reparations and war debts will fall due as from the 1st July next;

"Are of opinion, in order to permit the work of the Conference to proceed undisturbed, that, without prejudice to the solution which may ultimately be reached, the execution of the payments due to the Powers participating in the Conference in respect of reparations and war debts should be reserved during the period of the Conference, which the undersigned Governments intend should complete its work in the shortest possible time.

"It is understood that the service of market loans will not be affected by these decisions.

"The undersigned Governments declare that they, for their own part, are prepared to act on this understanding and they invite the other creditor Governments taking part in the Conference to adopt the same course."

In accordance with the invitation contained in the last paragraph of the said Declaration, the Governments of the Commonwealth of Australia, Canada, Greece, India, New Zealand, Poland, Portugal, Rumania, Czechoslovakia, the Union of South Africa, and Yugoslavia subsequently associated themselves therewith.

On the occasion of this Declaration certain Governments addressed to the President of the Conference letters which have been placed in the archives.

As a result of meetings held from June 16 to July 9, 1932, the following instruments were drawn up:

    I.—Agreement with Germany.
    II.—Transitional measures relating to Germany.
    III.—Resolution relating to non-German Reparations.
    IV.—Resolution relating to Central and Eastern Europe.
    V.—Resolution relating to a World Economic and Financial Conference.

The present Act, of which the English and French texts are both authentic, will remain deposited in the archives of the Government of the French Republic, which will deliver a certified copy to each of the Governments who have taken part in the Conference of Lausanne, and also to the other Governments who took part in The Hague Conference of 1929–1930.

Done at Lausanne in a single copy, the 9th day of July, 1932.

J. RAMSAY MacDONALD
President of the Conference

M. P. A. HANKEY
    Secretary-General

I

AGREEMENT WITH GERMANY

The Government of His Majesty the King of the Belgians, the Government of the United Kingdom of Great Britain and Northern Ireland, the Government of Canada, the Government of the Commonwealth of Australia, the Government of New Zealand, the Government of the Union of South Africa, the Government of India, the Government of the French Republic, the Government of the Greek Republic, the Government of His Majesty the King of Italy, the Government of His Majesty the Emperor of Japan, the Government of the Republic of Poland, the Government of the Republic of Portugal, the Government of His Majesty the King of Rumania, the Government of the Czechoslovak Republic and the Government of His Majesty the King of Yugoslavia (hereinafter described as the creditor Governments), and the Government of the German Reich,

Recognizing that the legal validity of the Agreements signed at The Hague on January 20, 1930,[1] is not in question.

But concerned by the economic difficulties resulting from the present crisis,

And being desirous to make, so far as they are concerned, the necessary efforts to ensure the confidence which is indispensable to the development of normal economic and financial relations between the nations.

The undersigned, duly authorized to that effect by their respective Governments,

Have agreed as follows:

Declaration

The Powers signatory of the present Agreement have assembled at Lausanne to deal with one of the problems resulting from the war, with the firm intention of helping to create a new order, permitting the establishment and development of confidence between the nations in a mutual spirit of reconciliation, collaboration and justice.

They do not claim that the task accomplished at Lausanne, which will completely put an end to Reparations, can alone assure that peace which all the nations desire. But they hope that an achievement of such significance and so arduously attained will be understood and appreciated by all the pacific elements in Europe and the world, and that it will be followed by fresh achievements.

These further successes will be more readily won if the nations will rally to this new effort in the cause of real peace, which can only be complete if it is applied both in the economic and in the political sphere and rejects all possibility of resort to arms or to violence.

The signatory Powers will make every effort to resolve the problems which exist at the present moment or may arise subsequently in the spirit which has inspired the present Agreement.

---

[1] Cmd. 3484.

Article 1

The German Government shall deliver to the Bank for International Settlements German Government 5 per cent. redeemable bonds, to the amount of three milliard reichsmarks gold of the present standard of weight and fineness, to be negotiated under the following arrangements:

(1) The Bank for International Settlements shall hold the bonds as trustee.

(2) The Bonds shall not be negotiated by the Bank for International Settlements before the expiry of three years from the signature of the present Agreement. Fifteen years after the date of the said signature the Bonds which the Bank for International Settlements has not been able to negotiate shall be cancelled.

(3) After the above period of three years the Bank for International Settlements shall negotiate the Bonds by means of public issues on the markets as and when possible, in such amounts as it thinks fit, provided that no issue shall be made at a rate below 90 per cent.

The German Government shall have the right at any time to redeem at par, in whole or in part, the Bonds not yet issued by the Bank for International Settlements. In determining the terms of issue of the Bonds, the Bank for International Settlements shall take into account the desirability of giving to the German Government the right to redeem the Bonds after a reasonable period.

(4) The Bonds shall carry interest at 5 per cent. and sinking fund at 1 per cent. as from the date on which they are negotiated. They shall be free of all German taxes, present and future.

(5) The proceeds of the Bonds, as and when issued, shall be placed to a special account, the allocation of which shall be settled by a further agreement in due course between the Governments, other than Germany, signatory to the present Agreement.

(6) If any foreign loan is issued by the German Government, or with its guarantee, at any time after the coming into force of the present Agreement, the German Government shall offer to apply up to the equivalent of one-third of the net cash proceeds of the loan raised to the purchase of Bonds held by the Bank for International Settlements. The purchase price shall be such that the net yield on the Bonds so purchased would be the same as the net yield of the loan so raised. This paragraph does not refer to loans for a period of not more than twelve months.

(7) If, after five years from the signature of the present Agreement, the Bank for International Settlements considers that the credit of the German Government is restored, but the quotations of its loans remain none the less below the minimum price of issue fixed under paragraph (3) above, the minimum price may be varied by a decision of the Board of the Bank for International Settlements, which decision shall require a two-thirds majority.

Further, at the request of the German Government, the rate of interest may be reduced below 5 per cent. if issues can be made at par.

(8) The Bank for International Settlements shall have power to settle all questions as to the currency and denomination of bonds issued, and also all questions as to charges and costs of issue, which it shall have the right to deduct from the proceeds of the issue. In considering any questions relating to the issue of Bonds, the Board of the Bank for International Settlements shall take the advice of the President of the Reichsbank, but decisions may be made by a majority vote.

Article 2

On its coming into force the present Agreement will put to an end and be substituted for the reparation régime provided for in the agreement with Germany, signed at The Hague on January 20, 1930,[1] and the agreements signed at London on August 11, 1931,[2] and at Berlin on June 6, 1932; the obligations resulting from the present Agreement will completely replace the former obligations of Germany comprised in the annuities of the "New Plan."

Article 3

Consequently, Articles 1, 2, 4, 5, 7, 8, 9, and 12 and Annexes I, III, IV, V, VA, VI, VIA, VII, IX, X and XA of the said agreement with Germany are definitely abrogated.

Article 4

The Protocol signed at London on August 11, 1931, and the Protocol supplementary thereto signed at Berlin on June 6, 1932, are abrogated. Consequently, the provisional receipts handed to the Bank for International Settlements by the German Railway Company under the said Protocol of August 11, 1931, will be returned to it.

Article 5

The debt certificate of the German Government and the certificate of the German Railway Company referred to in Article 7 and in Annexes III and IV of The Hague Agreement shall, with the coupons attached, be returned to the German Government and to the German Railway Company respectively.

Article 6

Nothing in the present Agreement alters or affects Article 3 (Liquidation of the past), Article 6 (so far as concerns the corporate existence of the Bank for International Settlements), or Article 10 (Immunities of the Bank for International Settlements) of The Hague Agreement.

Article 7

The Signatory Governments declare that nothing in the present Agreement diminishes or varies or shall be deemed to diminish or vary

---

[1] Cmd. 3763.   [2] Cmd. 3947.

the rights of the bondholders of the German External Loan, 1924, or of the German Government International 5½ per cent. Loan, 1930.

Any necessary adaptation of the machinery relating to the manner in which the obligations of the German Government with respect to the German External Loan, 1924, and with respect to the German Government International 5½ per cent. Loan, 1930, will be discharged will be subject to mutual arrangement between the German Government, on the one hand, and the Bank for International Settlements, Fiscal Agent of the Trustees of the German External Loan, 1924, and Trustee of the German Government International 5½ per cent. Loan, 1930, on the other hand.

Article 8

The present Agreement will, on its coming into force, be notified by the Government of the French Republic to the Bank for International Settlements with a view to the application by the Bank of the provisions which affect it; the said Government will also inform the Bank, for the purposes of its Statutes, that the "New Plan" is no longer in effect.

Article 9

Any disputes, whether between the Governments signatory of the present agreement, or between one or more of those Governments and the Bank for International Settlements, as to the interpretation or application of this Agreement shall be referred to the Arbitration Tribunal set up under Article 15 of The Hague Agreement with Germany. The relevant provisions of that Article and of Annex XII of the said Agreement will for this purpose be applicable.

Article 10

The present Agreement, of which the English and French texts are both authentic, shall be ratified, and the ratifications shall be deposited at Paris.

The Governments whose seat is outside Europe will be entitled merely to notify the French Government, through their diplomatic representatives in Paris, that their ratification has been given; in that case they must transmit the instrument of ratification as soon as possible.

As soon as the present Agreement has been ratified by the Governments of Germany, Belgium, France, Great Britain and Northern Ireland, Italy and Japan, it shall come into force between those Governments whose ratifications have been deposited or notified at that date. It shall come into force in respect of every other signatory Government on the date of notification or deposit of ratification.

The French Government will transmit to all the signatory Governments and to the Bank for International Settlements a certified copy of the *Procès-verbal* of the deposit of each ratification, and a certified copy of each notification.

Article 11

The present Agreement may be signed at any time up to the date on which it first comes into force in accordance with Article 10, by any Government signatory to the Agreement signed at The Hague on January 20, 1930.

After that date any of the said Governments may accede to the present Agreement by means of a notification addressed to the Government of the French Republic, which will transmit to the other Contracting Governments and to the Bank for International Settlements a certified copy of such notification. In that case the Agreement will come into force for the Government concerned on the date of such accession.

Done at Lausanne, the 9th day of July, 1932, in a single copy which will remain deposited in the archives of the Government of the French Republic, which will transmit certified copies to each of the signatory Governments.

> For the Belgian Government:
> > RENKIN.
> > PAUL HYMANS.
> > E. FRANCQUI.

> For the Government of the United Kingdom of Great Britain and Northern Ireland:
> > J. RAMSAY MACDONALD.
> > JOHN SIMON.
> > N. CHAMBERLAIN.
> > WALTER RUNCIMAN.

> For the Government of Canada:
> > G. H. FERGUSON.

> For the Government of the Commonwealth of Australia:
> > GRANVILLE RYRIE.

> For the Government of New Zealand:
> > THOMAS M. WILFORD.

> For the Government of the Union of South Africa:
> > C. T. TE WATER.

> For the Government of India:
> > JOHN SIMON.

> For the French Government:
> > E. HERRIOT.
> > GERMAIN-MARTIN.
> > JULIEN DURAND.
> > JOSEPH PAGANON.
> > GEORGES BONNET.

For the Greek Government:

For the Italian Government:
>   ALBERTO BENEDUCE.
>   ANTONIO MOSCONI.

For the Japanese Government:
>   SHIGERU YOSHIDA.
>   S. KURIYAMA.
>   J. TSUSHIMA.

For the Polish Government:
>   AUGUSTE ZALESKI.
>   JAN MROZOWSKI.

For the Portuguese Government:

For the Rumanian Government:

For the Czechoslovak Government:

For the Yugoslav Government:

For the German Government:
>   F. VON PAPEN.
>   C. VON NEURATH.
>   GRAF SCHWERIN VON KROSIGK.
>   WARMBOLD.

II

TRANSITIONAL MEASURES RELATING TO GERMANY

The duly authorized representatives of the Governments signatories of the Agreement concluded this day with Germany have agreed as follows:—

Article 1

As from to-day's date the effects of the Declaration of June 16, 1932, will be prolonged as regards the payments due by Germany under The Hague Agreement of January 20, 1930, the London Protocol of August 11, 1931, and the Berlin Protocol of June 6, 1932.

This prolongation will terminate on the coming into force of the Agreement with Germany signed to-day at Lausanne, or, failing this, on any one of the Governments of the following countries, Germany, Belgium, United Kingdom, France, Italy and Japan, notifying the Governments concerned that it has decided not to ratify.

Article 2

Negotiations will be entered into without delay between the German Government and the Bank for International Settlements in order that the arrangements contemplated in Article 7 (2) of the Agreement with Germany signed to-day may be prepared before its coming into force.

Article 3

As regards the execution, by means of deliveries in kind, of contracts and works in course of execution, a Committee, consisting of representatives of the German Government and the Governments concerned, shall be appointed to draw up such proposals as may be desirable in regard to such contracts and works.

Signed at Lausanne, the 9th day of July, 1932.

For the Belgian Government:
RENKIN.
PAUL HYMANS.
E. FRANCQUI.

For the Government of the United Kingdom of Great Britain and Northern Ireland:
J. RAMSAY MACDONALD.
JOHN SIMON.
N. CHAMBERLAIN.
WALTER RUNCIMAN.

For the Government of Canada:
G. H. FERGUSON.

For the Government of the Commonwealth of Australia:
GRANVILLE RYRIE.

For the Government of New Zealand:
THOMAS M. WILFORD.

For the Government of the Union of South Africa:
C. T. TE WATER.

For the Government of India:
JOHN SIMON.

For the French Government:
E. HERRIOT.
GERMAIN-MARTIN.
JULIEN DURAND.
JOSEPH PAGANON.
GEORGES BONNET.

For the Greek Government:

For the Italian Government:
      ALBERTO BENEDUCE.
      ANTONIO MOSCONI.

For the Japanese Government:
      SHIGERU YOSHIDA.
      S. KURIYAMA
            (*ad referendum*).
      J. TSUSHIMA.

For the Polish Government:
      AUGUSTE ZALESKI.
      JAN MROZOWSKI.

For the Portuguese Government:

For the Rumanian Government:

For the Czechoslovak Government:

For the Yugoslav Government:

For the German Government:
      F. VON PAPEN.
      C. VON NEURATH.
      GRAF SCHWERIN VON KROSIGK.
      WARMBOLD.

III

NON-GERMAN REPARATIONS

The undersigned Governments,

Animated by the same spirit as inspired the Declaration signed on June 16th by the Five Inviting Creditor Powers,

Are agreed and recommend to the Conference that a Committee consisting of one representative of each of the Governments concerned shall be set up to consider the group of questions known as "non-German Reparations" and cognate questions viewing them within the framework of a general settlement,

Are of the opinion that, in order to permit the work of the said Committee to proceed undisturbed, without prejudice to any question of principle or to the solutions which may ultimately be reached, the execution of the payments due in respect of the above-mentioned questions should be reserved until December 15th next failing a settlement before that date.

Signed at Lausanne, July 7, 1932, for the Governments of:

Australia:
GRANVILLE RYRIE.

Belgium:
PAUL HYMANS.

Bulgaria:
M. MOUCHANOFF.

Canada:
THOMAS A. STONE.

Czechoslovakia:
STEFAN OSUSKY.

France:
CHARLES RIST.

Greece:

Hungary:
L. GAJZAGO.

Italy:
ANTONIO MOSCONI.

Japan:
SHIGERU YOSHIDA.

New Zealand:
T. M. WILFORD.

Portugal:
TOMAZ FERNANDES.

Rumania:
SAVEL RADULESCO.

South Africa:
C. T. TE WATER.

United Kingdom:
N. CHAMBERLAIN.

Yugoslavia:
CONSTANTIN FOTITCH

India:
N. CHAMBERLAIN.

IV

RESOLUTION RELATING TO CENTRAL AND EASTERN EUROPE

In order to achieve the financial and economic reconstruction of Central and Eastern Europe, the Conference decides to appoint a Committee which will be entrusted with the duty of submitting to the Commission of Enquiry for European Union at its next session proposals as to measures required for the restoration of the countries of Central and Eastern Europe, and, in particular—

(a) Measures to overcome the present transfer difficulties of those countries and to make possible the progressive suppression, subject to the necessary safeguards, of the existing systems of exchange control;

(b) Measures to revive the activity of trade, both among those countries themselves and between them and other States, and to overcome the difficulties caused to the agricultural countries of Central and Eastern Europe by the low price of cereals, it being understood that the rights of "third countries remain reserved."

Accordingly, the Conference invites the Governments of Germany, Austria, Belgium, Bulgaria, France, the United Kingdom, Greece, Hungary, Italy, Holland, Poland, Rumania, Switzerland, Czecho-slovakia and Yugoslavia, each to appoint not more than two representatives on the Committee referred to above.

J. RAMSAY MacDONALD

President of the Conference

M. P. A. HANKEY

Secretary-General

V

RESOLUTION RELATING TO A WORLD ECONOMIC AND FINANCIAL
CONFERENCE

The Conference, apart from the questions already dealt with, has further undertaken to decide upon "the measures necessary to solve the other economic and financial difficulties which are responsible for, and may prolong, the present world crisis."

The main questions of this order which demand examination are as follows:

(a) *Financial Questions.*

Monetary and credit policy.

Exchange difficulties.

The level of prices.

The movement of capital.

(*b*) *Economic Questions.*

Improved conditions of production and trade interchanges, with particular attention to—

Tariff policy.

Prohibitions and restrictions of importation and exportation, quotas and other barriers to trade.

Producers' agreements.

The Conference emphasizes in particular the necessity of restoring currencies to a healthy basis and of thereby making it possible to abolish measures of exchange control and to remove transfer difficulties; further, the Conference is impressed with the vital need of facilitating the revival of international trade.

To achieve the above purposes—

The conference decides to invite the League of Nations to convoke at a convenient date and at a place to be fixed (not necessarily Geneva) a Conference on Monetary and Economic Questions.

The Conference decides to entrust the preliminary examination of these complex questions, which are closely interdependent, to an authoritative committee of experts.

The Conference therefore invites the Governments of Germany, Belgium, France, the United Kingdom, Italy and Japan each to appoint as members of the Committee two experts, one qualified to deal with economic questions, the other qualified to deal with financial questions. The Committee would divide itself into two sub-committees according to the two branches of the subject. The two sub-committees would naturally have discretion to meet in joint session whenever necessary, with the object of ensuring the necessary co-ordination in their labours.

The Conference further resolves to invite the Government of the United States of America to be represented on the committee on the same basis as the Governments of the States mentioned above.

Finally, the Conference invites the Council of the League of Nations to nominate three persons qualified by their financial competence, and three persons qualified by their economic competence. It would be desirable that these persons should be nationals of countries other than those mentioned above. They might seek assistance from the Directors of the Economic and Financial Sections of the Secretariat of the League. The Conference similarly seeks the collaboration of the Bank for International Settlements and decides to invite the latter to nominate two persons to participate in the work of the Sub-Committee on Financial Questions.

J. RAMSAY MacDONALD

President of the Conference

M. P. A. HANKEY
    Secretary-General

Lausanne, July 9, 1932

APPENDIX II

THE "GENTLEMAN'S AGREEMENT" [1]

No. 1

Procès-verbal

THE Lausanne Agreement will not come into final effect until after ratification as provided for in the Agreement. So far as the creditor Governments on whose behalf this *Procès-verbal* is initialled are concerned, ratification will not be effected until a satisfactory settlement has been reached between them and their own creditors. It will be open to them to explain the position to their respective Parliaments, but no specific reference to it will appear in the text of the agreement with Germany. Subsequently, if a satisfactory settlement about their own debts is reached, the aforesaid creditor Governments will ratify and the agreement with Germany will come into full effect. But if no such settlement can be obtained, the agreement with Germany will not be ratified; a new situation will have arisen and the Governments interested will have to consult together as to what should be done. In that event, the legal position, as between all the Governments, would revert to that which existed before the Hoover Moratorium.

The German Government will be notified of this arrangement.

> On behalf of Belgium:
> J. R.
>
> On behalf of Great Britain:
> N. C.
>
> On behalf of France:
> E. H.
>
> On behalf of Italy:
> A. M.

July 2, 1932

No. 2

Note to the Chancellor of the German Reich

Lausanne, July 9, 1932

Your Excellency,

We have the honour and we feel it our duty to transmit to you herewith for your information copy of a *procès-verbal* setting out an arrangement which we arrived at on the 2nd July.

We have the honour, &c.

---

[1] British White Paper, Cmd. 4129.

For Belgium:
PAUL HYMANS.

For Great Britain:
JOHN SIMON.

For France:
EDOUARD HERRIOT.

For Italy:
ANTONIO MOSCONI.

No. 3

German Chancellor to Sir John Simon

(Translation.)

German Delegation,
Lausanne, July 9, 1932

Your Excellency,

I have the honour to acknowledge receipt of the communication signed by yourself and by the heads of the Belgian, French and Italian delegations, which you caused to be conveyed to me to-day after the signature of the Lausanne Agreement.

The arrangement of the four delegations, dated the 2nd instant, which accompanied your communication, relates to the case of an eventual non-ratification of the Lausanne Agreement, and conse-quently refers to the same question which also formed the subject of discussion on the 8th instant between the heads of the delegations of the six inviting Powers.

In accordance with the understanding arrived at at this discussion, I addressed on the same evening to the President at the public session of the conference a question concerning the point at issue, which was immediately answered by him in the name of the inviting creditor Powers.

In these circumstances, I consider myself justified in proceeding on the assumption that the matter has been authoritatively explained in so far as Germany is concerned by my question to the President of the conference and by his reply.

I have, &c.
VON PAPEN

No. 4

Extract from the 4th Plenary Meeting of the Lausanne Conference held on July 8, referred to in No. 3

* * * * *

Herr von Papen (addressing the President of the Conference, Mr. Ramsay MacDonald: translation from the French): I should like to ask one question concerning the second paragraph of article 1 in Annex II.[1] In the event, which I recognize to be improbable, of one of the six Powers concerned not ratifying the Agreement, what procedure is proposed to be followed? I imagine that what is essential is that the Governments concerned should get together as soon as possible to consider the situation that has arisen, but I should like to have an assurance that that is the intention of the Conference.

PRESIDENT: I am happy to be able to put this on record. It would be most inadvisable, and very difficult, to embody it in the Annex, but the Declaration I am now making on behalf of the Inviting Powers will, I think, be sufficient. It is that in the event of any inability to fulfil this Agreement and its Annexes, a further Conference will be held.

*   *   *   *   *

No. 5

Letters from the Chancellor of the Exchequer to the French and Italian Ministers of Finance regarding French and Italian Debts to the United Kingdom.

Lausanne, July 8, 1932

Dear { Monsieur Germain-Martin,
       { Signor Mosconi,

His Majesty's Government in the United Kingdom would have been very glad if it had been possible for them to cancel the War Debt of France (Italy) as part of an all-round cancellation of War Debts and Reparations. In the actual circumstances they regret that they cannot enter into any definite commitments modifying the existing War Debt Funding Agreement.

They agree, however, that the suspension provided for by the Declaration of the 16th June should apply to the annuities due under the War Debt Funding Agreement and under Annex I of The Hague Agreement of the 31st August, 1929, until the coming into force of the Lausanne Agreement or until it has been decided not to ratify that Agreement.

In the event of non-ratification of the Lausanne Agreement, the legal position between all the Governments concerned would revert to that which existed under The Hague Agreement of the 20th January, 1930, and the War Debt Funding Agreements. In that case the British and French (Italian) Governments would have to examine together the *de facto* situation which would be created.

Believe me,
Yours sincerely,
N. CHAMBERLAIN

His Excellency M. Germain-Martin.
His Excellency Dr. Antonio Mosconi.

---

[1] See p. 10 of Cmd. 4126 (Final Act of the Lausanne Conference).

No. 6

Declaration made by the Foreign Secretary at the Plenary Meeting of the Lausanne Conference on the 9th July in regard to War Debts of Invited Powers. Declarations in identical terms were also made on behalf of the French and Italian Governments.

I desire to make the following statement on behalf of His Majesty's Government in the United Kingdom, in order to make clear the position as regards the War Debts due to Great Britain by Invited Powers:

"The effect of the Declaration of the Conference signed on the 16th June, 1932, is extended to cover the suspension of the payments due in respect of such War Debts until the Lausanne Agreement with Germany which we are signing to-day has come into force or until a decision has been notified that it will not be possible to ratify that Agreement."

DECLARATION ISSUED BY HIS MAJESTY'S GOVERNMENT IN THE UNITED KINGDOM AND THE FRENCH GOVERNMENT ON JULY 13, 1932, AS TO METHODS FOR PROMOTING FUTURE EUROPEAN CO-OPERATION, WHICH OTHER EUROPEAN GOVERNMENTS ARE INVITED TO ADOPT.[1]

IN the declaration which forms part of the Final Act of the Lausanne Conference the signatory Powers express the hope that the task there accomplished will be followed by fresh achievements. They affirm that further success will be more readily won if nations will rally to a new effort in the cause of peace, which can only be complete if it is applied both in the economic and political sphere. In the same document the signatory Powers declare their intention to make every effort to resolve the problems which exist at the present moment or may arise subsequently in the spirit which has inspired the Lausanne Agreement.

In that spirit His Majesty's Government in the United Kingdom and the French Government decided themselves to give the lead in making an immediate and mutual contribution to that end on the following lines:

1. In accordance with the spirit of the Covenant of the League of Nations they intend to exchange views with one another with complete candour concerning, and to keep each other mutually informed of, any questions coming to their notice similar in origin to that now so happily settled at Lausanne which may affect the European régime. It is their hope that other Governments will join them in adopting this procedure.

2. They intend to work together and with other Delegations at Geneva to find a solution of the Disarmament question which will be beneficial and equitable for all the Powers concerned.

3. They will co-operate with each other and other interested Governments in the careful and practical preparation of the World Economic Conference.

4. Pending the negotiation at a later date of a new commercial treaty between their two countries they will avoid any action of the nature of discrimination by the one country against the interests of the other.

---

[1] British White Paper, Cmd. 4131.

APPENDIX IV

THE AUSTRIAN PROTOCOL [1]

Preamble

CONSIDERING

That the Government of the Austrian Federal Republic has addressed to the League of Nations a request to be assisted in maintaining the work of economic and financial reconstruction undertaken in consequence of the decision of the Council of the League of Nations of October 4, 1922, and of the signature of the three Protocols of the same date;

That the Austrian Government reaffirms its intention of meeting punctually all its foreign obligations;

That the Governments

[*Governments which signed the first Protocol of October 4, 1922, and which sign the present Protocol.*]

are ready to grant further assistance to Austria for this purpose;

That the above Governments, including the Austrian Government, declare that such assistance is given on the basis of Protocol No. 1 signed at Geneva on October 4, 1922, and of all the undertakings resulting therefrom; the provisions of which Protocol are to be considered as here reproduced;

The Governments of

[*All the Governments willing to sign the present Protocol.*]

on the one hand, and the Government of the Austrian Federal Republic, on the other,

Have by common consent drawn up the following provisions:

Article 1

In order to assist the Austrian Government to borrow a sum in foreign currencies, freely and immediately available, the net amount of which shall be equivalent to a maximum of approximately three hundred million Austrian schillings, at the present legal gold parity, the Governments of

undertake to apply without delay for such authority as may be required under their municipal law to enable them either to guarantee, as hereinafter provided, the principal and interest part of such loan or to furnish the amount to the Austrian Government in another manner.

---

[1] League of Nations Document, C.539, M.270, 1932, II, A.

In case of an issue on their markets, they will grant facilities for the issue of the amount which they have guaranteed.

Article 2

(i) There will be no joint guarantee as between the Governments. Each Government shall be responsible solely for the share in the total operation which it is to guarantee or to provide. No guarantor Government will be liable for the service or the repayment of a bond of the loan not included in the portion guaranteed by it.

As regards the public issues, the Austrian Government will prepare separate bonds for the portions of the loan issued in each country, specifically stating which Government is the guarantor.

The various national issues shall, however, form parts of one single loan. No discrimination may be made by the Austrian Government in carrying out its obligations as regards these different issues of the loan. The service and the repayment of the whole of the loan shall be carried out on conditions to be laid down in the General Bond, under the control of one or more trustees appointed by the Council of the League of Nations, acting jointly.

(ii) The participating Governments shall, at the moment of signing, state the amounts which they undertake to guarantee or to provide.

(iii) The expenses of issue, negotiation and delivery of each issue shall be added to the capital of the issue.

(iv) The loan shall be for a term of twenty years. The Austrian Government reserves the right to repay the loan before the expiration of that period, after ten years, on conditions which will be fixed by the Committee of Guarantor States at the time the operation is concluded. Subject to the priorities attached to the Loan of 1923–1943, the Relief Credits and the 1930 Loan, the system of pledged assets by which the 1923–1943 Loan is secured shall be made to apply to the present loan. The manner in which this shall be done shall be settled in detail in the General Bond. The service of the interest and the repayment of the present loan shall be free of all taxes, dues or charges, present or future, for the benefit of the Austrian State or of any other Austrian authority.

(v) The terms of issue (rates of interest, expenses, issue prices, the form of guarantee, etc.) shall be submitted for approval to the Committee of Guarantor States created by the Austrian Protocol No. II of October 4, 1922, or to persons appointed by that Committee; and any reference to the League of Nations in the prospectus of issue shall similarly be approved by the Chairman of the Financial Committee. Those Governments which have signed the present Protocol without being parties to the Austrian Protocol No. II of October 4, 1922, shall be invited to send representatives to the Committee of the Guarantor States.

Article 3

The proceeds of the operation shall be utilized by the Austrian Government for the objects set out in Annex I, in agreement, as the case may be, with the representative of the League of Nations or the Adviser to the National Bank referred to in Article 7.

Article 4

The Austrian Government undertakes to take the necessary steps to restore without delay and to maintain complete equilibrium between the revenue and expenditure of the State; it similarly undertakes to take all steps necessary to re-establish without delay the financial equilibrium of the Austrian State Railways and, in particular, to carry out the programme of budgetary and financial reforms set out in Annex II.

Article 5

Austrian monetary policy will aim at the abolition as soon as possible, subject to the necessary safeguards, of the difference between the internal and external value of the schilling, and, in consequence, at the progressive removal of the existing control over exchange transactions and the resulting obstructions to international trade.

Article 6

(i) It is agreed that the settlement of the question of the Creditanstalt must form part of the programme of financial reforms which are the object of the present Protocol.

(ii) The Austrian Government will take all possible steps without delay to conclude an agreement with the foreign creditors of the Creditanstalt. This agreement will take account of the necessity for avoiding excessive pressure on the schilling.

(iii) The Austrian Government undertakes to effect a settlement of the debt of the Creditanstalt to the National Bank and to issue as soon as possible one or more internal loans of a total amount of not less than 200 million schillings for the partial reimbursement of the debt due by the State to the National Bank.

Article 7

The Austrian Government will request the Council of the League of Nations to appoint a representative of the League of Nations, and to nominate an Adviser to the National Bank of Austria, with the object of continuing the collaboration contemplated in the declarations made in September 1931 by the Austrian Federal Chancellor and in the provisions of the present Protocol and its Annexes.

Article 8

The Committee of Guarantor States shall continue to perform its functions until the loan provided for in the present Protocol has been entirely repaid.

Article 9

(i) All decisions to be taken by the Council of the League of Nations in virtue of the present Protocol shall be taken by a majority vote.

(ii) Any dispute as to the interpretation of the present Protocol shall be settled by the Council by a majority vote.

Article 10

(i) The present Protocol, of which the English and French texts are equally authentic, shall remain open to signature by all Governments which desire to accede thereto. The Protocol shall be ratified, and the ratifications shall be deposited with the Secretariat of the League of Nations.

(ii) The present Protocol shall be approved by the Council of the League of Nations. It shall enter into force as regards the Governments which have ratified it as soon as the ratifications of Austria, the United Kingdom, France and Italy have been deposited. In order to enable the Protocol to enter into force, the ratifications of the above-mentioned States must be deposited not later than December 31, 1932. The Protocol shall enter into force as regards each other of the signatory Governments on the date of deposit of that Government's ratification.

In faith whereof, the undersigned, duly authorized, have signed the present Protocol.

Done at Geneva, the fifteenth day of July, nineteen hundred and thirty-two, in a single copy which shall be deposited at the Secretariat of the League of Nations.

ANNEX I

UTILIZATION OF THE PROCEEDS OF THE OPERATION PROVIDED FOR BY THE PROTOCOL

1. The proceeds in foreign exchange shall be credited to a special account or accounts as directed by the Austrian Government in agreement with the representative of the League of Nations.

2. The advance of 100 million schillings made by the Bank of England to the Austrian Government shall be repaid out of the proceeds of the loan.

3. The Austrian Government shall sell the remaining foreign exchange to the Austrian National Bank on conditions to be fixed in agreement with the representative of the League of Nations.

4. The use to be made of the foreign exchange thus sold by the Austrian Government to the Austrian National Bank shall be decided in agreement with the Adviser to the Bank.

5. The amount in schillings resulting from such sales shall be credited to a special account of the Austrian Government at the National Bank;

this amount in schillings—with the exception, if necessary, of a sum to be determined in agreement with the representative of the League of Nations—shall be used to repay part of the internal floating debt of the State and of the Railways, on condition that the creditors who thus obtain repayment shall simultaneously reduce their indebtedness to the Austrian National Bank by corresponding amounts. The Government may only draw on the sums standing to the credit of this account in agreement with the representative of the League of Nations.

Annex II

PROGRAMME OF BUDGETARY AND FINANCIAL REFORMS

1. In conformity with the declaration made before the Financial Committee by the Austrian Chancellor in September 1931, the Austrian Government will take every step necessary to restore without delay and to maintain equilibrium between its revenue and expenditure.

In order to ensure the application of this principle from 1932 onwards, further permanent economies sufficient to secure the balancing of the budget for the current financial year, estimated on the basis of present figures at 45 million schillings, must be made during the second half of the current year, in addition to those provided for in the supplementary budget which has been submitted to the Council of Ministers.

In view of the special circumstances and having regard to the arrangements contemplated in Annex I for reducing the short-term debt of the State, the 100-million-schilling surplus provided in the present budget for the repayment of short-term obligations may be applied to current needs such as the deficit on the Railways.

2. The Austrian Government undertakes to carry out without delay the general programme of economies and reorganization contained in the report of Dr. Herold, the railway expert who was entrusted with the enquiry into the administration and policy of the Railway system, in conformity with the declaration made by the Chancellor last September.

An expert appointed by the Council of the League of Nations shall be invited by the Austrian Government to decide to what extent the capital outlays (*Investitionen*) of the Railways are really indispensable and to what extent they could, in view of the present financial difficulties, be postponed.

3. All borrowing operations of the Austrian State, whether external or internal (other than those under the standing authority to issue Treasury Bills up to 75 million schillings), remain subject to the approval of the Committee of Guarantor States. The Austrian State Railways shall for this purpose be regarded as part of the Austrian State and shall not be authorized to contract any loan unless the Minister of Finance certifies that the approval of the Committee of Guarantor States has been duly obtained.

As regards contracts on a credit basis for supplies or works which involve a substantial charge on future budgets, including the budget of the Railways, the representative of the League of Nations shall determine whether these operations present an exceptional character warranting recourse to the procedure provided for in the preceding paragraph.

Having regard to the provisions of Annex I, no issue of Treasury Bills or other similar short-term operation shall be carried out by the Austrian Government on the home market unless the prior consent of the representative of the League has been given.

4. In conformity with the declaration of the Chancellor made last September, the Austrian Government will use its existing powers in order to secure that the budgets of the "Länder" and of the Communes are balanced. It will come to an agreement with these local authorities with a view to obtaining such extension of its powers of control as may be necessary, particularly as regards borrowing; all such borrowing operations must in future be approved by the Austrian Government, which will give its consent on the motion of the Minister of Finance after previous consultation with the National Bank and the representative of the League of Nations.

5. Every proposed credit operation, either by a private individual or by a public or private corporation, which involves foreign indebtedness of more than one million schillings, must be brought to the knowledge of the Austrian National Bank before being carried out.

6. The Austrian Government will revise the general legislation on banks in conformity with the September declaration.

7. In conformity with the declaration made in September, and in view of the responsibility assumed by the Austrian Government in regard to the Creditanstalt, the Government will take the necessary steps to secure a reduction in the administrative expenses of that bank and of the other banks operating in Austria.

ANNEX III

LEAGUE OF NATIONS REPRESENTATIVE AND BANK ADVISER

1. The representative of the League of Nations and the Adviser to the Austrian National Bank appointed under Article 7 of the Protocol shall carry out the functions assigned to them in the present Protocol and its Annexes. They shall be responsible to the Council and removable by it.

2. The Austrian Government undertakes to collaborate with the representative of the League of Nations with regard to the execution of the programme of reforms contained in the declaration of September 1931 and in the present Protocol, and further to furnish him with all the information which he may require for the execution of his mission.

3. The representative of the League of Nations will report to the

League of Nations every three months on the execution of the programme of reforms. He will further address supplementary reports to the League of Nations whenever he thinks it desirable to bring any fact as a matter of urgency to the knowledge of the League.

4. The provisions concerning the functions of the Adviser, which formerly constituted Articles 124 to 129 of the Statutes of the Austrian National Bank as enacted by the Federal Law of November 14, 1922 (*Bundesgesetzblatt* No. 823), shall be re-incorporated in the Statutes, except that the words "Commissioner-General of the League of Nations" shall be replaced by the words "Council of the League of Nations."

5. The representative of the League of Nations shall provide himself with the necessary staff. His expenses and those of his office shall be approved by the Council and defrayed by Austria. The representative of the League of Nations shall enjoy diplomatic privileges; he and his staff shall enjoy fiscal immunities.

6. The adviser to the Austrian National Bank shall enjoy fiscal immunities.

7. If the Austrian Government considers that the representative of the League of Nations, or the Adviser to the National Bank, has abused his authority, it may appeal to the Council of the League of Nations.

8. The Council shall terminate the appointment of the representative of the League of Nations and of the Adviser to the Bank when it decides that their services are no longer required.

9. The Council shall have the right, if it considers it necessary having regard to the financial situation, to reappoint the representative of the League of Nations or the Bank Adviser, or both; but such a measure may only be taken if the funds borrowed either in virtue of the present Protocol or through the Guaranteed Loan of 1923–1943 have not been entirely repaid.

10. After the termination of the appointment of the representative of the League of Nations, contact shall be maintained between the Austrian Government and the Financial Organization of the League of Nations by the preparation and publication of periodical statements on Austrian public finances by the Financial Organization of the League of Nations. The Austrian Government agrees to send a Treasury representative to discuss the statements so prepared with the Financial Organization.

BIBLIOGRAPHY

A SELECTED bibliography on reparations was included in *Information on the Reparation Settlement,* by J. W. Wheeler-Bennett and Hugh Latimer. The following list is supplementary to this and consists of books and publications issued in 1930 and after.

OFFICIAL DOCUMENTS

GREAT BRITAIN: FOREIGN OFFICE.

Treaty Series, 1930.
> No. 4, 1930. *Agreement at the Hague Conference, January 1930.* Cmd. 3484. 1931. London: H.M.S.O. 8vo. 172 pp. 3s.

> *Hague Agreements, 1930.* Memorandum on the Receipts of the United Kingdom under the Hague Agreement. Cmd. 3598. 1930. London: H.M.S.O. 56 pp. 1s.

Treaty Series, 1931.
> No. 2, 1931. *International Agreements re Financial Obligations of Germany.* Cmd. 3763. 1931. London: H.M.S.O. 8vo. 285 pp. 4s. 6d.

> No. 3, 1931. *International Agreement re Financial Obligations of Austria arising out of the Peace Treaties.* Cmd. 3764. 1931. London: H.M.S.O. 10 pp. 2d.

> No. 4, 1931. *International Agreement re Financial Obligations of Czecho-Slovakia.* Cmd. 3765. 1931. London: H.M.S.O. 6 pp. 1d.

> No. 5, 1931. *Agreement between United Kingdom, New Zealand, India, and the Austrian Government regarding the Liquidation of Austrian Properties.* Cmd. 3762. 1931. London: H.M.S.O. 18 pp. 3d.

> No. 6, 1931. *International Convention re Bank for International Settlements.* Cmd. 3766. 1931. London: H.M.S.O. 41 pp. 9d.

> No. 7, 1931. *International Agreement re Geneva 5½ per cent. Loan, 1930.* Cmd. 3761. 1931. London: H.M.S.O. 24 pp. 4d.

> No. 12, 1931. *International Agreement re Financial Obligations of Bulgaria under Treaty of Neuilly.* Cmd. 3787. 1931. London: H.M.S.O. 13 pp. 3d.

> No. 21, 1931. *Agreement between the United Kingdom, New Zealand, India, and the Hungarian Government regarding the Liquidation of Hungarian Properties.* Cmd. 3845. 1931. London: H.M.S.O. 9 pp. 2d.

Treaty Series, 1931—(continued).

No. 30, 1931. *Internal Agreement* re *Financial Obligations of Hungary under Treaty of Trianon.* Cmd. 3910. 1931. London: H.M.S.O. 73 pp. 1s. 3d.

Miscellaneous, No. 19, 1931.
Report of International Committee of Experts re *Suspension of certain Inter-Governmental Debts—due June 30, 1932.* Cmd. 3947. 1932. London: H.M.S.O. 44 pp. 9d.

Miscellaneous, No. 1, 1932. Bulgaria.
Protocol providing for Suspension of Certain Payments due by Bulgaria. 1932. London: H.M.S.O. 16 pp. 3d.

UNITED STATES: SENATE.

"Hearings before Committee on Finance, December 16, 1931." *Postponement of Inter-Governmental Debt.* 1931. Washington: Government Printing Office. Large 8vo. 29 pp.

GENERAL WORKS

BONN (M. J.): *Der Neue Plan.* 1930. Munchen: Humblot. viii, 266 pp.

FISCHER-WILLIAMS (Sir J.): "Legal Footnote to the Story of German Reparations," in *British Year-Book of International Law,* 1932, pp. 9–39.

GRIBBLE (Francis): *What America Owes Europe.* 1932. Hurst & Blackett. xxxiii, 188 pp.

LITTER (F.): *Die Verfahransvorschrift für Sachleistungen nach dem Haager Abkommen von 20 Jan. 1930.* (Kommentar). 1930. Berlin: Reichsverbanden der Deutschen Industrie.

LLOYD GEORGE (David): *The Truth about Reparations and War Debts.* 1932. London: Heinemann. 150 pp.

McFADYEAN (Sir A.): *Reparations Reviewed.* 1930. London: Benn. 220 pp. 8s. 6d.

MOULTON (H. G.) and PASVOLSKY (L.): *War Debts and World Prosperity.* (Brookings Institute Publication No. 46). 1932. Washington: Brookings Institute. xx, 487 pp.

MOUSLEY (Edward): *A British Brief.* 1932. Hutchinson. 203 pp.

MYERS (D. P.): *The Reparation Settlement.* 1930. Boston: World Peace Foundation. 249 pp.

RAAB (F.): *Der Neue Plan.* 1930. Berlin: Reimar Hobbing. 206 pp.

Deutschlands Recht zur Einstellung der Reparationen. 1932. Dresden: Ehlermann. 107 pp. Bwl.

SALTER (Sir A.): *Recovery.* 1932. London: Bell. xvi, 326 pp.

SCHACHT (H.): *The End of Reparations*. 1931. London: Jonathan Cape, 248 pp.

STOPFORD (R. J.) and MENKEN (J.): in *Survey of International Affairs*. Oxford University Press:—

1929 (1930. vii, 545 pp.) "The History of German Reparations from the Dawes Plan to the Young Report," pp. 111–116.

1930 (1931. ix, 605 pp.) "The History of German Reparations from the Signing of the Young Report to the Coming into Force of the Hague Agreements," pp. 499–528.
"The German Economy and Reparations," pp. 528–552.

WHEELER-BENNETT (J. W.) and LATIMER (Hugh): *The Reparation Settlement*. 1930. Allen & Unwin. 253 pp.

INDEX

INDEX

289